African American History

In the

United States of America

An Anthology

Written, Compiled and Edited by: Tony Rose
Publisher of Amber Books

From Africa to
President Barack Obama

Volume 1

African American History

In the

United States of America

An Anthology

Written, Compiled and Edited by: Tony Rose
Publisher of Amber Books

From Africa to President Barack Obama

Volume 1

Amber Books
Phoenix, AZ
New York   Los Angeles

African American History in the United States of America
An Anthology
Written, Compiled and Edited by: Tony Rose
Publisher of Amber Books
From Africa to President Barack Obama
Volume I

Published by:
Amber Books
A Division of Amber Communications Group, Inc.
1334 East Chandler Boulevard, Suite 5-D67
Phoenix, AZ 85048
Amberbk@aol.com
WWW.AMBERBOOKS.COM

ISBN # 978-0-9824922-0-8
Library of Congress Control Number: 2009928748

Dedication

This book is dedicated to my wife Yvonne Rose, and all the cultures on planet Earth. May the people of America and the world one day live together in peace, harmony, prosperity and love, for we are all one people, one race.

Acknowledgments

To my wife Yvonne Rose who gets to hear all my passions and dreams right away, whether she wants to or not, and has supported all of them. Thank you.

To Eleanor Brockington, for the hard work and long hours you put into this anthology for me, thank you. To Yvette Johnson, Gail Thompson, Lisa Liddy and Yvonne Rose, thank you all for your wonderful work and input.

To my former neighbors at Province in Maricopa, Arizona, who by their desire for knowledge first inspired this book—Jay and Shelia Steinle, Mike and Connie Cleary, Dave and Nancy Bounds and especially Kyle and Georgia Engelking who were the first neighbors I talked to about doing this anthology. Thank you all for your wonderful discussions about politics and cultural differences during that beautiful and surreal spring, summer and fall 2008, when the wind was blowing in sweet Arizona and a change called 'Yes We Can' was moving fast across America.

To my Phoenix and Maricopa friends—Jack and Yvonne David, Claire Newton, Russell and Marcy Patterson, Nathan and Eleanor Brockington, Melvin Wilson and my barber, Cedric O. Neal. The conversations were great that winter, spring, summer, fall 08 and the food slammin'.

To The First lady of the United States of America, Michelle Obama, whom it seemed to me never wavered in her belief in her husband and in America for one moment; to Malia and Sasha Obama whom every time I saw them walk on stage or walk to a podium with their parents reinforced my belief that this could happen, and to The President of the United States of America Barack Obama who's campaign for the presidency, beginning to end, was the greatest run for anything I and billions of people from all over the world had ever seen in our lives.

Thank you for being the four bravest, most courageous people we have witnessed in a long time, for bringing America a voice and a song it has long needed. Thank you for bringing America together for one long moment in time, to say 'Yes We can', 'Yes We Can', 'Yes We Can' change. And to America, thank you!

—Tony Rose

About the Author

Tony Rose is the Publisher/CEO, of Amber Communications Group, Inc. and the **2013 NAACP Image Award Winner for Outstanding Literature** (Youth/Teens) for the title *Obama Talks Back: Global Lessons – A Dialogue for America's Young Leaders* by Gregory J. Reed, Esq. He is editor of numerous books and the co-author of the national best-seller, *Is Modeling For You: The Handbook and Guide For The Young Aspiring Black Model*, written with Yvonne Rose. He has penned the critically acclaimed, best-seller, *Before the Legend: The Rise of New Kids On The Block and A Guy Named Maurice Starr, The Early Years* and written compiled, edited and published, the award winning, best-seller, *African American History In The United States of America—An Anthology—From Africa To President Barack Obama, Volume One*, a Top Ten Best African American Book, and has recently penned the critically acclaimed *America: The Black Point of View (1950's and 1960's) – An Autobiography of Short Stories – Essays and Poems.*

Introduction

And so it happened on November 4th 2008 the 56th Quadrennial United States Presidential Election was held and an African American man, in the truest sense of that word, with the unusual name of Barack Obama was elected to be the President of The United States of America, and on January 20, 2009 President Barack Obama was inaugurated and sworn in as the 44th President of the United States of America.

During the course of that election cycle of 2007 and 2008, and especially as we got closer to the Democratic Party nomination process and final election period of summer and fall 2008, and because an African American was running for and then became the Democratic Party nominee for President and the front runner through September and October 2008, I and millions of other African Americans became the focus of attention from their European American neighbors, fellow workers, countrymen and women.

The invitations to dinner, in order to socialize and discuss African American culture abounded. The reason for this was clear…most African Americans know a great deal about European and European American culture. Through reading and through our American educational process, European and European American history is predominant. Through our pop culture of television, radio, newspapers and magazines, European American history—past, present and future—is told everyday.

Most European Americans know very little of the African and African American culture. They don't, for the most part, read our books and the African and African American educational process in American schools is limited, for the most part, to the civil rights era (Dr. Martin Luther King, Jr.) and that slavery once existed in America. Most European Americans see African American culture through movies, television, sports and music, and that's as close as it gets.

They don't know that since 1623 more laws have been written for the containment or well-being of the African and African American by Europeans and European Americans; in fact there are more laws written for or against the African American and Native American than any other culture in the United States of America.

So who are these Africans who came to America in 1619 and became African Americans when the Declaration of Independence from Britain was read in 1776? Who are these African ancestors and African Americans who have been in this country for three hundred and ninety years? Two hundred and forty six years as indentured servants and slaves. One hundred and forty nine years as a "people trying to make a way".

After all of the dinner invitations—and, I thank all of those good people, from those I accepted and those I couldn't accept—I realized that I could not and neither could the other millions of African Americans explain who we were in a one-hour discussion. That our European American countrymen and women would have to read our history in a comprehensive book in context to understand what happened and what was happening… and why.

So because I was a book publisher and a writer, I embarked upon the task of putting together, compiling and editing some of the greatest writers and historians of African and African American history in the United States of America.

What you are holding in your hand is Volume One of *African American History in the United States of America—From Africa to President Barack Obama, An Anthology.*

Volume One begins with the story of ancient Africa, the beginning of Homo Sapiens and African Civilizations, the coming of Europeans and slavery in the United States of America and tells the stories of early African and African American People who lived in seventeenth, eighteenth and nineteenth century America.

By the time you have read Volume One, you will understand that the only persons who have fully enjoyed Affirmative Action in this country—from its formation as a colony since 1619 and as a democracy called The United States of America since 1776, through education, jobs, and housing because of the color of their skins—have been middle to upper class Europeans and European American men.

I want to thank Lerone Bennett Jr., President Barack Obama, Jim Haskins, Brenda Wilkerson, Otha Richard Sullivan, Clinton Cox and Eleanora E. Tate for the privilege of reading, compiling, editing and putting into sequence their work in Volume One of *African American History In The United States of America—From Africa To President Barack Obama, An Anthology.*

What I have done here is not the "end all" or the "be all". There are tens of thousands of books on the African American culture and journey through the United States of America. A great deal of them reside at the New York Public Library Schomburg Center for Research In Black Culture. If anything, it is the beginning of all of our searches to find common ground in the United States of America. It is the beginning of a story, old and new. It is the beginning and the end of a pledge.

"I pledge allegiance to the flag of the United States of America, and to the Republic for which it stands One Nation Under God, Indivisible, with Liberty and Justice For All."

It is my hope that you will read this in its entirety, from beginning to end. Do not flip through it, do not skim it, do not read it out of context, for it is the only way that you can begin to understand your past, present and future.

Tony Rose, Publisher
Amber Books

Foreword

I have taken certain liberties in writing, compiling, and editing this book. Since the words "black race" and "white race", in my opinion, have no meaning, as do the words "white and black people" said in that context, they have been struck from the text.

Let me explain:

The black race and white race were words first used by European upper class scientists and noblemen during the 17th and 18th century to explain the differences between them and the Africans they were now beginning to, with the use of guns and cannons, exploit and subjugate through force the taking of men and women from Africa to Europe and the to the New World of America, into slavery.

Thus, to differentiate themselves from these "Africans" they came up with the language of race, the African being savage, inferior and sub-human and themselves superior, civilized and human. The African and the African American were sold to Europe and eventually to America as another race, the black race, sub-human and uncivilized; and the white race became civilized and human. The African had to be another species, another race, surely not related to Europeans and European Americans.

To further define my point you do not hear newscasters or politicians or the people of today say, "The yellow race did that or the red race did that or the brown race did this." It's only used in context, still today, for the black race and the white race.

My recommendation is that the language of white race and black race in the United States of America be changed to the African American Culture and the European American Culture, because as everyone knows now, there is only one race, the "Human Race"… everything else is culture. The African Culture, The European Culture, The Asiatic Culture, The Hispanic Culture and so on. And then you bring it down to specific countries and groupings of people. The Kenyan Culture, The English Culture, The Ghanaian Culture, The French Culture, The Irish Culture and so on, and then to people; The African American Culture, The European American Culture. And that brings us to "white and black people"…there is no such thing.

Before the enslavement of Africans in America began, there was no such thing as the white people of France, or the white people of England, there were only Frenchmen and Englishmen. Only in early America, after a time, did every person who was of European ancestry become known as a white man, not Englishman, Frenchman or Dutchman, to again differentiate themselves, gain numbers and unify against the Africans and Native Americans. In early America every person who was of African ancestry became known as negro, colored, black or worse. The white man superior, the Black man inferior.

So, I have changed us in this book to what we were, African and European men and women, and what we are today African American and European American men and women. Not white and black people.

It is my hope and dream that one day we can all call one another who we truly are—"Americans".

Tony Rose, Publisher
Amber Books

Contents

African American History in the United States

Before The Mayflower:
A History of Black America

Lerone Bennett Jr.

The African Past

Africa is now regarded as the place where mankind first received light.

From Olduval Gorge in East Africa, from caves in the Sahara and excavations in the Nile Valley come bits of bone and husks of grain that speak more eloquently than words of the trials and triumphs of the African ancestors of African Americans. The evidence from these and other areas can be summarized briefly under four headings.

Olduval Gorge: A series of astonishing discoveries in this Tanzanian canyon suggest that the most important and fascinating developments in human history occurred in Africa. Discoveries by Dr. L.S.B. Leakey and other archeologists indicate that humanity was born in Africa. A growing body of research from this and other African sites indicates further that toolmaking began in Africa and that this seminal invention spread to Europe and Asia.

The Nile Valley. Important finds in the Sudan and the Nile Valley prove that people of a Black African type were influential contributors to that cradle of civilization—ancient Egypt. Discoveries at excavations near Khartoum in the Sudan and at El Badari on the Nile indicate that Stone Age Black Africans laid the foundation for much of the civilization of the Nile Valley and manufactured pottery before pottery was made in the world's earliest known city.

Central and South America: European American and African American scholars, working primarily in the United States and Mexico, unearth new archeological evidence, including carbon 14-dated sculpture, which suggests that African mariners explored the New World before Columbus. This evidence and corroborative data from the diaries and letters of explorers, Arabic charts and maps and the recorded tales of African griots indicate that there was extensive pre-Columbian contact between ancient Africa and the Americas.

"An overwhelming body of new evidence," says Professor Ivan Van Sertima (They Came Before Columbus), "is now emerging from several disciplines." "The most remarkable examples of this evidence are the realistic portraitures of Black Africans in clay, gold and stone unearthed in pre-Columbian strata in Central and South America."

The Sahara: French explorer Henri Lhote discovers rock paintings which suggest to author Basil Davidson that "peoples of a Black African type were painting men and women with a beautiful and sensitive realism before 3000 B.C. and were, perhaps, the originators or naturalistic human portraiture."

The implications of all this are extensive, as W.M. Whitelaw pointed out on a general summary of the evidence. "Later discoveries," he wrote, "all the way from Kenya to Transvaal not only of early human remains but also of advanced anthropoid types have brought the historical anthropologists to a state of confused expectancy. Considerably more evidence will have to be brought to light, however, before even the main outlines of man's early history in Africa can be drawn. It is already reasonable, however, to believe that such evidence may be forthcoming as will require a radical change of perspective on African history, if not on history itself".

It is already reasonable, in fact, to believe that the African ancestors of African Americans were among the major benefactors of the human race. Such evidence as survives clearly shows that Africans were on the scene and acting when the human drama opened.

For a long time, in fact, the only people on the scene were Africans. For some 600,000 Years Africa and Africans led the world.

Civilization started in the great valleys of Africa and Asia, in the Fertile Crescent in the Near East and along the narrow ribbon of the Nile in Africa. In the Nile Valley that beginning was an African as well as an Asian achievement. African Blacks, or people who would be considered of African descent today, were among the first people to use tools, paint pictures, plant seeds and worship gods.

In the beginning, then, and for a long time afterwards, the Africans marched in the front ranks of the emerging human procession. They founded empires and states. They extended the boundaries of the possible. They made some of the critical discoveries and contributions that led to the modern world.

Looking back on that age from our own, one is struck by what seems to be an absence of color consciousness. Back there, in the beginning, Blackness did not seem to be an occasion for obloquy.

During this critical period in the evolution of humanity, African Blacks were known and honored throughout the ancient world. Ancient Ethiopia, a vaguely defined territory somewhere to the south of Egypt, was hailed as a place fit for the vacation of the gods. Homer praised Memnon, King of Ethiopia, and Eurybates:

Homer, Herodotus, Pliny, Diodorus and other classical writers repeatedly praised the Ethiopians. "The annals of all the great early nations of Asia Minor are full of them," Flora Louisa Lugard wrote. "The Mosaic records allude to them frequently; but while they are described as the most powerful, or most just, and the most beautiful of the human race, they are consistently spoken of as African, and there seems to be no other conclusion to be drawn, than that at that remote period in history, the leading race of the Western world was an African culture." The Ethiopians claimed to be the spiritual fathers of Egyptian civilization. Diodorus Siculus, the Greek historian who wrote in the first century B.C., said that "the Ethiopians conceived themselves to be of greater antiquity than any other nation; and it is probable that, born under the son's path, its warmth may have ripened them earlier than other men. They supposed themselves to be the inventors of worship, of festivals, of solemn assemblies, of sacrifices, and every religious practice."

Whatever may have been the spiritual influence of the ancient Ethiopians, it is established beyond doubt that Black Africans from somewhere were an important element among the peoples who fathered Egyptian civilizations. Badarian culture proves that Black Africans camped on the banks of the Nile thousands of years before the Egypt of the Pharaohs. Bodies were excavated at El Badari amid artifacts suggesting a date of about eight thousand B.C. In the intestines of these bodies were husks of barley which indicated that the dark-skinned Badarians had learned to cultivate cereals. The beautifully fashioned Badarian pottery was never surpassed, not even in Egypt's days of greatest glory.

"The more we learn of Nubia and the Sudan, "Dr. David Randall-MacIver said, "the more evident does it appear that what was the most characteristic in the predynastic culture of Egypt is due to intercourse with the interior of Africa and the immediate influence of that permanent Black African element which has been present in the population of Southern Egypt from the remotest times to our own day."

If Black African people were a major element among the peoples who fathered Egyptian civilization, who were the Egyptians?" The question bristles with thorns. The only thing that can be said with assurance is that they probably were not European. The evidence suggests that they were a black-, brown-, and yellow-skinned people who sprang from a mixture of Black African, Senitic and European stocks.

The Greek historian Herodotus, who visited the country some five hundred years before Bethlehem said the Egyptians were "black and curly-haired."

Ra Nehesi and several other Pharaohs have been identified as African Blacks by eminent scholars. So has Queen Nefertari, "the most venerated figure." Sir Flinders Petrie said, "of Egyptian history." Nefertiti, the wife of Aahmes I, Egypt's great imperial leader, and cofounder of the famous Eighteenth Dynasty, has been described as a Negress (sic) of great beauty, strong personality, and remarkable administrative ability."

There was long and intimate contact between the dark-skinned Egyptians and the dark-skinned Ethiopians. For fifty centuries or more they fought, traded and intermarried. During the Middle Empire, Ethiopia was a tribune-paying dependency of Egypt. Then, in the middle of the eighth century B.C., the Ethiopians turned the tables and conquered Egypt. A bold Ethiopian monarch named Kashta began the conquest which was completed by his son Piankhy. When Piankhy returned to his capital at Napiata, he had subdued sixteen princes and was master of both Egypt and Ethiopia. The legs of his enemies, he said, trembled "like those of women."

Piankhy was a master of the allegedly modern profession of public relations. The celebrated stellar in which he recounted his deeds of valor is one of the gems of Egyptology. A modern scholar, Sir Alan Gardiner, said it is "one of the most illuminating documents that Egyptian history has to show, and displays a vivacity of mind, feeling, and expression such as the homeland could no longer produce.

For more than a century Ethiopian kings occupied the divine office of the Pharaohs. Shahaka who succeeded Piankhy, attempted to restore the dwindling fortunes of Egypt. He sponsored a cultural revival, built a chapel at Karnak and restored a temple at Thebes. Diodorus Siculus said he "went beyond all his predecessors in his worship of the gods and his kindness to his subjects." Herodotus said he abolished capital punishment in Egypt.

Taharka, the greatest of the Ethiopian Pharaohs, ascended the throne about 6900 B.C. at the age of forty-two. He was, by all accounts, a remarkable leader who improved the economic and cultural life of his realm. Sir E.A. Wallis Budge and Taharka (the Tirhakah of the Bible) was "a capable and energetic king, and under his able rule the country, notwithstanding his wars with the Assyrians, enjoyed a period of prosperity for about twenty-five years."

When, in 667 B.C., Taharka was defeated by the Assyrians, he retired to Napata, where Ethiopians continued to rule for several centuries. The capital was later moved farther south to Meroe, where strong-willed queens called candaces ruled. One of these queens, a one-eyed woman "with masculine characteristics," led the Ethiopians in unsuccessful forays against the Romans.

Whatever the true origins of modern Ethiopia, there is no exaggeration in saying that it is one of the oldest countries in the world. The African kingdom, which traces its lineage back to the famous visit the legendary Queen of Sheba ("black but comely") paid Solomon some one thousand years before Christ, reached the height of its power in the fifth century, when Christianity became the official religion. With the rise of Islam, the Ethiopians of Azum were isolated and slept, historian Edward Gibbon wrote, "for nearly a thousand years, forgetful of the world by whom they were forgotten."

During the early Christian era, African Blacks were scattered to the four corners of the world. For many centuries African Black merchants traded with India, China and Europe. Other African Blacks were sold as slaves in Europe and Asia. By the beginning of the Islamic era, African Blacks—as merchants and merchandise—had integrated Europe, Asia and the Far East. By that time African Blacks were well known in Venice and the rest of Europe and in the deserts of Arabia.

Perhaps the best known of the Arabic Blacks was Antar, the impassioned lover-warrior-poet. The son of an attractive slave woman and an Arab nobleman, Antar became a famous poet and was immortalized after his death as the "Achilles of the Arabian Iliad." Fearless, impetuous, ready to fight, sing a lyric or drink wine, Antar won fame in the poetic contests that were common in pre-Islamic days. His fame spread and he was hailed as the greatest poet of his time.

Antar died about A.D. 615 and his deeds were recorded in literary form as *The Romance of Antar*. This book, Edward E. Holden wrote, "has been the delight of all Arabians for many centuries. The unanimous opinion of the East has always placed *The Romance of Antar* at the summit of such literature. As one of their authors well says: *The Thousand One Nights* is the amusement of women and children; *Antar* is a book for men."

As a religious ethic, Islam seems to have been unusually effective in cutting across culture lines. All Moslems, whatever their color, were brothers in the faith. "If an African slave is appointed to rule you," Mohammed said, "hear him and obey him, though his head be like a dried grape."

In this climate a man can be a slave today and a prime minister tomorrow. It is not at all surprising, therefore, that many African Blacks played heroic roles in the rise and spread of Islam—men like Mohammad Ahmad, the Sudanese Black who claimed to be the Messiah; Abu'l Hasan Alai, the African Black sultan of Morocco, and Bilal, the friend of Mohammed. There were also numerous African Black generals, administrators and poets. When, in the eighth century, the Arabs exploded and carried Islam across North Africa and into Spain, African Blacks went with them.

In the same period, three powerful states—Ghana, Mali, and Songhay—emerged in the western Sudan, a broad belt of open country sandwiched between the Sahara in the north and the rain forests of the Guinea Coast on the south. The peoples and rulers of these countries were African Blacks, some of whom were converted to Islam in the eleventh century. The extent of Moslem influence is debatable, but it seems probable that the upper classes and leaders, especially in the large cities, were African Black Moslems.

As political entities, Ghana, Mali and Songhay do not suffer in comparison with their European contemporaries. In several areas, in fact, the Sudanese empires were clearly superior. "It would be interesting to know." Basil Davidson wrote, "What the Normans might have thought of Ghana. Anglo-Saxon England could easily have seemed a poor and lowly place beside it."

The economic life of these states revolved around agriculture, manufacturing and international trade. Rulers wielded power through provincial governors and viceroys and maintained large standing armies. Chain-mailed cavalry, armed with shields, swords and lances, formed the shock troops of the armies, Ibn-Batuta, an Arab traveler who visited Mali in the fourteenth century, was impressed by the flow of life in these states. "Of all people," he said, "the African Blacks are those who most detest injustice. Their Sultan never forgives anyone who has been guilty of it."

Trade and commerce flourished in the great cities that sprang up in the Sudaneses savannah, and the intellectual life was brisk and stimulating. Jenne' and Timbuktu were known throughout the Moslem world as centers of culture and learning. Ibn-Batuta said the African Black women of these cities were "of surpassing beauty." They were neither downtrodden nor meek, these women. Ibn-Batuta said they were "shown more respect than the men," adding: "Their men show no signs of jealousy whatever" and the women "show no bashfulness before men and do not veil themselves."

The power and wealth of Ghana, Mali and Songhay stemmed from the trans-Saharan trade, which exerted a profound influence on Sudanese civilization. The basis of this trade was gold. From the north came caravans of twelve thousand or more camels, laden with wheat, sugar, fruit, salt and textiles, which were exchanged in the Sudan for gold and other products. In the power politics of that day, the country that controlled this trade controlled Sudan.

Ghana, which was old when the Arabs first mentioned it in A.D. 800, dominated the Sudan for almost three hundred years, flourishing in the ninth and tenth centuries and reaching the peak of its power in the early part of the eleventh century. The rulers of Ghana, which was one of the main suppliers of gold for North Africa and Europe, were fabulously wealthy. Al-Bakri, an Arab geographer who wrote in 1067, said the king owned a nugget of gold so large that he could tether his horse to it.

Tenkamenin, who ruled Ghana in the middle of the eleventh century, had an army of two hundred thousand men and lived in a castle decorated with sculpture and painted windows. "When he gives an audience to his people," Al-Bakri said, "to listen to their complaints he sits in a pavilion around which stand his horses caparisoned on cloth of gold; behind him stand ten pages holding shields and gold-mounted swords, and on his right hand are the sons of the princes of his empire, splendidly clad with gold plaited into their hair. The governor of the city is seated on the ground in front of the king, and all around him are his vizirs in the same position. The gate of the chamber is guarded by dogs of an excellent breed, which never leave the king's seat, they wear collars of gold and silver."

In the eleventh century Ghana fell to a band of Moslem zealots, and the torch of Sudanese civilization passed to Mali, which began as a small Mandingo state on the left bank of the upper Niger River. Although the history of this country goes back to the seventh century, it owes its fame to two men—Sundiata Keita and Mansa Musa. Keita transformed the small state into a great empire. Musa, the most celebrated ruler of the ancient Sudan, came to power in 1307 and put together one of the greatest countries of the medieval world. Musa is best known for a pilgrimage he made to Mecca in 1324. He went in regal splendor with an entourage of sixty thousand persons, including twelve thousand servants. Five hundred servants, each of whom carried a staff of pure gold weighing some six pounds, marched on before him. Eighty camels bore twenty-four thousand pounds of gold, which the Black monarch distributed as alms and gifts. Musa returned to his kingdom with an architect who designed imposing buildings in Timbuktu and other cities of the Sudan.

Mali declined in importance in the fifteenth century and its place was taken by Songhay, whose greatest king was Askia Muhammed, a general who had served as prime minister and who seized power in 1493, a year after the European "discovery" of America. He reigned for nineteen years and built the largest and most powerful of the Sudan states. His realm was larger than all Europe and included most of West Africa. "He was obeyed," a Sudanese writer said, "with as much docility on the farther limits of the empire as he was in his own palace, and there reigned everywhere great plenty and absolute peace."

A brilliant administrator and an enlightened legislator, Askin reorganized the army, improved the banking and credit systems and made Gao, Walata, Timbuktu, and Jenne' intellectual centers. Certain scholars, Alexander Chamberlain in particular, believe he was one of the greatest monarchs of this period. "In personal character, in administrative ability, in devotion to the welfare of his subjects, in open mindedness towards foreign influences, and in wisdom in the adoption of non-Black African ideas and institutions," Chamberlain said, "King Askia was certainly the equal of the average European monarch of the time and superior to many of them."

Timbuktu, during Askia's reign, was a city of some one hundred thousand people, filled with gold and dazzling women. One of the most fabled and exotic cities in the medieval world, the Sudanese metropolis was celebrated for its luxury and gaiety. The towering minarets of two great mosques dominated the face of the city. From the Great Mosque, flat-roofed houses (of wood and plaster) radiated in all directions. The older Sankore Mosque, to which was attached the University of Sankore, was the center of intellectual life. The mosque and the university were of cut stone and lime. Other buildings fronted the narrow streets; factories and shops where one could buy exotic goods from North Africa and faraway Europe. Leo Africanus, a

Christianized Moor who visited the city in the sixteenth century, said it "is a wonder to see what plenty of merchandize is daily brought hither and how costly and sumptuous all things be….Here are many shops of merchants and especially of such as weave linen."

In the narrow streets of this Sudanese metropolis, scholars mingled with rich Black African merchants and young boys sat in the shade, reciting the Koran. Visiting Arab businessmen wandered the streets, looking, no doubt, for the excitement for which the city was famed. Youths from all over the Muslim world came to Timbuktu to study law and surgery at the University of Sankore; scholars came from North Africa and Europe to confer with the learned historians and writers of the Black African empire. Es-Sadi, a Timbuktu intellectual who wrote a history of the Sudan, said his brother came from Jenne' for a successful cataract operation at the hands of a distinguished surgeon. Ex-Sadi, incidentally, had a private library of sixteen hundred volumes.

"In Timbuktu," Leo Africanus said, "there are numerous judges, doctors, and clerics, all receiving good salaries from the king. He pays great respect to men of learning. There is a big demand for books in manuscript, imported from Barbary. More profit is made from the book trade than from any other line of business." Since man first learned to write, few cities have been able to make such a claim.

The University of Sankore and other intellectual centers in Timbuktu had large and valuable collections of manuscripts in several languages, and scholars came from faraway places to check their Greek and Latin manuscripts.

Timbuktu was Paris, Chicago and New York City blended into an African setting. Shocked Songhay historians said most of the people amused themselves with parties, love and the pleasures of the cup. Music was the rage (orchestra with both male and female singers were preferred), and midnight revels were common. The dress of the women was extravagantly luxurious. Men and women were fond of jewels, and the women dressed their hair with bands of gold.

Dramatic displays, including dancing, fencing, gymnastics and poetic recitation, were popular. So was chess. The story is told of a Donghay general who bungled a military campaign and explained that he became so engrossed is a chess game that he paid no attention to the reports of his scouts. Askia—a liberal man who had several wives and one hundred sons, the last of whom was born when he was ninety— was disturbed by the free and easy life of Timbuktu and attempted, apparently without too much success, to curb the social excesses.

Timbuktu and the civilization of which it was a flower declined in the seventeenth century and the reign of the great West African states came to an end. Why did Sudanese civilization collapse? Du Bois says it fell before the triphammer blows of two of the world's great religions, Islam and Christianity. Other students cite the difficulties of defense in the open Sudanese savannah and the corrupting influence of the slave trade. Es-Sadi, who wrote the Tarikh al-Sudan in the dying days of the Songhay empire, advanced another reason—social dissolution. The people, he said, had grown fat and soft on luxury and good living. "At this moment," he said, "faith was exchanged for infidelity; there was nothing forbidden by God which was not openly done. . . Because of these abominations, the Almighty in his vengeance drew upon the Songhai the victorious army of the Moors."

The age of the great Sudan empires ended, but several states to the east and south, notably Mossi, Hausa, Kanem-Borna and Ashanti, retained political identities down to the eighteenth and nineteenth centuries. Great Zimbabwe and other stone cities in Southern Africa suggest that strong states flourished inland. Vigorous centers of culture also existed on the East Coast, where Black African and Arab merchants traded with India and China.

European penetration and the slave trade debased much that was vital in African culture. The popular myth depicts the conquering

European carrying the blessing of civilization to naked "savages" who sat under trees, filed their teeth and waited for fruit to drop into their hands. The truth is less flattering to the European ego. On the West Coast of Africa, from whence came most of the ancestors of African Americans, there were complex institutions ranging from extended family groupings to village states and territorial empires. Most of these units had all the structures of the modern state—armies, courts, and internal revenue departments. Indeed, more than one scholar has paid tribute to "the legal genius of the African." Not even the kingdoms of Peru and Mexico could mobilize resources and concentrate power more effectively than could some of these African monarchies, which are more to be compared with Europe of the Middle Ages than referred to the common conception of the 'primitive' state."

Agriculture was the basis of the economic life of these states, although herding and artisanship were important. Specialization was advanced, with one nation, for example, concentrating on metallurgy and bartering with another nation which specialized in weaving or farming. A money system based on the cowrie shell was in use before European penetration. Contemptuous of the concept of private property, West Africans believed that the land belonged to the community and could not be alienated.

Iron was known and used from the Atlantic Ocean to Ethiopia. With simple bellows and charcoal fires, the Africans smelted iron and manufactured beautiful implements. "It seems likely," Franz Boas said, "Neither ancient Europe, nor ancient western Asia, nor ancient China knew iron, and everything points to its introduction from Africa."

The core of West African society was the family which was organized in some tribes on a matrilineal basis—that is, descent was traced through the mother. Polygamy was common, although, in practice, the poor, like poor people everywhere, contented themselves with monogamy. Social life was well organized. The old, the sick, the infirm were cared for. Spinsters were rare; prostitution was unknown.

Some nations, incidentally, were acquainted with the allegedly modern practice of birth control. Bantu people said it was not good for a woman to give birth to more than one child in a three-year period. Some nations vaccinated for smallpox and said there was a cause-and-effect relationship between the mosquito and the malaria. A European traveler in Abyssinia reported that "the natives hereabouts say that Malaria is caused by the bite of the mosquito, but, of course, we know better—it is caused by the miasmas of the swamps!"

The West Africans were a bewildering mixture of various stocks. Centuries of contact and interbreeding had already produced different types. Some of the West Africans were short and broad-nosed. Some were tall with straight hair and aquiline noses. They were of all colors: chocolate, asphalt, café' au lait, persimmon, cream.

Although West Africans spoke many tongues, there was a common sub-stratum. Only four African languages were reduced to writing before the coming of the European: Egyptian, Ethiopian; a variety of Berber and an invention of the Vai people of Liberia. Though not all reduced to writing, African languages were far from simple. There is no better summary of the flavor of these languages than Mario Pei's analysis of Swahili, which, he said, "is a complete refutation of the rather general belief that languages of 'primitive' peoples are necessarily primitive, and consist largely of grunts, groans and mixed up ideas. Swahili has a euphony that is comparable to Italian, with clear, distinct sounds, vowel endings, and a most pleasing arrangement of syllables that consist for the most part of consonant-plus-vowel. It is capable of such absolute precision that the Swahili version of the Pentateuch contains fewer words than the Hebrew original, without the slightest loss or distortion of meaning. Its grammatical and syntactical structure is logical, almost to the point of being philosophical."

Of whatever tongue, of whatever color, Africans were a deeply religious people. For a long time their religion was written off as a form of animism. We know now that it was a great deal more complicated than that. Like advanced peoples everywhere. Africans wrestled with the big questions. What is man? What happens to him after death? Is life a gigantic box or has it purpose and meaning?

The answers Africans gave to these questions determined the form of their religion. There was, to begin with, a Supreme God who created the earth. There was also a pantheon of lesser gods, identified sometimes with terrestrial objects. Intertwined with these concepts were the cults of fate and ancestor worship. Undergirding all was the basic concept of "Life forces." The life force of the Creator was thought to be present in all things, animate and inanimate. This force, "a kind of individualized fragment of the Supreme Being itself," continued to exist, even after the death of the individual. It continued, the African said, in a pure and perfect state which could influence the lives of living things.

The sophisticated concept bears a striking resemblance to Henri Bergson's elan vital and other modern philosophies and theories. Bernard Fagg, an expert on these matters, found some parallels between African philosophy and modern subatomic physics, "African thought," he said, "is conditioned by their ontology, that is, their theory of the nature of things is thought of in terms of force or energy rather than matter; the forces of the spirit, human, animal, vegetable and mineral worlds are all consistently influencing each other, and by a proper knowledge and use of them a man may influence his own life and that of others."

Religion, to the African, was life. Every event was charged with religious significance, and the climax of life was death. The African's attitude toward death, anthropologists say, survived the Atlantic crossing and took root in the soil of African American life. Another religious root, spirit possession, thrives, they say, in the shouting and ecstasy complex of some African American churches.

Art, like religion, was a life expression. There were no art museums or opera houses in pre-European Africa. Art and aesthetic expression were collective experiences in which all the people participated. Art, in short, was not for art's sake, but for life's sale,

The different faces of beauty—line, color, sound, rhythm—fascinated the African ancestors of African Americans. And their plastic art—embedded in cubistic masks, terra-cotta pieces, gold figurines, three-dimensional objects and naturalistic representations of the human body, is one of the great flights of the human spirit. Fascinated by the abstract geometry of African art, Picasso and other modernists turned their backs on the Greco-Roman and Renaissance visions and adopted the vocabulary of Benin, life and other West African art centers. In 1907 Picasso altered the faces of his huge canvas, Les Demoiselles d'Avignon, to resemble African masks. This was the beginning of cubism, a turning point to Western art.

Before the coming of the European, music and rhythm were everyday things in Africa. Music was everywhere and it was grounded in two techniques which survived in the New World: polyrhythmic percussive technique and the call-and-response pattern (leader and chorus alternating). The poetry of tom-toms, the symphonies of synchronized bodies, these ebbed and flowed with the rhythm of life. Men and women danced because dancing had a social and religious meaning and because dancing *was* meaning, was life itself. This attitude came to America, too. The African American dances are rooted in an African mystique.

There was much, to be sure, that was mean and base in African life-slavery, for example, although it was a thousand times more moderate than American slavery and, of course, the use of humans by humans, Humans used other humans in Africa, as they did in Greece and Rome. The only thing that can be said for human exploitation in Africa is that it was as well organized as it was in "more advanced" cultures.

The individuals who emerged from this African chrysalis were courageous and creative. They were not soft; they were hard. They had fought the tsetse fly and hundreds of nameless insects, and they had survived. They had wrested from the hungry jungle gaps of land and had found time to think beautiful thoughts and to make beautiful things. They were used to hark work and they were accustomed to an elaborate social code.

If they were aristocrats or rich merchants or priests if, in short, they belonged to the upper classes, as did some who came to America in chains, they were used to political responsibility, to giving orders and taking them, to making and altering rules, to governing. In fine, as Stanley M. Elkins said, in an otherwise questionable essay, they were "the product of .... Cultural traditions, essentially heroic in nature."

It is obvious from this—from the evidence of the names, habits, religious practices and music of African Americans—that Africa's golden past is crucial to an understanding of African Americans. What is equally true and equally important is that Africa's past is crucial to an understanding of European Americans. For it is impossible to understand European Americans, it is impossible to understand Thomas Jefferson or George Washington or the U.S. Constitution without some understanding of Africa's gift to the New World. And what that means, on the level of history a well as on the level of reality, is that America, contrary to the generally accepted view, is an African as well as a European invention.

Part One

Dreams From My Father: A Story of Race and Inheritance

Barack Obama

Chapter One

Dreams From My Father

I asked Granny to start from the beginning, How did our grandfather Obama come to live in Kendu? Where did our grandfather work? Why did the Old Man's mother leave? As she started to answer, I felt the wind lift, then die. A row of high clouds crossed over the hills. And under the fanning shade of the mango tree, as hands wove black curls into even rows, I heard all our voices begin to run together, the sound of three generations rumbling over each other like the currents of a slow-moving stream, my questions like rocks rolling the water, the breaks in my memory separating the currents, but always the voices returning to that single course, a single story....

First there was Miriwu. It's not known who came before. Miwiru sired Sigoma, Sigoma sired Owiny, Owiny sired Onondi, Onondi sired Obongo, Obongo sired Okoch, Okoch sired Opiyo. The women who bore them, their names are forgotten, for that was the way of our people.

Oboth lived in Alego. Before that, it is known only that families traveled a great distance, from the direction of what is now Uganda, and that we were like the Masai, migrating in search of water and grazing land for great herds of cattle. In Alego, the people settled and began to grow crops. Other Luo settled by the lake and learned to fish. There were other tribes who spoke Bantu, already living in Alego when the Luo came, and great wars were fought. Our ancestor

3

Owiny was known as a great warrior and leader of his people. He helped to defeat the Bantu armies, but the Bantu were allowed to stay on and marry Luo, and taught us many things about farming and the new land.

Once people began to settle and farm, the land in Alego became crowded. Opiyo, son of Okoth, was a younger brother, so perhaps that is why he decided to move to Kendu Bay. When he moved there, he was landless, but in the custom of our people, a man could use any unused land. What a man did not use reverted to the tribe. So there was no shame in Opiyo's situation. He worked in the compounds of other men and cleared the land for his own farm. But before he could prosper, he died very young, leaving behind two wives and several children. One wife was taken in by Opiyo's brother, as was the custom then—she became the brother's wife, her children, his children. But the other wife also died, and her oldest son Obama was orphaned when still a boy. He, too, lived with his uncle, but the resources of the family were strained, and so as Obama grew older, he began to work for other men as his father had done before him.

The family he worked for was wealthy, with many cattle. But they came to admire Obama, for he was enterprising and a very good farmer. When he sought to marry their oldest daughter, they agreed and the uncles in this family provided the necessary dowry. And when this eldest daughter died, they agreed that Obama would marry the younger daughter, whose name was Nyaoke. Eventually, Obama had four wives, who bore him many children. He cleared his own land and became prosperous, with a large compound and many cattle and goats. And because of his politeness and responsible ways, he became an elder in Kendu, and many came to seek his advice.

Your grandfather, Onyango, was Nyaoke's fifth son. Dorsila, who sits here, was the last child of Obama's last wife.

This is the time before the European man came. Each family had their own compound, but they all lived under the laws of the elders.

Men had their own huts, and were responsible for clearing and culti-
vating their land, as well as protecting the cattle from wild animals
and the raids of other tribes. Each wife had her own vegetable plot,
which only she and her daughters would cultivate. She cooked the
man's food, drew water and maintained the huts. The elders regu-
lated all plantings and the harvests.

They organized families to rotate their work, so that each family
helped the other in doing these things. The elders distributed food to
widows or those who had fallen on hard times, provided cattle as
dowry for those men who had no cattle themselves, and settled all
conflicts. The words of the elders were law and strictly followed—
those who disobeyed would have to leave and start anew in another
village.

The children did not go to school, but learned alongside their parents. The girls would accompany their mothers and learn how to
grind the millet into porridge, how to grow vegetables and pack clay
for the huts. The boys learned from their fathers how to herd and
work pangas and throw spears. When a mother died, another would
take the child in and suckle him as her own. At night, the daughters
would eat with their mothers, while the sons would join their father
in his hut, listening to stories and learning the ways of our people.
Sometimes a harpist would come, and the entire village would come
to listen to his songs. The harpists sang of great deeds of the past, the
great warriors and wise elders. They would praise men who were
good farmers or women who were beautiful, and rebuke those who
were lazy or cruel. All were recognized in those songs for their contributions to the village, good and bad, and in this way the traditions of
the ancestors stayed alive in all who heard. When the children and
women were gone, the men in the village would gather together and
decide on the village affairs.

Even from the time that he was a boy, your grandfather Onyango was
strange. It is said of him that he had ants up his anus, because he
could not sit still. He would wander off on his own for many days,

and when he returned he would not say where he had been. He was very serious always—he never made jokes. He was always curious about other people's business, which is how he learned to be an herbalist. You should know that an herbalist is different from a sharman— what the European and European American calls a witch doctor. A sharman casts spells and speaks to the spirit world. The herbalist knows various plants that will cure certain illnesses or wounds, how to pack a special mud so that a cut will heal. As a boy, your grandfather sat in the hut of the herbalist in his village, watching and listening carefully while the other boys played, and in this way he gained knowledge.

When your grandfather was still a boy, we began to hear that the Europeans had come to Kisuma town. It was said that these Europeans had skin as soft as a child's, but that they rode on a ship that roared like thunder and had sticks that burst with fire. Before this time, no one in our village had seen Europeans—only Arab traders who sometimes came to sell us sugar and cloth. But even that was rare, for our people did not use much sugar, and we did not wear cloth; only a goatskin that covered our genitals. When the elders heard these stories, they discussed it among themselves and advised the men to stay away from Kisuma until this European was better understood.

Despite this warning, Onyango became curious and decided that he must see these Europeans for himself. One day he disappeared, and no one knew where he was gone. Then, many months later, while Obama's other sons were working the land, Onyango returned to the village. He was wearing the trousers of a European, and a shirt like a European, and shoes that covered his feet. The small children were frightened, and his brothers didn't know what to make of this change. They called Obama, who came out of his hut, and the family gathered 'round to stare at Onyango's strange appearance.

"What has happened to you?" Obama said. "Why do you wear these strange skins?" Onyango said nothing, and Obama decided that

Onyango must be wearing trousers to hide the fact he was circumcised, which was against Luo custom. He thought that Onyango's shirt must be covering a rash, or sores. Obama turned to his other sons and said, "Don't go near this brother of yours. He is unclean." Then he returned to his hut, and the others laughed and shunned Onyango. Because of this, Onyango returned to Kisumu, and would remain estranged from his father for the rest of his life.

Nobody realized that the European intended to stay in the land. We thought that they had come only to trade their goods. Some of their customs we soon developed a taste for, like the drinking of tea. With tea, we found that we needed sugar, and teakettles and cups. All these things we bought with skins and meat and vegetables. Later , we learned to accept the European's coin. But these things did not affect us deeply. Like the Arabs, the European remained small in number, and we assumed they would eventually return to their own land. In Kisumu, some Europeans stayed on and built a mission. These men spoke of their god, who they said was all-powerful. But most people ignored them and thought their talk silly. Even when the Europeans appeared with Rifles, no one resisted because our lives were not yet changed by the death such weapons could bring. Many of us thought the guns were just fancy ugali stirrers.

Things began to change with the first of the European wars. More guns arrived, along with a European who called himself district commissioner. We called this man Bzama Ogalo which means "the Oppressor" . He imposed a hut tax that had to be paid in the European's money. This forced many men to work for wages. He conscripted outright many of our men into his army to carry provisions and build a road that would allow automobiles to pass. He surrounded himself with Lucs who wore clothes like the European to serve as his agents and tax collectors. We learned that we now had chiefs, men who were not even in the council of elders. All these things were resisted, and many men began to fight. But those who did so were beaten or shot. Those who failed to pay taxes saw their huts burned to the ground. Some families fled farther into the countrywide to start new villages. But most people stayed and learned to live with this new institution, although we now all realized that it had been foolish to ignore the Europeans arrival.

During this time, your grandfather worked for the European. Few people could speak English or Spanish in those days—men didn't like to send their sons to the European's school, preferring that they work with them on the land. But Onyango had learned to read and write, and understood the European's system of paper records and land titles. This made him useful to the European, and during the war he was put in charge of road crews. Eventually, he was sent to Tanganyika, where he stayed for several years. When he finally returned, he cleared land for himself in Kendu, but it was away from his father's compound and he rarely spoke to his brothers. He didn't build a proper hut for himself, but instead lived in a tent. People had never seen such a thing and they thought he was crazy. After he had staked his claim, he traveled to Nairobi, where a European had offered him a job.

In those days, few Africans could ride the train, so Onyango walked all the way to Nairobi. The trip took him more than two weeks. Later he would tell us of the adventures he had during his journey. Many times, he chased away leopards with his panga. Once he was chased into a tree by an angry buffalo and had to sleep in the tree for two days. Once he found a drum lying in the middle of the forest path and when he opened it, a snake appeared and slid between his feet into the bush. But no harm came to him, and he eventually arrived in Nairobi to begin his work in the Europeans house.

He was not the only one who moved to town. After the war, many Africans began working for wages, especially those who had been conscripted or lived near cities or had joined the European missions. Many people had been displaced during and immediately following the war. The war had brought famine and disease in its wake, and it brought large numbers of European settlers who were allowed to confiscate the best land.

The Kikoyo felt these changes the most, for they lived in the highlands around Nairobi, where European settlement was heaviest. But the Luo also felt the European's rule. All persons had to register with the colonial administration and hut taxes steadily increased. This pressured more and more men to work as laborers on the large European farms. In our village, more families now wore the Europeans clothes, and more fathers agreed to send their children to mission school. Of course, even those who went to school could not do the things the European did. Only Europeans were allowed to buy certain land or run certain businesses. Other enterprises were reserved by law for the Hindus and the Arabs.

Some men began to try to organize against these policies, to petition and hold demonstrations. But their numbers were few, and most people just struggled to live. Those Africans who did not work as laborers stayed in their villages, trying to maintain old ways. But, even in the villages, attitudes changed. The land was crowded, for with new systems of land ownership, there was no longer room for sons to start their own plots—everything was owned by someone. Respect for tradition weakened, for young people saw that the elders had no real power. Beer, which once had been made of honey, and which men drank only sparingly, now came in bottles and many men became drunks. Many of us began to taste the European man's life, and we decided that compared to him, our lives were poor.

By these standards, your grandfather prospered. In his job in Nairobi, he learned how to prepare the European's food and organize the European's house. Because of this, he was popular with employees and worked in the estates of some of the most important Europeans, even Lord Delamere. He saved his wages and bought land and cattle in Kendu. On these lands, he eventually built himself a hut. But the way he kept his hut was different from other people. His hut was so spotless, he would insist that people rinse their feet or take off their shoes before entering. Inside, he would eat all his meals at a table and chair, under mosquito netting, with a knife and fork. He would not touch food that had not been washed properly and covered as soon as it had been cooked. He bathed constantly, and washed his clothes every night. To the end of his life, he would be like this, very neat and hygienic, and he would become angry if you put something in the wrong place or cleaned something badly.

And he was very strict about his property. If you asked him, he would always give you something of his—his food, his money, his clothes, even. But, if you touched his things without asking, he would become very angry. Even later, when his children were born, he would tell them always that you do not touch other people's property.

Part Two

Before the Mayflower:
A History of Black America

Lerone Bennett Jr.

Chapter Two
Before the Mayflower

She came out of a violent storm with a story no one believed, a name no one recorded and a past no one investigated. She was manned by pirates and thieves. Her captain was a mystery man named Jope, her pilot an Englishman named Marmaduke, her cargo an assortment of Africans with sonorous Spanish names—Antoney, Isabella, Pedro.

A year before the arrival of the celebrated *Mayflower,* 113 years before the birth of George Washington, 246 years before the Thirteenth Amendment, this ship sailed into the harbor at Jamestown, Virginia, and dropped anchor into the muddy waters of history. It was clear to the men who received this "Dutch man of Warr" that she was no ordinary vessel. What seems unusual today is that no one sensed how extraordinary she really was. For few ships, before or since, have unloaded a more momentous cargo.

From whence did this ship come?

From somewhere on the high seas where she robbed a Spanish vessel of a cargo of Africans bound for the West Indies. Why did she stop at Jamestown, the first permanent English settlement in America? No one knows for sure. The captain "pretended," John Rolfe noted, that he was in great need of food and offered to exchange his human cargo for "victualle." The deal was arranged. Antoney, Isabella, Pedro and seventeen other Africans stepped ashore in August, 1619. The history of African Americans in America began.

It began, in a way, with Antoney. And it began with a love story. Antoney, who had no surname, fell in love with Isabella and married her. In 1623 or 1624 Isabella gave birth to the first African American child in English America. The child, a boy named William, was baptized in the Church of England.

There were other ships, other Williams, other Antoneys and other Isabellas—millions after millions. This is a story about those millions and the way they came to the Americas. This is a story about the merchandising and marketing of human beings. This is a story about the "greatest migration in recorded history."

The story of Antoney and Isabella is only one act in a larger drama—the European slave trade— which began in 1444 and continued for more than four hundred years. During this period Africa lost an estimated forty million people. Some twenty million of these men and women came to the New World. Millions more died in Africa during and after their capture or on the ships and plantations.

These figures, though instructive, do not say anything meaningful about the people involved. The slave trade was not a statistic, however astronomical. The slave trade was people living, lying, stealing, murdering, dying.

The slave trade was an African man who stepped out of his house for a breath of fresh air and ended up, ten months later, in Georgia with bruises on his back and a brand on his chest.

The slave trade was an African mother suffocating her newborn baby because she didn't want him to grow up a slave.

The slave trade was a "kind" captain forcing his suicide-minded passengers to eat by breaking their teeth, though, as he said, he was "naturally compassionate."

The slave trade was a bishop sitting on an ivory chair on a wharf in the Congo and extending his fat hand in wholesale baptism of slaves who were rowed beneath him, going in chains to the slave ships.

The slave trade was a greedy king raiding his own villages..

The slave trade was a pious captain holding prayer services twice a day on his slave ship and writing later the famous hymn, "Amazing Grace."

The slave trade was deserted villages, bleached bones on slave trails and people with no last names. It was Caesar African, Angelo African and African Mary.

Above all, it was Captain Tomba, who came to America, and Nealee, who didn't.

> Nealee started out but she couldn't or wouldn't make it. She was being driven to the West African coast for sale when she became ill and refused to walk another step. Mungo Park, who was one of the last persons to see Nealee, said she was put on an ass "but the ass was so very unruly, that no sort of treatment could induce him to proceed with his load; and as Nealee made no exertion to prevent herself from falling, she was quickly thrown off, and had one of her legs much bruised.
>
> Every attempt to carry her forward being thus found ineffectual, the general cry of the coffle [slave caravan] was, *kangtegi, kang-tegi,* 'cut her throat, cut her throat'; an operation I did not wish to see performed, and therefore marched onwards with the foremost of the coffle. I had not walked above a mile when one of Karfa's [the leader] domestic slaves came up to me, with poor Nealee's garment upon the end of his bow and exclaimed, 'Nealee *affeeleeta.*' (Nealee is lost.) I asked him whether the Slatees had given him the garment as a reward for cutting her throat; he replied that Karfa and the schoolmaster would

not consent to that measure, but had left her on the road; where undoubtedly she soon perished, and was probably devoured by wild beasts.

Captain Tomba, who came to America, was first seen in a slave pen in Sierra Leone. John Atkins, a surgeon who saw him there, said he was a handsome man "who scorned looking at us, refusing to rise or stretch out his limbs, as the master commanded." A few days later Captain Tomba and a companion led a revolt on a slave ship and killed three sailors before they were subdued.

What happened to Captain Tomba?

"Why," John Atkins wrote, "Captain Harding weighing the Stoutness and worth of the two slaves [Captain Tomba and a companion] did, as in other countries they do by rogues of dignity, whip and scarify them only; while three others, Abettors, but not actors, nor of strength for it, he sentenced to cruel deaths; making them first eat the heart and liver of one of them killed. The woman he hoisted up by the Thumbs, whipp'd, and slashed her with Knives, before the other Slaves till she died."

Captain Tomba living, Nealee dying, John Newton praying, the King of Barsally stealing, the fat bishop baptizing, Captain Harding torturing—these personalities and millions like them made the slave trade one of the cruelest chapters in human history.

This chapter started in the fifteenth century, but it can't be understood if it is not placed in the flow of history from which vantage point it will appear that slavery is not a disgrace peculiar to African Americans but a universal phenomenon that has been practiced in almost all countries.

Slavery was old when Moses was young. In Plato's Athens and Caesar's Rome, humans—White, Black and Brown—were bought and sold. Slavery existed in the Middle Ages in Christian Europe and in Africa. In the ancient world almost anyone might become a slave.

Slavery was so prevalent, in fact, that Plato said every person has slaves among his ancestors.

There was a crucial difference, however, between ancient slavery and modern slavery. Ancient slavery, which had little or nothing to do with race/culture, was justified primarily by the rules of war. Christians and Moslems added a new dimension to this ancient institution, capturing and enslaving one another for religious reasons. The same rationale served both groups when economic interests and improved technology focused world attention on Africa.

The Moslems got there first. For several decades before the opening of the European trade, Moslem merchants dragged dark captives across the hot Sahara sands. Then, in the fifteenth century, Portugal diverted this trade to the Atlantic. The prime mover in this development was a devout and covetous prince named Henry the Navigator. Excited by stories of the great wealth of Africa and Asia he ordered his ships to explore the coast of Africa where, on a fateful day in 1444, his men came upon the first group of Africans. The Europeans tiptoed through the high grass and crept to the edge of the village and then, said a contemporary, "they looked towards the settlement and saw that the Moors, with their women and children, were already coming as quickly as they could out of their dwellings, because they had caught sight of their enemies. But they, shouting out 'St. James,' 'St. George,' 'Portugal', attacked them, killing and taking all they could."

The pious Portuguese captured seventy more Africans, including a girl they found sleeping in a deserted village, and sailed home, where they baptized the captives and enslaved them. Within ten years Portugal was importing one thousand Africans a year. A century later Africans outnumbered Europeans in some sections of Portugal, where there was a big demand for African domestics, stevedores and agricultural laborers, especially in the southern section. "By the middle of the sixteenth century," Mary Wilhelmina Williams commented, "the inhabitants of the Algarve were largely Ethiopians, and even as far north as Lisbon, Africans outnumbered Europeans..

17

There was no marked color line, and the blood of the two races mingled freely, resulting eventually in African/Negroid physical characteristics in the Portuguese nation."

This phase of the slave trade was relatively unimportant economically. There was no widespread demand for slaves in Europe, and the number of Africans captured was relatively small. As a consequence the European monologue quickly became an African-European dialogue based on a trade in humans and goods and ideas.

Africa just then was in a state of highly unstable equilibrium. The continent had emerged from the Golden Age of the Great Empires with a number of critical problems, including climatic changes which pushed the Sahara south, triggering massive migrations and isolating large sections from the dominant currents of the age. No less obvious and ominous was the absence of modern firepower (Guns), a fact that would prove decisive in the coming confrontation with Europe.

Despite these problems, life in some African states compared favorably with life in some European states. (Europe's eminence, one must remember, came in large part after the fall of Africa and as a direct result of that fall.) In fact, in some areas, Africans were a step or two ahead. The Sudanese empire, with its showplace of Timbuktu, had passed its peak, but the ancient continent could still show Europe a thing or two.

There were large empires and populous cities, some as large as all but the largest European cities, along the coasts, and Benin and other African centers were thriving inland. In the sixteenth century, when the whole of America was a howling wilderness and large sections of the European peasantry had been reduced to beggary, Benin City was a dazzling place, twenty-five miles wide, with imposing boulevards and intersecting streets, flanked by substantial houses with balustrades and verandas.

Impressed by these and other evidences of African power, the first European emissaries greeted Africans as allies and partners in trade The letters and diaries of traders show that down to the eighteenth century they had no conception of Africans as racial pariahs. On the contrary, many of these traders said Africans were their equals and superior to many of their countrymen back home.

Africans were of substantially the same mind. They did not consider themselves inferior to Europeans. If anything, they considered themselves superior to the odd-looking men with pale skins We are told that the king of Dahomey seldom shook hands with Europeans and that when he did it was a "very uncommon mark of royal condescension." A French trader complained in 1660 that the Fanti were "so proud and haughty that a European trader there must stand bare to them."

Standing up to each other, as equals and partners in trade and commerce, both Africans and Europeans profited. Plenipotentiaries were exchanged, and bright young men of the ruling stratum went to Lisbon and Rome to study and observe. African and European kings exchanged letters filled with terms of royal endearment ("my fellow brother and my fellow queen"). They also exchanged gifts and mistresses of various hues and dispositions. On May 15, 1518, one hundred years before the Jamestown landing, Henry of the Congo led a mission to the Vatican, formally addressed the Pope in Latin and was appointed bishop of the Congo. In Rome, Lisbon and other European centers, Africans rose to high positions in the church including and state. (Editors note; In the previous centuries Africans had served as Popes in the Roman Catholic church)

In the fervor of worldwide exploration and the commingling of peoples from different lands and cultures, new vistas opened up for both Africans and Europeans It seemed for a spell that Christianity would have the same fertilizing influence in Africa in the sixteenth century that Islam had had in the eleventh and twelfth centuries. But it was not to be. While the bright young Africans were feasting in the courts of Lisbon, while the eager African priests were genuflecting in the courts of the Vatican, events were happening in the outer world that would destroy the dream and change Europe and Africa forever.

The most important of these events was the European discovery of America and the opening of the New World. It is a point of paradoxical interest that descendants of the first African captives— African Christians born in Spain and Portugal—were with the first European explorers and settlers.

Black African explorers, servants slaves, and free men, accompanied Spanish and Portuguese explorers in their expeditions in North and South America. They were with Pizarro in Peru, Cortes in Mexico and Menendez in Florida. Thirty Africans were with Balboa when he discovered the Pacific Ocean. Typical of the early African explorers in America was Estevanico, who opened up New Mexico and Arizona for the Spaniards. Other Africans, W.E.B. Du Bois said, "accompanied DeSoto and one of them stayed among the Indians in Alabama and became the first settler from the Old World."

Spaniards, who took the lead in the exploration, attempted at first to enslave Indians. But they died so fast that a famous missionary named Bishop Bartolome Las Casas recommended in 1517 the importation of Africans, a recommendation he lived to regret.

The development of large-scale sugar planting created a demand for men that casual kidnapping couldn't supply. In the wake of that development, the vision of European monarchs shifted, and the African-European dialogue became a monologue focused almost exclusively on a trade in men. Within a few years hundreds of thousands of Africans were crossing the Atlantic each year, and the soil of Africa and America was drenched with their blood. "Strange," said Eric Williams, "that an article like sugar, so sweet and necessary to human existence, should have occasioned such crimes and bloodshed!"

More than a million of these slaves found their way to the land that became the United States of America. But the first African immigrants (Antoney, Isabella, and the Jamestown group) were not slaves. This is a fact of critical importance in the history of African America. They came, these first Africans, the same way that most of the first European immigrants came, under duress and pressure. They found a system (indentured servitude) that enabled poor Europeans to come to America and sell their services for a stipulated number of years to planters.

Under this system, thousands of European paupers, ne'er-do-wells, religious dissenters, waifs, prisoners and prostitutes were shipped to the colonies and sold to the highest bidder. Many were sold, as the first Africans were sold, by the captains of ships.

Some were kidnapped on the streets of London and Bristol, as the first Africans were kidnapped in the villages of Africa.

In Virginia, then, as in other colonies, the first African settlers fell into a well-established socioeconomic groove that carried with it no implications of racial inferiority. That came later. But in the interim, a period of forty years or more, the first African settlers accumulated land, voted, testified in court and mingled with Europeans on a basis of equality. They owned other African servants, and certain Africans imported and paid for European servants whom they apparently held in servitude.

During these fateful forty years, the African population of the Virginia colony grew by natural additions and importations. In 1621 the *James* arrived from England with a number of immigrants, including an African man named Antonio. In 1623 the *Swan* arrived with still another African from England, a man named John Pedro. In 1623 or 1624, as we have seen, Isabella, the wife of Antoney, gave birth to what was probably the first African child born in America. The new child, the first of a long African line that would swell to millions, was christened William in the Church of England, and a new account was opened in the ledge book of history.

At that juncture, according to the first detailed census of 1624-25, Africans constituted about 2 percent of the total population of

1,227. The twenty-three African American pioneers—eleven males, ten females, and two children—lived in six of the twenty-three settlements in Virginia.

We can only imagine the feelings of these seminal Africans. The record burns with their presence but is strangely silent on their reactions. The African American founding fathers and mothers enter history thus: faceless men and women uprooted from Africa and flung into a maelstrom of history.

Nothing in the record indicates that the cultural shock was great for either the Europeans or Africans. There were skilled farmers and artisans among the first group of Africans, and there were indications in the record that they were responsible for various innovations later credited to English immigrants An early example of this was reported in Virginia, where the governor ordered rice planted in 1648 on the advice of "our Africans," who told the Europeans that conditions in Virginia were as favorable to the production of the crop as "in their Country."

There is furthermore the testimony of Washington Irving, who made the following observation in a contemporary satirical skit: "These Africans, like the monks of the Dark Ages, engross all the knowledge of the place, and being infinitely more adventurous and more knowing than their masters, carry on all the foreign trade; making frequent voyages in canoes, loaded with oysters, buttermilk and cabbages. They are great astrologers predicting the different changes of weather almost as accurately as an almanac."

A large proportion of the first generation of Africans entered America with Spanish names. For reasons that are not readily apparent, many Africans males were called Antonio, a name that quickly became Antoney or Anthony. Other popular names of the period were Michaela, Couchaxello, Mingo, Pedro, Francisco, Jibina, Maria, Wortello, Tomora, Angola, and Tony Kongo. Shortly after their arrival in America, many Africans discarded African and Spanish names and adopted English titles. Thus within the span of a generation the African soul moved from Africa to England to Spain to America—from the X of the severed African family tree to Antonio and the William X or the William ? of the first native American African, who apparently had no surname at the time of his christening.

During the next forty-odd years, hundreds of Africans made that extraordinary cultural leap.

In 1625 Brase, another victim of piracy, was brought into the colony. Four years later, in 1629, there was a substantial increase in the African population when the first ship from Africa arrived at Port Comfort, bringing Africans captured from a Portuguese ship off the coast of Africa In the 1630s and 1640s approximately 160 Africans were imported. By 1649 colonial officials were able to report that "there are in Virginia about fifteen thousand English, and of Africans brought thither, three hundred good servants."

The "good servants" came from different backgrounds with different experiences. Quite a few, as we have noted, came from England, where Africans had lived since the middle of the sixteenth century. Many came from Spain, Portugal and the West Indies. Significantly, many were Christians, baptized either in Spain or Portugal or on the high seas. In 1624 John Phillip testified in a Jamestown court and his testimony against a European man was admitted because he had been "christened in England twelve years since..."

In a limited but nonetheless significant sense, then, the Jamestown experience was an open experience which provided unusual opportunities for individual African.

This comes out most clearly in the life and times of Anthony Johnson, who came to America in 1621 or thereabouts from England. Like many other Africans of the period, Johnson quickly worked out his term of indenture and started accumulating property. In 1651, according to official records, he imported and paid for five servants, some of who were European, and was granted 250 acres of land on the basis of the headright system, which permitted planters to claim fifty acres of land for each individual brought to the colony.

The abstract of the deed reads as follows:

> ANTHONY JOHNSON, 250 acs. Northampton Co., 24 July 1651.....At great Naswattock Cr., being a neck of land bounded on the SW by the maine Cr. & on W.E. & N.W. by two small branches issuing out of the maine Cr. Trans. of 5 pers: Tho. Bemrose, Peter Bughby, Antho. Cripps, Jno. Gesorroro, Richard Johnson.

In the years that followed, Johnson and his relatives established one of America's first African communities on the banks of the Pungoteague River. In 1652 John Johnson, who was probably Anthony Johnson's son, imported eleven persons, most of them European American males and females, and received headrights for 550 acres adjacent to Anthony Johnson. Two years later Richard Johnson imported two European indentured servants and received one hundred acres. Here are the records of the deeds:

> JOHN JOHNSON, 550 acs. Northampton Co., 10 May 1652.....At great Naswattocks Cr., adj. 200 acs.
>
> granted to Anthony Johnson. Trans. of 11 pers: John Edward, Wm. Routh, Tho. Yowell, Fra. Maland,
>
> William Price, John Owen, Dorothy Rily, Richard Hemstead, Law, Barnes, Row. Rith Mary Johnson.
>
> RICH. Jnoson (Johnson—also given as John) African American, 100 acs.Northampton Co., 21 Nov. 1654.....
>
> On S. Side of Pongoteague Riv., Ely. upon Pocomock Nly. upon land of John Jnoson., African,
>
> Wly. upon Anto. Jnoson, African, & Sly. upon Nich. Waddilow. Trans. of 2 pers: Wm. Ames,
>
> Wm. Vincent.

The Johnson settlement at its height included only a handful of African with large holdings. Other Africans lived in integrated communities in other areas of the colony. In 1656, for instance, Benjamin Doyle received a patent for three hundred acres in Surry County.

In 1668 John Harris bought fifty acres in New Kent County; and Phillip Morgan, reflecting the optimism of the age, leased two hundred acres in York County for ninety-nine years.

One can hardly doubt, in the face of this clear evidence, that the first generation of African Americans had, as J.H. Russell noted, "about the same industrial or economic opportunities as the free European American servant."

Additional evidence of the relatively high status of the first African is to be found in colonial documents which indicate that they voted and participated in public life. It was not until 1723, in fact, that African Americans were denied the right to vote in Virginia.

According to Albert E. McKinley, Africans voted in South Carolina until 1701, in North Carolina until 1715, and in Georgia until 1754. Not only did pioneer African Americans vote, but they also held public office. There was an African American surety in York County, Virginia, in the first decades of the seventeenth century, and an African American beadle in Lancaster County, Virginia.

Nor was this sort of thing confined to Virginia. The first Africans in Massachusetts arrived in 1638 on the *Desire,* America's first slave ship, and were apparently assigned the status of indentured servants. In his classic work, *The Negro in Colonial New England,* Lorenzo J. Greene said that "until almost the end of the seventeenth century the records refer to the Africans as 'servants' not as slaves.' For some time no definite status could be assigned to incoming Africans. Some were sold for a period of time only, and like the European, indentured servants became free after their indenture."

The available evidence suggests that most of the first generation of Africans worked out their terms of servitude and were freed. A very interesting and instructive case in point is that of Richard Johnson, an African carpenter who came to Virginia in 1651 as a free man and signed a contract of indenture. Within two years Johnson was a free man. Within three years he was acquiring pounds and property and servants.

In addition to Johnson and other Africans who were freed as a matter of course, the record lists other cases in which colonial courts freed African servants Such a case was that of Andrew Moore, who migrated to Virginia and bound himself out for a term of five years. In October 1673, the General Court "ordered that the Said Moore be free from his said master, and that the Said Mr. Light pay him Corne and Clothes according to the Custome of the Country and four hundred pounds tobac and Caske for his service done him Since he was free, and pay costs."

Looking back on that age from our own, one is struck by what can only be called equality of oppression. Not the least among the things that startle us in this period is that the colony's power structure made little or no distinction between African and European servants, who were assigned the same tasks and were held in equal contempt. This has caused no end of trouble for latter-day European American historians, who have tried to explain away a record that is understandably astonishing in view of the later practices of some European Americans.

Many European American historians, for example deny that European women worked in the fields. But contemporary witnesses tell us in no uncertain terms that European women not only worked in the fields but were also flogged at colonial whipping posts. There are also court records in which European American women asked the courts to relieve them of this burden. Historian Philip A. Bruce conceded this point and commented with disapproval: "The class of European women who were required to work in the field belonged to the lowest rank in point of character; not having been born in Virginia and not having thus acquired from birth a repugnance to associations with Africans upon a footing of social equality, they yielded to the temptations of the situations in which they were placed."

There is contradictory testimony which indicates that character, Bruce to the contrary notwithstanding, had little or nothing to do with the status of European servants. "They became in the eyes of the law" J.B. McMaster said, "a slave and in both the civil and criminal codes were classed with the African and the Indian. They were worked hard, were dressed in the cast off clothes of their owners, and might be flogged as often as the master and mistress thought necessary." There is also the testimony of T.J. Wertenbaker, who said that "the indentured servants....were practically slaves, being bound to the soil and forced to obey implicitly those whom they served."

Working together in the same fields, sharing the same huts, the same situation, and the same grievances, the first African and Europeans, aristocrats accepted, developed strong bonds of sympathy and mutuality. They ran away together, played together and revolted together. They mated and married, siring a sizeable mixed population. In the process African and European servants, the majority of the colonial population, created a racial wonderland that seems somehow un-American in its lack of obsession about race and color.

There was, to be sure, prejudice then, but it was largely English class prejudice, which was distributed without regard to race, creed or color. There were also, needless to say, prejudiced individuals in the colony, but—and this is the fundamental difference between prejudice and racism—their personal quirks and obsessions were not focused and directed by the organized will of a community. The basic division at that juncture was between servants and free people, and there were Europeans and Africans on both sides of the line.

Of all the improbable aspects of this situation, the oddest to modern African Americans and European Americans is that European people did not seem to know that they were white. It appears from surviving evidence that the first European colonists had no concept of themselves as white people. The legal documents identified whites as Englishmen and/or Christians. The word *White*, with its burden of arrogance and biological pride, developed late in the century, as a direct result of slavery and the organized debasement of Africans.

The same point can be made from the other side of the line. For a long time in colonial America, there was no legal name to focus European anxiety. The first Africans were called Blackamoors, Moors, Negers and Negars. The Word *Negro,* a Spanish and Portuguese term for black, did not come into general use in Virginia until the latter part of the century.

A similar course of development was roughly characteristic of New York, where the African settlement preceded the English and the name *New York.* There are records from 1626 identifying eleven Africans, about 5 percent of the non-Indian population, who were servants of the Dutch West Indian Company. The eleven African pioneers were males, Responding to the pleas of these males, the Dutch imported three women, identified as "Angolans," in 1628.

In 1644, some eighteen years after their arrival, the "Dutch Negroes," as they were called, filed a petition for freedom, the first African American legal protest in America. The petition was granted by the Council of New Netherlands, which freed the Africans because they had served the Company seventeen or eighteen years and had been "long since promised their freedom on the same footing as other free people in New Netherlands." The eleven Africans cited in the petition were Paul d'Angola, Big Manuel, Little Manuel, Manuel de Gerrit de Rens, Simon Congo, Anthony Portuguese, Gracia, Peter Santome, John Francisco, Little Anthony and John Fort Orange. All received parcels of land in what is now Greenwich Village.

What is essential to grasp about the first Africans in New York is that they stood on the same footing as European indentured servants from the very beginning. "They had almost full freedom of motion and assembly," James Weldon Johnson wrote in *Black Manhattan*. "They were allowed to marry; wives and daughters had legal protection against the lechery of masters, and they had the right to acquire and hold property."

What has been outlined above with reference to New York and Virginia holds good also though with minor variations for other colonies, including Pennsylvania, where the system of African indentured servitude was so deeply rooted that African American servants outnumbered African American slaves at the time of the Revolution.

There were no accurate figures on the number of Africans who came to America in this period. In 1715, according to one estimate, there were 2,000 Africans and 96,000 Europeans in Massachusetts, 4,000 Africans and 27,000 Europeans in New York, 2,500 Africans and 45,800 Europeans in Pennsylvania, 9,500 Africans and 40,700 Europeans in Maryland, 23,000 Africans and 72,000 Europeans in Virginia, and 10,500 Africans and 6,250 Europeans in South Carolina.

Who were these first generation African Americans?

The answer is simple. They were *Africans*. This fact, is so big and obvious that it is easily overlooked or assumed without question. And yet it is the key to an understanding of the first and the tenth generation of African Americans. They were *Africans*: that's the fact. They were former citizens of states and principalities on the West Coast of Africa.

It is scarcely possible to understand the history of African America unless we make at the least an effort to understand that fact and the further fact that the Africans brought their mind and ethos to America with them. The important point here is that the first generation of African Americans were carriers of an African world view. They had ideas about social organization and the nature of the forces that controlled the universe. They also had technical skills, especially in the area of agriculture, which was well developed in Africa.

Although the African immigrants came from the same historical space and shared certain cultural and philosophical presuppositions, they were far from homogenous. Some came by way of Europe or the West Indies, and others came from different sections of Africa. Not only did they come from different countries and different kinship groups but they also spoke different languages. Most apparently were ordinary citizens, but some were warriors and some were from the highest ranks of African society.

This fact was noted by a number of contemporary witnesses, including Hugh Jones, who said that Africans "that have been kings and gentlemen [in their countries] are generally lazy, haughty, and obstinate." Discounting the obvious bias in that statement, it appears from this and other testimony that not a few "great men" were among the founding fathers of African American America.

There is corroborative evidence on this point from John Josselyn, an English traveler who visited Samuel Maverick of Massachusetts in 1639 and made this observation:

> The second of October, about 9 of the clock in the morning, Mr. Maverick's African woman came to my chamber window, and in her own Country language and tune sang her song very loud and shrill. Going out to her, she used a great deal of respect towards me, and willingly would have expressed her grief in English; but I apprehended it by her countenance and deportment, whereupon I repaired to my host, to learn of him the cause, and entreat him in her behalf, for that I understood before, that she had been a Queen in her own Country, and observed a very humble and dutiful garb used towards her by another Negro who was her maid.

> Mr. Maverick was desirous to have a breed of Africans, and therefore seeing she would not yield by persuasion to company with an African young man he had in his use, he commanded him, wil'd she nill'd she, to go to bed with

her, which was no sooner done, but she kicked him out again, this she took in high disdain beyond her slavery and this was the cause of her grief.

In this anonymous queen from an unnamed country, we catch a glimpse of the many people of differing ranks who were forced by history to sing their "own Countrey language and tune" in a strange land.

The dominant note in that tune from the seventeenth century to the end of slavery was resistance to European oppression.

An English traveler named Edward Kimber said it was extremely difficult to break the will and spirit of new African immigrants. "To be sure," he said, "*a new African,* if he must be broke, either from Obstinacy, or, which I am more apt to suppose, from Greatness of Soul, will require more hard Discipline than a young Spaniel; You would really be surpriz'd at their Perseverance; let an hundred Men shew him how to hoe, or drive a Wheelbarrow, he'll still take the one by the Bottom, and the other by the Wheel: and they often die before they can be conquer'd."

It was no less difficult to destroy the cultural heritage of Africans, manifested most notably in the widely reported "feasts and burials" of colonial African Americans. In 1680 the Virginia Assembly said that "the frequent meetings of considerable numbers of African American slaves under pretence of feats and burials is judged of dangerous consequence."

One of these funerals was witnessed by Henry Knight, who said it was customary in that day for African American Virginians to "sing and dance and drink the dead to his new home, which some believe to be in old Guinea."

Though the evidence is not as firm as one could with, there are indications that Africans hoped for more than a century that a miracle would enable them to return to Africa. As the years went by, with no sign of the intervention of African gods, many abandoned hope and began the long process of adapting themselves to a new situation.

The adaptation was made with a facility that gives point to Kenneth Stampp's observation that the first generation of African Americans was as prepared for freedom as the tenth generation. In addition to the Virginia cases already cited, we might add the case of the African woman who became a member of a Dorchester, Massachusetts, church three years after her arrival on the *Desire.*

By that time, 1641, there were at least forty African members of Bouweire Chapel in New Amsterdam. In the same year, two Africans, Antony van Angola and Lucie d'Angola, were married in the Dutch church in New Amsterdam. These cases were instructive, as are several others, for the light they shed on the activities of the first generation of Africans, who were slowly and painfully shaping the foundations of the African American family.

Not all Africans welcomed the newfangled rites. Large numbers, especially in the South, wooed and wed in feasts and weddings that synthesized African and European forms. An early instance of an improvised African American wedding in North Carolina was reported by Thomas Brickell, who said, with some bias, that "their marriages were generally performed among themselves, there being very little ceremony use upon that Head; for the Man makes the Woman, a Present, such as a Brass Ring or some other Toy, which she accepts of, becomes his wife...."

Such was the system called into life by the establishment of European and African fragments on the American mainland. For at least forty years—until the 1660s—this system contained the seeds of at least four alternatives. Indentured servitude could have been continued for African and European servants or both groups could have been reduced to slavery. Other options were Indian slavery and a free labor system for Africans and European, Indians and immigrants. Socioeconomic forces—a worldwide demand for sugar and tobacco and the development of capitalist planting techniques based on the use of gang labor—tilted the structure in the direction of African American slavery.

To understand this fact in its fullness, we have to notice first that the rulers of the colonies were not overly scrupulous about the color or national origin of the work force. They tried Indian slavery, and they tried to enslave European men and women. When these attempts failed, the spotlight fell on Africans, who were tried and found not wanting. How explain this?

The explanation is to be found in the situations that defined Africans and Europeans and Indians.

Europeans, to begin with, were under the protection of recognized governments; they could appeal to a monarch or to European public opinion. Europeans, moreover, were White: they could escape and blend into the crowd. Indians, too, could escape; they knew the country and their brothers were only a hill or a forest away. The European rules of the colonies also said and apparently believed that Indians tended to sicken and die under conditions of slavery.

Africans, from the standpoint of the colonial ruling class, did not have these disadvantages. They were strong: one African, the Spanish said, was worth four Indians. They were inexpensive: the same money that would buy an Irish or English servant for seven years would buy an African for life. They were visible: they could run, but they could not blend into the European crowd. Above all else, they were unprotected. And the supply, unlike the supply of Irishmen and Englishmen, seemed to be inexhaustible. The rulers of the colonies fell to thinking. Why not?

In the fateful sixties of the seventeenth century the men who ran the colonies, egged on by the slave-trading royalists of London, made a decision that would lead, step by step, to the fateful sixties of the nineteenth century and the fateful sixties of the twentieth. Heedless of the consequences, these men decided to base the American economic

system on human slavery organized around the distribution of mela-
nin in human skin. Virginia and Maryland led the way, enacting laws
in the 1660s that forbade intermarriage and made African Americans
slaves for life. Under the new dispensation, which was adopted with
minor modifications by other colonies, children born of African
women were ruled bond or free, according to the status of the mother.

Thus, European America and African America crossed a great divide.
And European America, finding itself on the other side of that
divide, found it necessary almost immediately to take two additional
steps. The first was the creation of an ideology of Racism that justified the subordination of Africans. The second, flowing with and out
of the first, was the destruction of the bonds of community between
African and European servants,

Who constituted the majority of the population. Who was responsible for this policy?

The planters, the aristocrats, the parsons, the lawyers, the founding
fathers—*the good people:* they sowed the seeds of the bitter harvest in
a painful and protracted separation movement that continued for
more than a century.

Astonishingly enough, the first rationalization for this policy was
religion. Africans, it was said, were good material for slavery because
they were "heathens." The limitations of this ideology were obvious
to almost everyone. It was not permanent; people could become
Christians, and since many more became Christians in the colonies,
planters and planter ideologists set about to find a more enduring
mark, something that could not be changed

But before this step could be taken, it was necessary to clear up certain theological difficulties. Was it not a sin to baptize slaves? This
question was debated with passion, and the Scriptures were searched
for supporting and dissenting opinions. Finally, to the surprise of
almost no one, it was decided that it was a Christian duty to bring
heathens into the fold of Christian civilization so their souls could be

cleansed and "whitened." Thus, God and profits were reconciled, as Virginia noted in its law of 1667: "The conferring of baptisme doth not alter the condition of the person as to his bondage or freedom."

After that it was easy. A series of laws stripped African slaves of all rights of personality and made color a badge of servitude. The African populations, which had grown slowly during the twilight interim of freedom, now lunged forward. In 1710 the number was fifty thousand.

When the Declaration of Independence was signed, there were a half-million.

When the Civil War opened, the twenty African seeds of Jamestown had become four million.

Where did these people come from? How did they come? Why did they come?

Most of the slaves came from an area bordering a 3,000-mile stretch on the West Coast of Africa. They came, chained two by two, left leg to right leg, from a thousand villages and towns. They came from many racial stocks and many tribes, from the spirited Hausas, the gentle Mandingos, the creative Yorubas, from the Ibos, Efiks and Krus, from the proud Fantins, the courageous Ashantis, the shrewd Dahomeans, the Binis and Senegalese. Some of these slaves were captured in African wars and sold to slave merchants, who sold them to Europeans. Many were kidnapped by Europeans and Africans. Some were sold into slavery for infractions of African laws.

Certain captives made forced marches of five hundred miles to the coast, w here they were examined like cattle and packed into the holds of ships. They came, on these forced marches, across rivers and over mountains, barefooted and naked to their enemies, with chains on their ankles, burdens on their heads and fear in their hearts.

Were they—these African people who gave to the world the African American—were they the dregs of society? No. The strong came and the weak, too. Priests, princes, warriors, merchants, and nobles came. Slave traders said that it was not at all unusual for an African to sell an African today and to be captured and sold tomorrow. The story is told of a major slave merchant who sold a parcel of slaves and unwisely accepted a social drink to seal the transaction. One drink led to another and to America. The slave merchant woke up the next morning with a hangover and a brand on his chest. He was in the hold of a slave ship with his victims and over him stood the captain, laughing to beat the band.

This story underlines a rather obvious fact: Africans as well as Europeans were involved in the slave trade. There has been a systematic attempt, however, to overemphasize the degree of African involvement. The picture of a whole continent of Africans kidnapping and selling one another for rum, guns and gewgaws is wide of the mark. It is true that some Africans, corrupted by Europe's insatiable desire for human flesh, sold their countrymen.

But many Africans, like King Almamm and Captain Tomba, loathed the whole business and forbade their subjects to take part in it. To cite only one example, Mani-Congo, the ruler of a Congo state, tried to end the trade in 1526. In a strong letter to John III of Portugal, he said "we need from [your] kingdoms no other than priests and people to teach in schools, and no other goods but wind and flour for the hold sacrament; that is why we beg of Your Highness to help and assist us in this matter, commanding the factors that they should send here neither merchants nor wares, because it is our will that in these kingdoms [of the Congo] there should not be any trade in slaves or markets for slaves."

This would be a different world in Mani-Congo's plea for "Point IV aid" had been heeded in the sixteenth century. But Europe was impervious to such pleas. She was only interested in the gold of African bodies, and she forced that obsession on Africa—to the undoing of both Europe and Africa.

European nations fought one another for the privilege of managing this trade. Portugal, which ran the first leg, was ousted by Holland which in turn surrendered supremacy on the African coast to France and England. Portugal, one trader said, "served for setting dogs to spring the game." Once the game was sprung, all Europe rushed to the playing field. Spain, barred from Africa by a papal bull which gave her most of the New World, made money by giving other powers a contract to supply her colonies with slaves. This contract, the infamous asiento, was the national status symbol of the day, indicating commercial and political supremacy. In the eighteenth century, when England held the asiento, the slave trade was the basis of European commerce, the cause of most of her wars and the prize politicians competed for.

An intricate set of trading arrangements existed on the Guinea Coast (the West Coast of Africa) for processing Africans bought and stolen. Europeans—French, Swedish, Danish, Portuguese, Dutch, English and Prussian traders—dotted the coast with forts and factories. Each fort and factory had a dungeon or "Negroe House," where slaves were confined until shipment. Into these factories Europeans poured a steady stream of goods—colorful cloth, trinkets, rum and "other strong water," blankets, old sheets—that were converted into human beings. Europeans, operating as representatives of powerful companies or as private entrepreneurs, bartered these goods for men and women. A woman might change hands for a gallon of brandy and six beads. A man might bring eight guns, a wicker bottle, two cases of whiskey and twenty-eight old sheets.

Slaves were purchased from brokers at the forts and factories or in open markets. An appalling report on conditions in these open markets has come down to us. "As the slaves come down to Fida from the inland country," trader John Barbot said, "they are put into a booth, or prison, built for that purpose, near the beach, all of them together; and when the Europeans are to receive them, they are brought out into a large plain, where the surgeons examine every part of every one of them, to the smallest member, men and women being all stark naked.

Such as are allowed good and sound are set on one side, and the others by themselves; which slaves so rejected are there called Mackrons, being above thirty-five years of age, or defective in their limbs, eyes or teeth; or grown grey, or that have the venereal disease, or any other imperfection. These being so set aside, each of the others, which have passed as good, is marked on the breast, with a red-hot iron, imprinting the mark of the French, English or Dutch companies....In this particular, care is taken that the women, as tenderest, be not burnt too hard."

The newly purchased slaves, properly branded and chained, were then rowed out to the slave ships for the dreaded Middle Passage across the Atlantic. They were packed like books on shelves into holds, which in some instances were no higher than eighteen inches. "They had not so much room," one captain said, "as a man in his coffin, either in length or breadth. It was impossible for them to turn or shift with any degree of ease." Here, for the six to ten weeks of the voyage, the slaves lived like animals. Under the best conditions, the trip was intolerable. When epidemics of dysentery or smallpox swept the ships, the trip was beyond endurance.

"On many of these ships," a contemporary said, "the sense of misery and suffocation was so terrible in the 'tween-decks—where the height sometimes was only eighteen inches, so that the unfortunate slaves could not turn round, were wedged immovably, in fact, and chained to the deck by the neck and legs—that the slaves not infrequently would go mad before dying or suffocating. In their frenzy some killed others in the hope of procuring more room to breathe. Men strangled those next to them, and women drove nails into each other's brains." It was common, John Newtown said, to find a dead slave and a living slave chained together. So many dead people were thrown overboard on slavers that it was said that sharks picked up ships off the coast of Africa and followed them to America.

Not all Africans came this way. There was a trickle of free immigrants from the West Indies, and some Africans got on boats in Africa and paid their way to America. In 1772, for instance, the governor of Georgia issued a certificate to Fenda Lawrence, "a free African American woman and heretofore a considerable trader in the river Gambia on the coast of Africa [who] hath voluntarily come to be and remain for some time in this province." The certificate gave Miss Lawrence permission to "pass and repass unmolested within the said province on her lawful and necessary occasions." Fenda Lawrence, of course, was an exception. Most Africans came by the millions and millions in chains, followed by wise and greedy sharks.

The survivors of this grueling ordeal were sold either on the ships or in slave markets in American ports. In New England, where there was a large "retail" demand, slaves were sold in taverns, stores and warehouses. They were also "shown," as the ads put it, in the homes of merchants. It was common for merchants to sell Africans and Europeans, liquor and clothing. A typical advertisement of the times indicates the general tendency:

> "Several Irish Maid Servants time/most of them for Five Years one/Irish Man Servant—one who is a good/Barber and Wiggmaker/also Four or Five Likely African boys."

The price of men, like the price of butter, fluctuated. In 1754 George Washington bought a male slave for $260. But when he went to the market ten years later, he had to pay $85. Slaves were sold for small down payments and "on reasonable terms." An advertisement of 1726 noted that "the Buyer shall have 3,6,9 or 12 months Credit." There was also a mail-order business. One New Englander made the following entry in his diary: "I wrote Mr. Salmon of Barbadoes to send me an African."

The human factories in Africa struggled to keep up with the demand. In the eighteenth century between fifty thousand and one hundred thousand slaves crossed the Atlantic each year. The greatest number, by far, went to the West Indies and Brazil. At least two million were shipped to the West Indies. Joao Pandia Calogeras, the Brazilian historian, said at least eighteen million were shipped to Brazil.

Large blocks of slaves were dropped off in Spanish colonies in the Caribbean and in Central and South America. As early as 1553 there were twenty thousand Africans in Mexico. Some two hundred thousand slaves were imported before slavery was abolished in Mexico in the first quarter of the nineteenth century.

Hundreds of thousands of slaves were scattered over the areas of present-day Panama, Columbia, Ecuador, Chile, Peru, and Venezuela. In 1810 Venezuela had some 500,000 Africans in a total population of 900,000. In 1847 there were 496,000 Africans and only 418,000 Europeans in Cuba. In the same year there were 4,400,000 Africans in Brazil's population of 7,360,000.

Because of widespread amalgamation and unreliable census data, it is difficult to assess the impact of these millions on South American life. But in some South American countries people with "African blood" still comprise a considerable proportion of the population.

What Gilberto Freyre, the Brazilian sociologist and philosopher said of Brazil is true for large areas of the New World: "Every Brazilian, even if he is light skinned and has fair hair, bears in his soul…the shadow or the mark of the native or the African….The influence of the African is direct or vague and remote. In our way of expressing tenderness, in our excessive mimicry, in our Catholicism which is a delight of the senses, in our way of walking and talking, in the songs which cradle our childhood, in short in all the sincere expressions of our life, the African influence is patent."

For the human beings involved, the slave trade was a stupendous roulette wheel. The boats fanned out from Africa and scattered human freight over the Western Hemisphere. Around and around the wheel went, stopping here and there, sealing, wherever it stopped, the fate of mothers and fathers and their children to the ninth generation.

It made a great deal of difference to the slaves where the dice of fate fell, whether they landed, for example, in a country where the word was the Spanish *yo* or the French *je* or the English I, slavery, to be sure, was a form of hell wherever it existed. But there were gradations of hell, Dantesque circles, as it were, within circles. By all accounts, the British-Protestant colonies were the deepest pit. The French and Spanish could be cruel, and often were. But they didn't seem to be driven by the same demons that pursued the English Puritans.

For this reason, among others, African religious practices and other elements of African culture were not as vigorously opposed in Roman Catholic colonies as they were in the Protestant colonies. The Protestant colonies, with an instinct for the jugular vein, rode herd on tom-toms and joyful noises unto the Lord. The difference this made in social cohesion is roughly the difference between the successful Haitian Revolution and abortive Nat Turner insurrection. The final meeting of the Haitian Revolution was held at a voodoo ceremony and the signal went out by tom-toms. Another difference, minor perhaps, but important to the people involved, was the texture of the different societies. The Catholic colonies were gay and colorful; the Protestant colonies, by comparison, were a dull shade of gray.

One of the dominant characteristics of the Roman Catholic colonies was the relative absence of color prejudice. One result was that the life of a slave in these colonies was less hopeless and unhappy than the life of a slave in, say South Carolina. There were other differences

Manumission was easier in Brazil and Spanish America, and a manumitted slave inherited the rights and privileges of citizens. There were several ways in which a slave could win freedom in these colonies. If he earned his purchase price, he could walk up to his master and hand him the money and the master had to accept it. Another means of salvation was childbearing. If slave parents had ten children in Hispanic America, the whole family was freed.

The difference between Hispanic America and Protestant America reduced itself, as so many racial problems do, to the problem of sex. The Spanish and Portuguese were willing to marry Africans. In America, European American men drew the line—at marriage, that is.

Surface differences apart, slavery was a dirty business in both Hispanic and Protestant America. In both areas slaves were given a new conception of themselves—according to the different lights of their captors. This process, whether it took place in liberal Brazil or harsh South Carolina, was a painful, mind-reversing operation in which two or three out of every ten died.

In one form or another, every slave from Africa went through this "breaking-in" period. During this period, which varied from one to three years, the slave was taught pidgin English or French or Spanish. He got a new name and began to look at himself and others in a different manner. Yahweh took the place of Olorum; Legba became St. Peter; the Mass or hymnal replaced African rituals.

The strain was too much for tens of thousands, who died of old and new diseases and the shock of physical mutilation. But millions of others, testifying to physical and spiritual strength that transcended the heroic, survived. And, surviving, they ensured the survival—and prosperity—of America, which fashioned out of their misery the take-off capital that made American capitalism possible. Many of the first great American fortunes, in fact, were founded on the slave trade and its allied industries. By the American Revolution, as Dr. Lorenzo J. Greene has shown, the slave trade "formed the very basis of the economic life of New England; about it revolved, and on it depended, most of her other industries."

The same situation obtained in England, France, Holland, Spain, and Portugal. In these countries, as in New England, the slave trade provided direct returns to financiers and investors and stimulated the growth of ancillary industries, such as shipbuilding and distilleries.

"This contribution of the African," Eric Williams wrote, "has failed to receive adequate recognition...England and France, Holland, Spain and Denmark, not to mention the United States, Brazil and other parts of South America are all indebted to African labor."

Africans helped build Liverpool, Nantes, and Newport. They helped finance the Industrial Revolution. They helped clear the forest in America. They made these enormous contributions, but the price—to them and to American and Europeans—was frightfully high, and it was not paid without protest.

Protests began in Africa, where mutinies on ships were common, and continued in America, where revolts were common. "The Africans," Captain Thomas Phillips said, "are so willful and loth to leave their own country, that they have often leap'd out of the canoes, boat and ship, into the sea, and kept underwater where they were drowned, to avoid being taken up and saved by our boats, which pursued them; they having a more dreadful apprehension of Barbadoes than we can have of hell, tho' in reality they live much better there than in their own country; but home is home, etc."

Home being home, etc., many slaves revolted, brained the captain and crew and escaped to the shore. Rebellions on ships were so common that a new form of insurance, insurrection insurance was introduced.

Many slaves refused to eat when well and refused to take medicine when ill. One man, for instance, attempted to cut his throat. After the wound was sewed up, he ripped out the sutures with his fingernails. He was patched up again but refused to eat and died ten days later of starvation.

This resistance—desperate, doomed, definitive—continued throughout the slaving period. A long series of conspiracies and revolts culminated in the great Haitian Revolution, which played an important part in the abolition of the trade. Pushed by fear of the unmanageable slaves and pulled by humanitarian motives stemming from the American and French revolutions, politicians abolished the trade in the first decades of the nineteenth century. It continued surreptitiously, However, until the abolition of slavery in the United States.

The slave trade left a blood-stained legacy. During the four hundred years the trade was pursued, it wrecked the social and economic life of Africa, set nation against nation and village against village. The trade was no less disastrous in Europe and America where it left a legacy of ill will and guilt and a potentially explosive racial/cultural problem.

"Raphael painted, W.E.B. DuBois said, "Luther preached, Corneille wrote, and Milton sang; and through it all, for four hundred years, the dark captives wound to the sea amid the bleaching bones of the dead; for four hundred years the sharks followed the scurrying ships; for four hundred year America was strewn with the living and dying millions of a transplanted race; for four hundred years Ethiopia stretched forth her hands unto God."

Chapter Three
Behind the Cotton Curtain

For two hundred and forty six years African and African American men and women were held in bondage in America. During these years "a social system as coercive as any yet known" was erected on the framework of "the most implacable race consciousness yet observed in virtually any society." A curtain of cotton rang down on some four million human beings.*It became a crime to give them a Bible.

Behind this cotton curtain four million human beings were systematically deprived of every right of personality. Vice, immorality, and brutality were institutionalized. The sanctity of the family was violated; children were sold from mothers, and fatherhood, in effect, was outlawed. The rape of a sale woman, a Mississippi court ruled, is an offense unknown to common or civil law. The "father of a slave," a Kentucky court ruled; "is unknown to our law."

Out of this system came the African American and though some would like to forget it, the

European American; for everyone, African and European, free and slave, slaveholder and non slaveholder, was stained by it. And it is not possible to know much about Africans and Europeans unless one knows a little about those terrible two hundred and forty six years through which they came together. "The pro-slavery theory of the ante-bellum South," Gunnar Myrdal said, "is basic to certain ideas, attitudes, and policies prevalent in all fields of human relations even at the present time."

It is fashionable, for many years to view this era through the astigmatic lenses of Gone with the Wind.

A radical reevaluation in Scholarly circles has largely destroyed that myth. Although a number of European American scholars have tried to pump new life into the old and discredited myth with computer printouts and other scholarly sleight of hand, it is established by irrefutable evidence that the story of slave resistance was a moving and instructive chapter in the history of mankind.

Historian Kenneth M. Stampp, whose book (*The Peculiar Institution*) helped shape the new interpretation, said: "The record of slave resistance forms a chapter in the story of the endless struggle to give dignity to human life. Though the history of southern bondage reveals that men can be enslaved under certain conditions, it also demonstrates that their love of freedom is hard to crush. The subtle expressions of this spirit, no less than the daring thrusts for liberty comprise one of the richest gifts the slaves have left to posterity

Let us go back in time to the peculiar institution which stamped these people.

Let us feel the lash which broke their skins and sing the Spirituals that soothed their hearts:

Let us visit the houses and fields where the trouble started.

The big White house stands in colonnaded splendor on a hill which overlooks field fleeced with cotton or lined with tobacco or sugar cane or rice. Near this house, which oftentimes was neither big nor very White, huddle two rows of "log-and-daub" cabins. Other houses and buildings dot the landscape; the overseer's quarters, the stables, the corn cribs, the gin and press. The center of this agricultural factory is the "big house." From it radiate like spokes the fields and gardens: the sweet potato field, the watermelon patch, the cornfield, the pews of cotton or sugar cane or tobacco or rice.

This is a plantation. This is where the trouble started.

Not all African Americans were slaves; there was a substantial free population even in the South.

Nor did all slaves work on plantations; some five hundred thousand worked in cities as domestics, skilled artisans and factory hands. But they were exceptions to the general rule. Most African Americans were slaves on plantations-sized units in seven states of the Deep South.

Plantations and planters varied. There were small farmers with two or three slaves, planters with ten to thirty slaves and big planters who owned a thousand or more slaves. Scholars generally agree that slaves received better treatment on small farms and plantations that didn't employ overseers or general managers. But almost half of the slaves lived, worked and died on plantations where the owners delegated much of their authority to overseers. Of much more pointed social relevance is the fact that the plantation and its fleecy flower, King Cotton, gave tone and direction to the whole society.

The plantation was a combination factory, village and police precinct. Its most conspicuous external characteristic was totalitarian regimentation. One manifestation of this, to begin with slave children, was a communal nursery that prepared slave children for slavery and made it possible for their mothers to work in the fields. The woman who cared for African American children was commonly designated "aunty" to distinguish her from the "mammy," the nurse of European American children. Sometimes one woman cared for both European American and African American children.

Children, boys and girls, flopped around in a state of near-nudity until they reached the age of toil. On some plantations they were issued two-linen shirts; on others they wore guano bags with holes punched in them for the head and arms. Children were never issued shoes until they were sent to fields, usually at the age of six or seven. Young workers were broken in as water boys or in the "trash gang." At the age of ten or twelve, children, boys and girls, were given a regular field routine.

"Children had to go to the fiel' at six on our place," a former slave recalled. "Maybe they don't do nothin' but pick up stones or tote water, but they got to get used to bein' there. Uncle Zack…had a twisted leg Used to set in the shade lookin' at the children goin' to the field and mutter, 'Slave young, slave long.'"

Cooking, in many instances, was also a collective project. On most plantations food was prepared in a common kitchen and sent to the workers in the field. In most cases, however, slaves were expected to cook the evening meal in their cabins.

The food, which was issued once a week, was generally coarse and lacking in variety. The usual allocation was peck of corn and three or four pounds of bacon or salt pork. Fractional amounts, usually one-half, were allotted to each child in the family. Most slaves supplemented this meager fare by trapping coons and opossums in the fields or by "stealing" corn from the master's corn cribs and chickens from his chicken coops. Slaves, it should be noted, made a distinction between "taking" and "staling." It was considered right and proper to "take anything that belonged to European American folk." It was considered wrong to "steal" the property of other slaves.

Twice a year the regimented slave was issued a clothes ration. A South Carolina planter described a typical allowance in his plantation manual: "Each man gets in the fall 2 shirts of cotton drilling, a pair of woolen pants and a woolen jacket. In the spring 2 shirts of cotton shirting and 2 pr. of cotton pants.…Each woman gets in the fall 6 yds. of woolen cloth, 6 yds. of cotton drilling and a needle, skein of thread and 1/2 dozen buttons. In the spring 6 yds. of cotton shirting and 6 yds. of cotton cloth similar to that for men's pants, needle thread and buttons. Each worked gets a stout pr. of shoes every fall, an a heavy blanket every third year.

Clothes came in two sizes, large and small, and women and men were apparently issued the same kind of shoes. Former slaves said "the slave brogans" burned and blistered in the summer and "got stiff as a board in cold weather." On some plantations the same man shod slaves and horses. West Turner, who was a slave in Virginia, remembered Old Black Jack Fly, a Blacksmith, who would "trace yo' foot in the dirt with a stick, but it didn't do no good, 'cause he ain't never made the shoes like the dirt say."

Most slaves lived in family-type cabins, but some lived in large barracks "literally alive with slaves of all ages, conditions and size." Some of the family cabins were two-and three-room brick or frame structures with windows and brick fireplaces. The vast majority, however, were rickety structures, built flat on the ground. It was a common procedure to put five or six slaves into one room. "Everything," a former slave said, "happened in that one room—birth, sickness, death—everything."

There was considerable specialization on larger plantations. The basic division in the work force was between field slaves, who, as the name implies, worked in the fields, and house slaves, who worked in and around the house (maids, cooks, butlers) or performed services as specialists (nurses, gardeners). Although work in and around the house was generally lighter, it brought disadvantages, including constant surveillance by European Americans and the psychic tension of wearing a public mask.

For this reason, and others as well, many slaves preferred field work to house work, a fact noted by Frederick Law Olmsted, who said: "Slaves brought up to house work dread to be employed at field-labor, and those accustomed to the comparatively unconstrained life of the African American-settlement detest the close control and careful movements required of the house-servants. It is a punishment for a lazy field-hand to employ him in menial duties at the house… and it is equally a punishment to a neglectful house-servant, to banish him to the field-gangs."

In addition to house slaves and field slaves, there was another and different layer composed for the most part of highly skilled technicians, such as engineers, millwrights and master carpenters. From this layer came the men who were largely responsible for the construction and maintenance of antebellum mansions and plantation mills and machinery.

"Such slaves," according to the Atlanta University study, *The Negro Artisan*, "were especially valuable and formed usually a privileged class, with a larger degree of freedom…Many if not most of the noted leaders of the African American in earlier times belonged to this slave mechanic class, such as [Denmark] Vesey, Nat Turner, Richard Allen and Absalom Jones. They were exposed neither to the corrupting privileges of the house servants nor to the blighting tyranny of field work and had large opportunity for self development." There is furthermore the testimony of J.D. Smith, an engineer who learned his trade from a slave engineer: "One only needs to go down South and examine hundreds of old Southern mansions, and splendid old church edifices, still intact, to be convinced of. the cleverness of the African American artisans, who constructed 90% of them."

At the apex of the European American-imposed slave structure was an ambiguous figure called the driver, an unambiguous title which pointed to the function, driving slaves in the fields and maintaining order in the quarters. Feared and detested by most slaves, the driver was an integral part of the plantation command structure, holding a position roughly comparable to a master sergeant under a lieutenant (overseer), under a captain (slaveholder).

When there were two or more drivers, one was named head driver. "The head driver," one planter said, "is the most important African American on the plantation, and is not required to work like other hands. He is to be treated with more respect than any other African

American by both master and overseer…He is to be required to maintain proper discipline at all times; to see that no slave idles or does bad work in the field, and to punish it with discretion.

The operative words here are "with discretion." Real, that is to say, instructive punishment was administered and/or supervised by the slave master or overseer. The usual punishment was thirty-nine lashed with a cow skin whip. It was not unusual, however, for slaves to receive one hundred or more lashes. And few slaves, no matter how obedient or humble, reached old age without receiving at least one lashing. As one would expect, psychotic and sadistic masters added embellishments. But even "kind" slave masters whipped the skin off the backs of slaves and washed them down with brine.

The most common "offense" was impudence. And what was impudence? "Impudence," Frederick Douglass said, "might mean almost anything, or nothing at all, just according to the caprice of the master or overseer at the moment. But, whatever it is, or is not, if it gets the name of 'impudence,' the party charged with it is sure of a flogging. This offense may be committed in various ways; in the tone of an answer; in answering at all; in not answering; in the expression of the countenance; in the motion of the head; in the gait manner of the slave."

There was method in this seeming madness, which was designed, at least in part, to keep slaves off balance. And the method was reinforced by the bells, horns and military formations of plantation life. One need only read Charley Williams's classic description to pick up the tempo of that life.

"When the day begin to crack, the whole plantation brake out with all kinds of noises, and you could tell what was going on by the kind of noise you hear.

"Come the daybreak you hear the guinea fowls start potracking down at the edge of the woods lot, and then the roosters all start up round the barn, and the ducks finally wake up and join in. You can smell the sowbelly frying down at the cabins in the Row, to go with the hoecake and the buttermilk.

"Then pretty soon the wind rise a little, and you can hear a old bell donging way on some plantation a mile or two off and then more bells at other places and maybe a horn, and pretty soon yonder go Old Master's old ram horn with a long toot and then some short toots, and here come the overseer down the row of cabins, hollering right an left, and picking the ham outen his teeth with a long shiny goose-quill pick."

"Bells and horns! Bells for this and horns for that! All we knowed was go and come by the bells and horns!"

Generally speaking, the horn (that old fo' day horn) or bell sounded about four in the morning. Thirty minutes later the field hands were expected to be out of their cabins and on the way to the fields. Stragglers and late sleepers were lashed with the whip. An eyewitness recalled seeing women scurrying to the field "with their shoes and stockings in the hands, and a petticoat wrapped over their shoulders, to dress in the fields the best way they could." Overseers and drivers, armed with whips, drove the work force. The overseer sometimes carried a bowie knife and a pistol. He often rode a horse, accompanied by a vicious dog.

Solomon Northup, a free African American who was kidnapped and sold into slavery, said the hands worked steadily and "with the exception of ten or fifteen minutes, which is given them at soon to swallow their allowance of cold bacon, they are not permitted to be a moment idle till it is too dark to see, and when the moon is full, they often labor till the middle of the night." Another former slave said that it seemed that the fields stretched "from one end of the earth to the other."

Men, women and children worked in these fields. Women cut down trees, dug ditches, and plowed. The old and the ailing worked, oftentimes in the yards, feeding poultry, cleaning up, mending clothes and caring for the infants and the sick.

Male and female, the quick and the halt worked the traditional hours of slavery—from can (see) to can't (see).

What happened at the end of the day?

Former slaves said the day never really ended. After work, to quote Northup again, "each must then attend to his respective chores. One feeds the mules, another the swine—another cuts the wood, and so forth…Finally, at a late hour, they reach the quarters, sleepy and overcome with the long day's toil. then a fire must be kindled in the cabin, the corn ground in the small handmill, and a supper, and dinner for the next day in the field prepared…By this time, it is usually midnight."

"The same fear of punishment…possesses them again on lying down to get a snatch of rest. It is the fear of oversleeping in the morning. Such an offense would certainly be attended with not less than twenty lashes. With a prayer that he might be on his feet and wide awake at the first sound of the horn, he sinks to his slumbers nightly."

Fear, toil, the lash, hard words, a little ash cake and bacon, and fields stretching "from one end of the earth to the other"—such was life for most slaves, day in and day out, season after season, with a half-day off on Saturday perhaps and a whole day off on Sunday. Small wonder that the burdened bondsmen eased his weary frame down and addressed God in stark eloquence:

> *Come day,*
> *Go day,*
> *God send Sunday.*

If all this was designed to rush the spirit of the slaves, it had precisely the opposite effect.

For the slaves, in the most astonishingly creative act in our history, transcended their environment, creating a new structure of meaning and putting their oppressors and the world in their debt. No one can read the record of that transcendence without a sense of awe at the audacity of the slaves' hope.

This hope was clearly visible in the concentric circles of community that started in the family and radiated in larger and larger circles that enveloped the whole of Slave Row. From that community came the rhythmic, spiritual and psychic piles that bottomed the new synthesis called African America. The results—the Spirituals, the blues, the rhythmic tonality of African America—point to and guarantee the medium, which was a community of passion and creativity.

This community was a product of the plantation, but it was neither defined nor contained by the plantation. On the contrary, it was defined by difference, by the fact that it contradicted and called into question the values and institutions of the plantation. The fundamental difference was orientation.

The community of slaves was a communal entity characterized by a collective orientation stemming partly from the African past and partly from the exigencies of the situation. Unlike the slaveholder community, it was orientated toward freedom, toward freedom of the body and soul, which were not defined as two different things but as two aspects of the same thing.

Although the slave community was located in Slave Row, the prototype of the Harlems and South Sides of today, it was not defined by the geography of any one Slave Row. Like the invisible church of slavery, the community was everywhere and nowhere, which is to say that it was a being which inhabited the slave and move with him through time and space. Unwittingly and with the worst of motives, slaveowners furthered and deepened this reality by selling and shipping slaves from one Slave Row to another, from one state or region to another.

Because the bridges of the slave community were stronger than the chasms of plantation society, all slaves, house and field, artisan and laborer, participated in this reality. These bridges were based on the strongest of all human needs, the imperative need for a home place for the heart. No matter how many airs the house slaves might put on, they knew, and their slavemasters knew, that the only real home they had on the plantation was in the quarters, where they could drop their masks and stretch out their legs and souls.

"House servant and field hand might meet there," the authors of *The Negro in Virginia* wrote, "and the testimony of the living ex-slave does not support the tradition of animosity between the two. House servants would regale other members of the 'row,' some of whom had never set foot in the 'big house,' with tales of 'master' and 'missus,' would 'take them off' in speech and gesture so faithful that the less privileged would shake with laughter."

The words *less privileged* are questionable in view of the fact, already noted, that many slaves didn't consider it a privilege to work in the house. And it appears from this quotation and from the contemporary views of slaves and slaveowners that many house slaves realized the limitations of their alleged privileges. The evidence for this is chiefly in the fact that house slaves ran away and attacked slavemasters directly with blows and indirectly with poison and fire.

Subject to the same oppression and sharing the same interests, slaves of all ranks were bonded together by a common commitment to a common cause. This was clear to both African American and European American contemporaries. In 1842, for instance, a hostile European American witness named Charles C. Jones noted:

> "The African Americans are scrupulous on one point: they make common cause, as servants, on concealing their faults from their owners. Inquiry elicits no information; no one feels at liberty to disclose the transgressor; all are profoundly ignorant; *the matter assumes the sacredness of a 'professional secret'*; for they remember that they may hereafter require the same concealment of their own transgressions from their fellow servants, and if they tell

upon them now, they may have the like favor returned them; besides, in the meantime, having their names cast out as evil from among their brethren; and being subjected to scorn, and perhaps personal violence or pecuniary injury (emphasis added)."

There is corroboration on this point in a Tennessee court case of a slave named Jim, who killed a slave named Isaac for betraying him after his escape. At the trial the judge noted that "Isaac seems to have lost caste....He had combined with the European folks...no slight offense in their eyes; that one of their own color, subject to a like servitude, should abandon the interests of his caste, and betray African American folks to the European American people, rendered him an object of general aversion."

In this case, as well as in the acts and words of both slaves and slaveholders, we find most conclusive proof of the dominating influence of the counter-community of the slaves.

The status hierarchy of this community was composed of ascending levels that paralleled and challenged the plantation-imposed hierarchy. Although slavemasters tried to make drivers the leading figures of Slave Row, the influence of these functionaries seldom exceeded the circles of European American power they reflected. The slaves instead looked to natural leaders who received their credentials from age, wisdom, strength, and the world of the spirits.

One slaveholder said it was a "a notorious fact" that "on almost every large plantation of African Americans, there is one among them who holds a kind of magical sway over the minds and opinions of the rest; to him they look as their oracle....The influence of such an African American, often a preacher, on a quarter is incalculable." Such a person was "Old Abram" a plantation patriarch who was said to be "deeply versed in such philosophy as is taught in the cabin of the slave."

The slaves also had their own specialists in matters of decorum, dress, worship, and marriage.

Significantly, the slave community was totally democratic in the sense that the highest roles were open to female talent. A Louisiana planter noted that a slave woman called Big Lucy was an indigenous leader who "corrupts every young African American in her power." On a South Carolina plantation, a leader named Sinda prophesied the end of the world and for a long time no slave on the plantation would work.

There was also an interesting and significant circle of elders, who occupied a position in slave society roughly equivalent to the position of the elders in West African society. The influence of this institution was mot clearly visible in the status of older slaves, commonly called uncle or aunt, who were revered and respected on almost all plantations. The best description of the institution is in the narrative of Frederick Douglass:

> "These mechanics were called 'Uncles' by all the younger slaves, not because they really sustained that relationship to any, but according to plantation etiquette, as a mark of respect, due from the younger to the older slaves. Strange, and even ridiculous as it may seem among a people so uncultivated, and with so many stern trials to look in the face, there is not to be found, among any people, a more rigid enforcement of the law of respect to elders…A young slave must approach the company of the elder with hat in hand, and woe betide him if he fails to acknowledge a favor, of any sort, with the accustomed 'tankee' etc."

The roles in the slave community were organized into institutions or proto-institutions. There were institutions, i.e., organized patterns of behavior, for maintaining community standards, for dealing with the slavemaster, for inducting new members into the group, and for expressing the soul and style of the people. Some of thee institutions were more or less direct translations of African institutions. Others were creative blending of African and European forms. Still others were free improvisations on European themes.

The energies flowing through these forms organized themselves around three axial forces. The first, of course, was the axis of the spirit. In this realm, as in others, the slaves reinterpreted European American patterns, weaving a whole new universe around biblical images and giving a new dimension and new meaning to Christianity. This enormous achievement, which astonished Arnold J. Toynbee and other historians, contradicted the religion taught the slaves. That religion was a censored pablum which dwelt almost always on the duties of patience and obedience. J.W. Fowler of Coahoma County, Mississippi, told his overseer that he had no objection to his slaves hearing the gospel if they heard it in its "original purity and simplicity." What did this mean? Ephesians 6:5, usually: "Servants, be obedient to them that are your masters....

American slaves, with few exceptions, rejected this version of Christianity. Their God was the God who delivered the Israelites.

> *Didn't my Lord deliver Daniel,*
> *And why not every man.*

In a total and passionate quest for this God, the slaves, tempered and toughened by the annealing heat of adversity, turned American Christianity inside out, like a glove, infusing it with African-oriented melodies and rhythms and adding new patterns, such as the ring shout, ecstatic seizure and communal call-and-response patterns. The seeds sown here produced a new synthesis, which colored and changed the European original. The new creation surfaced first in the invisible church of slavery, which centered in the portable "hush-harbors."

We get a glimpse of these "hush-harbors" in a description in Peter Randolph's book, *From Slave Cabin To Pulpit*:

> "Not being allowed to hold meetings on the plantations, the slaves assembled in the swamps, out of reach of the patrols. They have an understanding among themselves as to the time and place of getting together. This is often

one by the first one arriving breaking boughs from the trees and bending them in the direction of the selected spot. Arrangements are then made for conducting the exercises. They first ask each other how they feel, the state of their minds, etc.

The male members then select a certain space, in separate groups, for their division of the meeting. Preaching in order, by the brethren; then praying and singing all around, until they generally feel quite happy. The speaker usually commences by calling himself unworthy, and talks very slowly, until, feeling the spirit, he grows excited, and in a short time, there fall to the ground twenty or thirty men and women under it's influence."

Important as this institution was, it is necessary to perceive it in proper perspective. For it was only one element in a complex world view that included spirits that were not visible to European American Christians. And so, to mention only the most obvious fact, many American slaves believed in Jesus and an overlapping world of spirits who could be manipulated and persuaded to serve the living. Hence, the widespread belief in "haunts," charms and taboos.

Undergirding all this, undergirding everything, in fact, was the second great axis of music and rhythm. This axis, which informed every element of slave life, was characterized by the so-called "blues" tonality and a rhythmic, collective and emotional orientation. The same elements are evident in slave folklore and philosophy, especially the Brer Rabbit, Brer Fox and Old John cycles.

The expressions of this orientation were as varied as the people and included cries, hollers, work songs, devil songs, Spirituals and blues. There have been repeated attempts by latter-day students to separate these expressions, and the people who created them, into blues archetypes and Spiritual archetypes. But the slave world view was anti-dichotomies and recognized no such distinction, and it is almost certain that both the Spirituals and the blues were products of a common blues-Spiritual matrix.

This totality—America's only original contribution to the world of music—was a collective product, but was shaped by creative geniuses, by men and women of large vision and even larger voices, men and women immortalized by James Weldon Johnson in the poem, "O Black and Unknown Bards."

The mood and meaning of the products they created varied, as we can see if we look for a moment at the Spirituals. There were coded Spirituals of protest and defiance, based on the passion and eventual triumphs of the Hebrew slaves of Egypt.

> *Oh, Mary, don't you weep, don't you moan;*
> *Pharaoh's Army got drowned.*

There were joyful sounds unto the Lord:

> *I went down in the valley to pray.*
> *My soul got happy and I stayed all day.*

And regrets:

> *Don't know what my mother wants to stay here for.*
> *This old world ain't been no friend to her.*

And tears.

> *I know moon-rise, I know star-rise,*
> *Lay this body down.*
> *I walk in the moonlight, I walk in the starlight,*
> *To lay this body down.*
> *I'll walk in the graveyard, I'll walk through the graveyard*
> *To lay this body down.*
> *I'll lie in the grave and stretch out my arms;*
> *Lay this body down.*
> *I go to the judgement in the evenin' of the day,*
> *When I lay this body down;*

And my soul and your soul will meet in the day
When I lay this body down
I'll lie in the grave and stretch out my arms.

The words made shivers run down Thomas Wentworth Higginson's back.

"Never," he said, "it seems to me, since man first lived and suffered, was his infinite longing for peace uttered more plaintively than in that line."

This longing was also expressed, though in different language, in the jubilations of the slaves. These temporary releases from toil—on Saturday nights and holidays, notably Christmas—were rare, and slaves made the most of them, holding dances and parties in barns, open fields and Slave Row shacks. On these festive occasions the slaves did jigs, shuffles and "set de flo." They danced to the fiddle or the banjo and beat out rhythms with sticks and bones or by clapping their hands and stomping their feet.

The slaves had a word for it, even then. A "cool cat" in those days was a "ring-clipper." If the slave was aware, or, in the jazz idiom, if he was hip, he was no "bug-eater."

On most plantations there were comely lasses like Miss Lively, a Louisiana belle who had a "well-earned reputation," Solomon Northrup said, "of being the 'fastest gal' on the bayou."

The third great axis was the extended family. In interpersonal relationships, as in the fields of music and religion, the slaves triumphed by transcending and transforming the institutions of their oppressors. We can see this in its purest form in the field of family relations, for the slave family had no standing in law and was the focus of some of the strongest pressures of the slave regime. In all slaves states, the wife or husband or children could be separated and sold to other slaveholders in other counties and regions. Worse yet, certain slaveholders sanctioned polygamy and polyandry and bred slaves for the market.

Apologists for the slave regime deny that slave breeding—sustained efforts to produce the maximum number of slave children— occurred, but there is abundant evidence to the contrary. The subject was bruited about by men and women, African American and European American. Travelers in the South, Harriet Martineau, Frederick Law Olmsted and others, frequently mentioned the subject.

Olmsted, a perceptive observer, believed that slave breeding was common.

"Most gentlemen of character," he wrote, "seem to have a special disinclination to converse on the subject...It appears to me evident, however, from the manner in which I hear the traffic spoken of incidentally, that the cash value of a slave for sale, above the cost of raising it from infancy to the age at which it commands the highest price, is generally considered among the surest elements of a planter's wealth.... That a slave woman is commonly esteemed least for her laboring qualities, most for those qualities which give value to a brood-mare, is, also, constantly made apparent."

Southerners admitted as much. In a letter to Olmsted a slaveholder said that "in the states of Md., Va., N.C., Ky., Tenn. and Mo., as much attention is paid to the breeding and growing of African Americans as to that of horses and mules. Further South, we raise them both for use and for market. Planters command their girls and women (married or unmarried) to have children; and I have known a great many African American girls to be sold off, because they did not have children. A breeding woman is worth from one-sixth to one-fourth more than one that does not breed."

Advertisements listing slave women for sale were brutally frank. A South Carolina advertisement of 1796 offered fifty prime African Americans for sale. "They were purchased," the advertisement said, "for stock and breeding African Americans, and to any Planter who particularly wanted them for that purpose, they are a very choice and desirable gang."

Another advertisement of May 16, 1838, offered a slave "girl of about 20 years of age [who] is very prolific in her generating qualities and affords a rare opportunity for any person who wishes to raise a family of strong and healthy servants...."Other advertisements relied on suggestive terminology; "She is a No. 1 girl," "This is truly a No. 1 woman."

"Breeding slaves," "child-bearing women," and "breeding period" were also stock advertising terms.

The African American family in America was shaped by this system—and by a breathtakingly creative response to the system. For in the violence and humiliation of one of the vilest systems created by man, American slaves, males and females, created unique mating and marriage patterns that made it possible for the African American spirit to survive and grow.

By far the most ingenious of these patterns was the slave marriage, which was generally organized around the proverbial broomstick. We don't know, we may never know, the symbolic importance of this ceremony, but former slaves said couples usually celebrated their marriage by jumping over a broomstick. Georgianna Gibbs, who was a slave in Virginia, said the slaves jumped "a broom three times," but the procedure in Kentucky, another former slave said, was for the man to jump the broom while the woman stood still.

At any rate, it was necessary, according to almost all observers, to jump high, for, according to Jeff Calhoun, who was a slave in Alabama, "to stump our toe on the broom meant you got trouble comin' 'tween you."

A revealing portrait of one of these marriages was drawn by Carolina Johnson Harrison, who was a slave in Virginia, and was married by "Ant Sue," one of the leaders of Slave Row.

> "Didn't have to ask Marsa or nothin'," she said, "Just go to Ant Sue an' tell her you want to get mated. She tell us to

think 'bout it hard for two days, "cause marryin' was sacred in the eyes of Jesus. After two days Mose an' I went back an' say we done thought 'bout it an' still want to get married.

Then she called all the slaves after tasks to pray fo' the union that God was gonna make. Pray we stay together an' 'have lots of children an' none of em gets sold way from the parents. Then she lays a broomstick cross the sill of the house we gonna live in an' join our hands together. Fo' we step over it she ask us once mo' if we was sho' we wanted to get married. 'Course we say yes.

Then she say, 'In the eyes of Jesus step into the holy land of matrimony.' When we step cross the broomstick, we was married. Was bad luck to touch the broomstick. Folks always stepped high 'cause they didn't want no spell cast on 'em—Ant Sue used to say whichever one touched the stick was gonna die first."

Everything indeed suggests that slave marriages were resilient institutions, unencumbered by traditional considerations of property and paternalism. In almost all cases, the bride was a worker who toiled in the fields with her husband and other males. She thus entered marriage as a free spirit (within the confines of a system of equality of oppression) and she was free to opt out when she wanted to. The marriage she and her mate consummated was thus a love match in the true sense of the word.

It was customary until recently to suggest that slave men and women lived a life of riotous debauchery. But a path finding study by Professor Herbert G. Gutman (*The Black Family in Slavery and Freedom*) destroyed that myth and established four points that are central to an understanding of the slave community and the African American family:

1. Most slaves lived in family units headed by a father and mother, and "large numbers of slaves lived in long marriages," some of thirty or more years.

2. Fathers were strong and respected members of the family circle, and male children were often named for their fathers.

3. Premarital sex was fairly common, although the slave community expected a premarital pregnancy to be followed by marriage. The slave community was more open—and more honest—about sex, but it did not approve or condone indiscriminate mating and begetting. More than that, the slave community expected males and females to remain faithful after marriage. Robert Smalls, who later served in the U.S. Congress, told the American Freedmen's Inquiry Commission in 1863 that "if a woman loses her husband, she mourns for him and will not marry for a year and a half unless she is driven to it by want and must have somebody to help her."

4. In slavery, and afterwards, Black marriage was buttressed by extended family groupings that included a wide range of personal relationships.

This was the inner reality within the veil that American slaves created behind the cotton curtain. Within this internal veil, the slaves created a community with its own values and orientation. It was this community that sustained them as they struggled, day in and day out, to maintain a sense of humanity and expectancy in a European-dominated world bounded by fields and fences and the seasons of the year.

Largely because of the existence of the slave community, the struggle continued behind the lines of slavery until the end of slavery.

Men and women nourished and sustained by the slave community pressed that struggle on several levels. Militants, as we shall see, organized and led revolts and conspiracies. Activists, aided by members of the community, who provided food and medicine and kept their mouths shut, ran away to Canada or to Indian reservations on the

Underground Railroad. It has been estimated that at least 100,000 slaves escaped from the South during this period.

Besides these more or less organized forces there was resistance and pressure from runaways who remained in the South and raided nearby plantations from their bases in the swamps. Frederick Law Olmsted was told that escaped slaves lived, bred and died in the swamps. "What a life it must be!" he wrote, "born outlaws: educated self-stealers, trained from infancy to be constantly in dread of the approach of a European man as a thing more dreaded than wildcats or serpents, or even starvation."

A typical instance of this was reported in Virginia. A deputy, sent out to capture a runaway slave, saw his man standing neck deep in a dangerous recess of the swamp. The deputy went back to the courthouse and scratched the slave's name off the book. He wrote across the warrant: "Seeable but not Comeatable."

Another runaway, cornered by his pursuers, chose death. A contemporary newspaper account says that when pursuers found him he was standing "at bay upon the outer edge of a large raft of driftwood, armed with a club and a pistol. In this position he bade defiance to men and dogs—knocking the latter into the water with his club, and resolutely threatening death to any man who approached him.

Finding him obstinately determined not to surrender, one of his pursuers shot him. He fell at the third fire, and so determined was he not to be captured, that when an effort was made to rescue him from drowning he made battle with his club, and sunk waving his weapon in angry defiance at his pursuers.

A further complication was added by African American rebels who attacked the system from within, using poison and the torch. As early as 1723, fifty-three years before the Declaration of Independence, Boston was terrorized by a series of fires. On April 18, 1723, the Rev. Joseph Sewell of Boston preached a sermon on "The Fires that have Broken out in Boston, supposed to be set purposely by ye Africans."

Fires and rumors of slave-set fires convulsed Southern cities until the end of slavery. Beyond any question the antebellum South was a high-risk area. An official of the American Fire Insurance Company of Philadelphia sent the following letter to a Savannah, Georgia, man on February 17, 1820:

> "I have received your letter of the 7th instant respecting the insurance of your house and furniture in Savannah. In answer thereto, I am to inform you, that this company, for the present, decline making insurance in any of the slave states."

Arrayed against rebellious slaves was a police apparatus of unparalleled severity. Each slave state had a slave code which was designed to keep slaves ignorant and in awe of European American power. Under the provisions of these codes, slaves were forbidden to assemble in groups of more than five or seven away from their home plantation. They were forbidden to leave plantations without passes and could not blow horns, beat drums or read books.

Slave preachers were proscribed and hemmed in by additional restrictions; and slaves were forbidden to hold religious meetings without European American witnesses. Other provisions forbade slaves to raise their hands against European Americans and gave every European American person police power over every African American, free or slave.

A free African American, when challenged by a European American person, was obliged to produce papers proving that he was free. the presumption in most slave states was that an African American person was a slave. Slave patrols or "paderollers," as the slaves called them, were authorized to make periodic searches of slave cabins and to chastise bondsmen found off plantations without passes.

The police power of the state, the state militia and the U.S. Army stood behind these totalitarian laws. But power alone could not uphold them. More was needed: the slave, if slavery was to be successful, had to *believe* he was a slave. Anticipating the devious tactics of the modern police state, masters laid hands on the minds of their human chattel.

Each slave was taught, by various methods and with varying success, that he was totally helpless and that his master was absolutely powerful. Each slave was taught that he was inferior to the meanest European American man and that he had to obey every European American man without thinking, without questioning. Finally, if these lessons were learned, the slave looked at himself through the eyes of his master and accepted the values of the master.

Masters, with few exceptions, recognized the necessity of mind control. A Louisiana planter told Olmsted that he wanted to buy the land of poor European Americans who lived near his plantation. "It was better," he said, "that they [slaves] never saw anybody off their own plantation; they should, if possible, have no intercourse with any other European American man than their owner or overseer; especially, it was desirable *that they should not see European American men who did not command their respect, and whom they did not always feel to be superior to themselves, and able to command them.*"

That some slaves succumbed to this assault on the mind is not unusual. Faced with absolute power in a closed system, European American men and Europeans succumbed in concentration camps in Korea and Germany. What was surprising was not that some African Americans succumbed to the pressure of slavery—It was rather that so many with so few resources never stopped fighting back. Many rebels who could not and would not be whipped by one man were overpowered by groups and killed.

Some were sent to "professional African American breakers" and broken. Several "persisted in their folly." They poisoned masters and mistresses with arsenic, ground glass and "spiders beaten up in buttermilk." They chopped European Americans to pieces with axes and burned their houses and bars to the ground. Not a few "bad African Americans" were women.

Court records speak for the "bad African Americans" some historians would like to forget.

One slave said: "He would be damned if he did not kill his master, if he ever struck him again."

Another was ecstatic as he dug his master's grave. "I have killed him at last." Patrick vowed revenge. "Their master had attempted to whip Patrick....and it took five persons to hold him. That Patrick said he was not done yet, that he was a good African American when he was let alone, but if he was raised he was the devil."

A woman slave prodded a timid male. "If she, the witness, were a man, she would murder her master."

Another woman was frank. "If old mistress did not leave her alone and quit calling her a bitch and a strumpet, she would take an iron and split her brains out."

The court records yield ample evidence that a large number of slaves refused to play the game of slavery; they would neither smile nor bow. Other slaves bowed but would not smile. Still others, perhaps the majority, went through the ritual of obedience.

What about them?

What did they think of slavery? What they thought can be inferred from what they did.

African American and European American historians have uncovered a mass of material on their passive "day-to-day resistance" to slavery.

These slaves, who smiled sometimes and bowed sometimes, used a variety of techniques to indicate their dissatisfaction with the system.

They staged deliberate slowdowns and sit-down strikes. They broke implements and trampled the crops In a now visible, now invisible underground struggle which continued until the end of slavery, they quietly, subtly and deliberately sabotaged the system from within.

By resisting, maintaining, enduring and abiding, by holding on and holding fast and holding out, they provided one of the greatest examples of history of the strength of the human spirit in adversity.

Part Three

African American Military Heroes

Jim Haskins

Introduction

Throughout American history, most African Americans have been eager to participate equally in society, and that has included defending their country. Despite centuries of being shut out from full participation in the rights of citizenship, African Americans have loyally served their country in uniform in every major war.

During the Revolutionary War, 5,000 free African Americans joined the Continental army. They often fought side by side with European Americans. But when the war was over, the new Congress of the United States barred African Americans from joining state militias. Neither the navy nor the marines would let African Americans enlist. An era of exclusion had begun. Several hundred African American sailors saw action in the War of 1812 against the British, but between the War of 1812 and the start of the Civil War in 1861, few African Americans served in the military. The Southern states that dominated the nation's military believed in rigid segregation. Northern states also placed many restrictions on African Americans. Only a handful served in the conflict between the United States and Mexico (1846-1848), known as the Mexican War. From 1850 until the Civil War, the peacetime army and navy were exclusively European American.

When the Civil War broke out in 1861, African Americans rushed to take part. But even though the fight was largely about slavery, the Union forces would not admit them. That changed after President Lincoln issued the Emancipation Proclamation freeing slaves in the South. The Union needed African American manpower to win. Before the war was over, nearly 180,000 African American men— and at least one African American woman in disguise— served in the Union army and navy, and nearly 40,000 died for the cause.

Reconstruction followed the Union victory in 1865. Congress passed civil rights acts and amendments to the United States Constitution guaranteeing African Americans full citizenship. That included the right to serve in the military, although African Americans were restricted mainly to cavalry and infantry regiments on the western frontier. Nicknamed "Buffalo Soldiers" by the Indians, they patrolled the frontier and skirmished with the Indians. African American units also fought in the Spanish-American War (1898).

The United States declared war on Germany in 1917. Almost 400,000 African Americans enlisted or were drafted. More than 10 percent of American servicemen were African American. But most worked in labor and stevedore battalions. In France, African American troops under French commanders fought bravely, were well respected and were awarded many medals for their sacrifices.. But European American officers hated and scorned African American troops under their command. The U.S. Army banned African Americans from its combat divisions —-the air, artillery, engineers, signal, and tank corps. The navy and marines excluded African Americans from all service except that of messmen in the kitchen.

In spite of continuing discrimination, a million African Americans joined the military when the United States entered World War II (1941-1945). Many saw combat and distinguished themselves for their courage and fighting ability. The army formed African American units. The Army Air Corps trained 1,000 African American pilots, the famous Tuskegee Airmen. Almost 4,000 African American women served in the Women's Army Corps. Although the navy allowed African Americans to serve only as messmen, three African Americans won the Navy Cross, the navy's highest military honor, (Dorey Miller was one of only two men who shot down (two) Japanese planes at Pearl Harbor). But segregation began to break down when there were not enough European American men available to fight and the United States once again needed African Americans in regular units.

A quiet revolution occurred after the war. In July 1948, President Harry S. Truman signed Executive Order 9981, which called for equality for all persons in the armed services. The new Department of the Air Force was the quickest to respond. At last, the army began to integrate. Many African Americans enlisted to fight in the Korean War (1950-1953). By the fall of 1954, integration in the military was complete.

In the spring of 1954, the United States Supreme Court handed down a watershed decision in the history of race relations. *Brown v. Board of Education, Topeka*, declared separate-but-equal schools unconstitutional. The decision triggered violence and conflict. Integration elsewhere in America would not be as peaceful as it had been in the military.

The Vietnam War (1954-1975) was the first war in U.S. history where African Americans served in every type of military unit and fought in every major battle on land, on sea, and in the air. Today, in the words of General Colin Powell, the armed forces have become "the most democratic institution in America where [you] rise or fall on merit"

The people profiled in this book are only a few of the many courageous and dedicated African Americans who have beaten the odds and succeeded in their quest to defend our country. The actual number could fill many more such collections.

Chapter Four
Private Peter Salem

(1750 - 1816)

The 5,000 African Americans who served in the Revolutionary War had good reason to fight—they got their freedom when they enlisted in the Continental army. Among them was Peter Salem, who was also called Salem Middleux. Born a slave in Framingham, Massachusetts, he belonged, according to some sources, to Captain Jeremiah Belknap. Belknap sold him to Major Lawson of Buckminster, Massachusetts, a town near Boston.

In 1775, the American colonists' Continental army prepared to face the British occupying troops. The people of Boston readied for battle, and so did Peter Salem. He enlisted in the First Massachusetts Regiment as a private in Captain Simon Edgel's company and was granted his freedom.

Salem was at the April 1775 Battle of Lexington, against British Major John Pitcairn. He was also at Concord. Those battles marked the beginning of the Revolutionary War. On June 17, 1775, the colonists and British redcoats squared off at Bunker Hill. More than twenty-five African Americans were in the colonial ranks. Private Peter Salem was among them—as a servant to Lieutenant Grosvenor, who was facing Major Pitcairn a second time.

As the British advanced, colonial officers rode back and forth among the troops. "Don't fire until you see the whites of their eyes!" they urged. Peter Salem obeyed orders as long as he could. The king's soldiers charged a third time. Leading the charge, Major Pitcairn called out, "The day is ours!" Then a bullet from Private Peter Salem's gun shot him through. The colonists eventually drove the British from the hill and showed their enemy that they were a force to be reckoned with.

Although some observers said that several bullets brought Major Pitcairn down, most regarded Peter Salem as the hero. According to one report, they took up a collection to send Salem to General George Washington as the man who had slain Pitcairn.

The artist John Trumbull witnessed the battle from Roxbury, across the harbor from Bunker Hill, and possibly met Salem within the next few days. Trumbull painted the climactic scene ten years later, in London. He worked from memory and probably used a black model in his studio to represent Peter Salem. In the lower right section of the painting, Salem stands close behind Lieutenant Grosvenor, holding a French Charleville musket of the sort that fired the fatal bullet into Pitcairn.

Salem stayed with the Continental army, participating in the critical Battle of Saratoga in 1777, among others. With the American victory over the British in 1783, Salem left the army. That same year he married Katie Benson and settled in Leicester, Massachusetts, as a basket weaver. Eventually, he returned to Framingham, where he died in the town's poorhouse on August 16, 1816.

For some years, after the Revolutionary War, engravings based on John Trumbull's painting included Peter Salem in a prominent position. But by 1855, according to William C. Nell, an African American historian of the time, Salem was less visible: "In more recent editions, his figure is *non est inventus*. A significant but inglorious omission."

In 1882, the citizens of Framingham built a monument to the memory of Peter Salem. For many years, the Freedman's Bank of Boston printed his picture on their banknotes. The Daughters of the American Revolution bought Salem's home in 1909 and turned it into a historic site. In 1968, the federal government made a commemorative stamp of the Trumbull painting that included Peter Salem.

Long before the first shots at Lexington and Concord, bands of colonists openly defied the redcoats, as the British soldiers were known. Crispus Attucks, the son of an African and a Native American, was the first patriot killed in one of those protests. He had been born a slave in 1723 in Framingham, Massachusetts, Peter Salem's birthplace. As a boy, he ran away to become a sailor. Attucks learned to read and write, and he grew devoted to the cause of freedom. Meeting with other protesters, near the Boston courthouse on March 5, 1770, he died when British soldiers fired their muskets in the crowd. The incident became known as the Boston Massacre. A monument on the Boston Commons honors Attucks's memory.

Chapter Five
Private Austin Dabney

(? - ?)

Peter Salem had voluntarily enlisted in the Continental army, but Austin Dabney was sent in his master's stead. Born a slave in North Carolina, the son of a slave woman and her master, Dabney was owned by a Georgia colonist named Aycock. At the time, a colonist who did not wish to serve in the army could send a slave or servant in his place. Aycock sent Austin Dabney.

Dabney served as an artilleryman in the Battle of Battle Creek, Georgia. On February 4, 1779, a musket ball ripped through his thigh. Left on the battleground, he was found by a European American soldier named Harris, who took him home and cared for him until he recovered. According to legend, Dabney never forgot Harris's kindness and served the family faithfully for years afterward. Much later, the Harris family's eldest son found a way to thank Dabney for his loyalty and self-sacrifice.

When the Harris family moved to Madison County, Georgia, Dabney went with them. His hard work and saving made it possible for the eldest Harris son to go to Franklin College. When young Harris got a job in the office of state legislator Stephen Upson, he sought Upson's help for Dabney. Upson persuaded the Georgia Assembly to award Dabney a pension for his service in the Revolutionary War.

In 1819, the government held a lottery for land. It was only for Revolutionary War veterans. Although a pensioner, Dabney was not allowed in the lottery because he was an African American. After protests from Harris and others, the Georgia Assembly cited Dabney's "bravery and fortitude" in "several engagements and actions," and passed an act awarding Dabney 112 acres of land in Walton County, Georgia. But a group of European Americans in Madison County protested the award, claiming "it was an indignity to European American men, for a mulatto to be put upon an equality with them in the distribution of the public lands."

To collect his pension, Dabney traveled once a year to Savannah. On one occasion he encountered the governor of Georgia, who recognized him and invited him into his home as an honored guest. Dabney prospered. He owned fine horses an attended races and bet on horses, and when the young Harris moved away from Madison County, Dabney went with him. Dabney died in Zebulon, Georgia.

Another African American patriot, James Armistead, became an undercover agent for the Continental army. For his service he received a commendation from the Marquis de Lafayette of France.

Chapter Six
Private Lemuel Haynes

(1753 - 1833)

"When I was five months old, I was carried to Granville, Massachusetts, to be a servant to Deacon David Rose till I was twenty-one. He was a man of singular piety. I was taught the principles of religion," recalled Lemuel Haynes about his life before the Revolutionary War. His mother was a European American woman, and his father was an African American man whom he never knew. Born on July 18, 1753, in West Hartford, Connecticut, Haynes was given up as a baby.

The Roses were farmers, and young Lemuel helped them clear land and plant crops. There was little time left over for school. When he did go, he attended a common school with European American children. He loved reading and spent his evenings pouring over the Bible and books of psalms by the light of the fire. As he grew older, he read to the Rose family in the evenings. One night, he slipped a sermon he had written in the book and read it to the family. Deacon David Rose was impressed. Since the parish had no minister, Rose asked his young servant to conduct the service and read an approved sermon, sometimes written by Lemuel.

By 1774, clouds were gathering on the horizon of the British colonies in North America. Haynes stood up for his belief in what was right and joined the Minute Men, the colonial militia established by the Massachusetts provincial congress. Every week, he and his comrades practiced for battle in case they were needed. Soon enough, they were. After the Battle of Lexington, Massachusetts, in April 1775, Hayes accompanied Captain Lebbeus Ball's militia company to join the Continental army at Roxbury Massachusetts. In 1776, Haynes marched in the expedition to Fort Ticonderoga, where with Ethan Allen and the Green Mountain Boys, he helped to take the fort from British General Burgoyne's army.

Forty years later, in a sermon delivered on George Washington's birthday, Haynes would remind his listeners of his service in the Revolution: "Perhaps it is not ostentatious in the speaker to observe, that in early life he devoted all for the sake of freedom and independence, and endured frequent campaigns in their defense...." Returning home from the war, Haynes put down his gun and took up the Bible again. In 1779, a clergyman in New Canaan, Connecticut, helped him learn Latin. Another supporter got him a teaching job and tutored him in Greek. Now Haynes could read the New Testament as originally written.

On November 29, 1780, after taking an examination in languages, sciences, and the gospel, Haynes became a preacher. A Congregational church in Middle Granville invited him to be its pastor, and

he served that church for several years. While in Granville, Hayes married Elizabeth Babbitt, a European American former schoolteacher. They had ten children—seven girls and three boys. In 1785, Hayes was officially ordained a minister of the gospel by an association of ministers in Litchfield, Connectiut.

That same year, he accepted a position as pastor at a church in Torrington, Connecticut, becoming the first African American pastor of a European American church in the United States. One parishioner kept his hat on in church as a sign of disrespect. When the self-confident Reverend Hayes approached the pulpit, he either did not see or did not pay attention to the slight but began preaching. According to Haynes's biographer, Timothy Cooley, the parishioner later recalled, "My hat was instantly taken off and thrown under the seat, and I found myself listening with the most profound attention." But others did not come around, and the snubs of a determined clique in the congregation forced Haynes to leave Torrington after two years.

In March 1788, Haynes accepted a pastorship with a church in Rutland, Vermont, where he remained for thirty years.

He was active in political and church circles throughout New England, speaking out on the moral wrong of slavery. "I am pointing you to the poor Africans among us," he wrote in 1801. "What has reduced them to their present pitiful, abject state? Is it any distinction that the god of nature hath made in their formation? Nay—but being subjected to slavery, by the cruel hands of oppressors, they have been taught to view themselves as a rank of beings far below others, which has suppressed in a degree, every principle of manhood and so they become despised, ignorant, and licentious. This should fill us with the utmost detestation against every attack on the rights of men...."

In 1804, Haynes was presented with a master of arts degree from Middlebury College in Vermont, thus becoming the first African American person to receive an honorary degree from a European American college in the United States.

Eventually, Haynes returned to Granville, Massachusetts. There, he spent the last eleven years of his life. He died on September 28, 1833, at the age of eighty.

Chapter Seven
Deborah Sampson

(1760 - 1827)

At least one African American woman fought in the Revolutionary War, disguised as a man and able to keep her secret. Deborah Sampson wanted to be part of the events that affected her land, and she had the courage to do so.

Sampson was born on December 17, 1760, in Plymouth, Massachusetts, one of several children. Her father, Jonathan Sampson, was a sailor who disappeared at sea. Her mother, unable to care for the children, sent them to different families. Five-year-old Deborah lived first with a cousin, who died when Deborah was about eight. Then Deborah spent two years with the wife of a local pastor.

At the age of ten, Sampson was sent out as a servant to Benjamin Thomas of Middleborough, Massachusetts. For eight years, she not only did domestic chores, but she also worked in the fields, cared for the farm animals, and did carpentry. In addition, she managed to attend the local public school part-time. The Thomas children taught her what they knew. An avid reader, she was especially fond of newspapers and studied the major issues of the day.

Sampson was just thirteen years old at the time of the Boston Tea Party in 1773, the first major rebellion by American colonials against Great Britain. When the colonies declared their independence and the Revolutionary War began, she could not get enough of the news.

When Sampson was eighteen years old, her bondage to the Thomas family ended. She taught for six months at the same public school that she had attended. How she made her living after that is not known. In November 1780, she joined the First Baptist Church of Middleborough, but soon encountered problems. Accused of dressing in male clothing and engaging in conduct unbecoming a respectable lady, she was banished by the congregation.

Sampson chafed against the restrictions of life in that Massachusetts town when such exciting events were taking place elsewhere. At some point, she determined to volunteer for the Continental army. Sampson was above average in height for a woman. Years of hard work for the Thomas family had made her strong. She purchased fabric and sewed a man's suit for herself. Then she walked to Billingham, Massachusetts. Using the alias Robert Shurtleff, she enlisted in the Continental army. Mustered into service at Worcester, Massachusetts, on May 23, 1782, she was assigned to Captain George Webb's company in the Fourth Massachusetts Regiment.

Sampson first served at White Plains, in the colony of New York, then moved with her company to Tarrytown, New York. In the battle at Tarrytown, she was wounded three times: a sword cut on the head and two musket balls in one leg.

At the Battle of Yorktown, Pennsylvania, four months later, Sampson was shot through the shoulder. During the march north after the battle, she succumbed to the extreme cold and other deprivations suffered by the soldiers of the Continental army and collapsed.

Although Deborah Sampson was seriously wounded at Tarrytown, New York, she was afraid to go to a field hospital, because her true identity might be discovered. Despite her protests, her fellow soldiers carried her six miles to the nearest hospital.

Sampson was unconscious when she arrived at the field hospital operated by Dr. Barnabas

Binney, a Philadelphia physician. In fact, it was first thought that she was dead. But Dr. Binney discerned a pulse, and in the course of treating her, he discovered that she was a woman. He kept this knowledge to himself, and when she was well enough to leave the hospital, he arranged for her to recuperate in his own home.

While in the hospital Sampson reported only the head wound, which she knew she could not hide. She did not mention the two musket balls in her leg. While at the hospital, she somehow managed to get hold of surgical instruments and to remove one of the musket balls herself. the other was too deep to retrieve and remained in her leg. As soon as she had recovered sufficiently, she returned to the company.

Formally and honorably discharged from the army by General Henry Knox at West Point on October 23, 1783, Sampson returned to New England and went to live with an uncle in Sharon, Massachusetts. There, she seems to have had no problems fitting into the community. She married a farmer named Benjamin Gannett on April 7, 1784. The couple had three children, a boy and two girls. They adopted another girl whose mother had died.

Sampson was proud of her service in the Continental army and, after her discharge, never tried to hide the truth of her daring deception. She sought, and with the help of Revolutionary Was hero Paul Revere who wrote a letter of support, she was successful in securing, a government pension for her service. This event attracted the attention of Henry Mann, who became fascinated with her story and wrote a highly romanticized biography of Sampson, which was published in 1797. Mann also helped Sampson write a lecture about her experiences, which she first delivered at the Federal Street Theater in Boston on March 22, 1802. Thereafter, she lectured as often as she could, for her fees helped the family, who were not doing well at farming.

Sampson died on April 29, 1827, and was buried in Rockridge Cemetery in Sharon, Massachusetts. Carved on the back of her tombstone were these words: "Deborah Sampson Gannett, Robert Shurtleff, The Female Soldier: 1781 - 1783."

Several years later, her husband, Benjamin Gannet, petitioned Congress to collect his late wife's pension. Gannett argued that caring for her during her long and protracted illnesses resulting from her wounds in the Revolutionary War had left him in severe economic distress. In 1837, Congress granted Gannett a pension of $80 a year for the rest of his life.

Chapter Eight

Seaman John Bathan Vashon

(1792 - 1854)

The Revolutionary War ended with the signing of the Treaty of 1783. Yet U. S. troubles with Great Britain continued, especially on the high seas. Embroiled in the Napoleonic Wars, Britain had a great need for sea power. It had the ships but often had difficulty finding the crews.

To man its ships, Britain resorted to pressing deserters and criminals into service. British subjects who had adopted America as their country were also pressed into service, at that time

England did not recognize the right of a person to change his or her nationality. British naval captains often used the search for British subjects as an excuse to intercept American ships. Once they had succeeded in boarding an American ship, they and their officers were none too careful about whom they took away. American resentment over British impressments of its citizens was one of the causes of the War of 1812.

The War of 1812 was primarily a naval war, and since the U.S. Navy admitted very few African Americans at the time, African Americans had little opportunity to serve their country during this conflict. But while small in number, African Americans again contributed to America's defense. John Bathan Vashon was among them.

Vashon was born in Norfolk, Virginia, the son of a mulatto mother. His father was Captain George Vashon, a European American of French ancestry. George Vashon was an Indian agent under General George Washington and later under President Martin Van Buren. Like his father, John Vashon had set out as a young man looking for great adventure. He was twenty years old when the War of 1812 began.

One of the few African Americans accepted into the United States Navy, Vashon enlisted as a seaman and embarked on the USS *Revenge.* The *Revenge* was sailing off the coast of Brazil when it was engaged in battle by a British ship. The British force proved to be superior and took Vashon and other members of the crew of the *Revenge* prisoner. Luckily, they were later released in a prisoner exchange.

Discharged from the navy after the war ended in 1815, Vashon returned to Virginia, married, and started a family. Around 1822, he moved to Carlisle, Pennsylvania, where he ran a saloon for seven years. He then moved to Pittsburgh, where he became active in the anti-slavery movement. Vashon had found another worthy crusade.

Joining forces with the European American abolitionist William Lloyd Garrison, he became a member of the Temperance and Moral Reform societies. He also helped organize and served as one of the vice presidents of the National Convention of Colored Men in Rochester, New York, in July 1853.

Vashon stayed in touch with other veterans of the War of 1812.

Ironically, he was attending a Convention of 1812 War Veterans in Philadelphia when he had a heart attack and died on January 8, 1854.

Chapter Nine
Major Martin Robison Delany

(1812 - 1885)

For a quarter century after the Mexican War (1846—1848), the United States benefited from international peace. It expanded westward. New territories, including Texas, became states. The southern plantations prospered, finding huge markets for their cotton in Europe. Northern manufacturing grew steadily. It seemed that people everywhere wanted U.S.-manufactured products. But while prosperous, the United States was far from peaceful. Slavery was causing deep divisions between northern and southern states, and this and other issues led to civil war.

For the first year and a half of the war, African Americans waged their own struggle to get into the fight. Among those who fought most forcefully for the right to defend the Union was a physician named Martin Robison Delany, who became a major in the Union army. Born of a free mother and a slave father in Charlestown, Virginia, on May 6, 1812, Delany learned early to be proud. His father, the son of an African chief, managed to gain his freedom.

Seeking education for their children, the family moved to western Pennsylvania. Delany attended schools in Pittsburgh. He studied nights at an African American church while also working during the day. He received medical training from two local physicians. When he moved for a time to the Southwest in the late 1830s, he worked as a physician's assistant and dentist. Years later, Delaney decided to pursue formal medical studies.

He was one of the first African Americans admitted to Harvard Medical School. He did not graduate, however, because his fellow students petitioned successfully for his dismissal. After leaving Harvard, Delany returned to Pittsburgh, where he became a prominent physician as well as a leader of the African American community.

In Pittsburgh, Martin Delany started a weekly newspaper, *The Mystery*. He published it from 1843 to 1846. In its pages, he championed equal rights for both African Americans and women. He also worked to move fugitive slaves north and to restore the vote to African Americans in Pennsylvania.

Through his work, Martin Delany became friendly with the noted abolitionist Frederick Douglass. Even the great Douglass noticed Delany's fierce pride. Douglass said, "I thank God for making me a man simply, but Delany always thanks Him for making him an African American man." In 1847 Douglass invited Delany to be an editor of Douglass's weekly newspaper *North Star* published in Rochester, New York. Delany was listed on the masthead as an editor until 1849.

During the 1820s, the movement to abolish slavery grew in the North. One northern state after another outlawed slavery. In Congress, representatives from these states fought to admit new territories as states only if they, too, outlawed slavery. But southern representatives in Congress were just as determined that new states would be slave states. In contested territories like Kansas, armed conflict broke out between pro-and anti-slavery forces.

In 1860, the nation was like a tinderbox, ready to catch fire. The election of Republican Abraham Lincoln, who was not an abolitionist but who worried pro-slavery forces, provided the spark. It ignited armed rebellion. In 1861, seven southern states seceded from the

Union and formed a new nation, the Confederate States of America. The federal government was determined to preserve the Union. The Civil War began.

Delany despaired that even European Americans who favored abolition would never accept African Americans as equals. So he broke with Frederick Douglass and other abolitionists who believed African Americans could be integrated into American society, and began to give serious thought to the idea of African Americans leaving the United States.

Perhaps they could seek a life of peace and equality elsewhere. At first, he advocated emigration to Haiti or Central America, later to Africa. In 1854, he had organized a National Emigration Convention of 100 men and women.

In 1856, in protest against oppressive conditions for African Americans in the United States, Delany moved to Canada, where he continued his medical practice. In 1858, he presided over an emigration convention in Chatham, Canada. The convention appointed Delany as chief commissioner of a Niger River exploring party.

Accompanied by Robert Campbell, a young schoolteacher from Philadelphia, Delany spent nine months in Africa, exploring the Niger River delta region. He made an agreement with the rulers of Ahbeokuta, in present-day Nigeria, for an African American settlement there. For his leadership of this expedition, and for his writings on African American equality, Delany became known as the Father of African American Nationalism. In 1861, Delany returned to the United States and joined Douglass and others urging President Lincoln to enlist African Americans to fight in the Civil War. Meeting personally with Lincoln, Delany proposed an army of African Americans commanded by African Americans. At first, the president did not agree.

At last, in 1863, the War Department mustered the all-African American Fifty-fourth Massachusetts Volunteer Regiment. Delany, among those most actively recruited, served as its surgeon.

In February 1865, Delany became the first African American man to receive a regular army commission.

Major Delany traveled to Hilton Head Island, South Carolina, to recruit and organize former slaves for the North. But his efforts were cut short.

The war ended in April with the surrender of Confederate General Robert E. Lee at Appomattox Court House, Virginia. The federal government quickly sent occupying troops into the former Confederate states and established a period of Reconstruction during which the Confederate states would write new constitutions.

These would guarantee equal rights to the former slaves when the southern sates were readmitted to the Union. The government also established a Freedmen's Bureau to help the former slaves. Delany served on the bureau in South Carolina.

In July 1865, Major Delany delivered a fiery speech to freedmen at the Brick Church, St. Helena Island. Delany urged his audience to be careful of trusting Yankees, to deal only with genuine government agents. He promised them that he would do all he could to work with the officers of the federal troops to see that the former slaves received their own plots of land to farm.

After an honorable discharge, Delany served with the Freedmen's Bureau in South Carolina for three more years. In 1874, he ran unsuccessfully as an Independent Republican for the office of lieutenant governor of South Carolina. He later became a customs inspector and trial justice in Charleston.

In his later years, Delany continued his scientific studies, publishing *Principia of Ethnology: The Origin of Race and Color* in 1879. Major Delany died in Xenia, Ohio on January 24, 1885.

Chapter Ten

Lieutenant Peter Vogelsang

(1815 - 1887)

Like Martin Delaney, Peter Vogelsang became a commissioned officer in the all-African American Fifty-fourth Massachusetts Volunteer Regiment. Born on August 21, 1815, in New York City, Vogelsang was working as a clerk when the Civil War broke out in April 1861. At age forty-eight, Peter Vogelsang was by far the oldest recruit in the Fifty-fourth. Steady and serious, he soon became a father figure, particularly in Company H, one of the ten units into which the men were organized.

Vogelsang would have made a good commissioned officer from the start. But the army was firmly against the recruits becoming officers. Governor Andrew of Massachusetts wrote to Secretary of War Stanton, asking for African American officers such as surgeons and a chaplain to be placed in African American regiments. But both Stanton and President Lincoln feared that appointing African American officers would outrage European Americans. The average European American Northerner was against slavery in principle, but had no interest in African Americans having equal rights of citizenship.

No one could keep the determined African Americans out of the war. Leading abolitionists like Martin Delany and Frederick Douglass continually pressed the cause. Escaped slaves made their way to Union lines and freedom. Union generals on the battlefields of the South found themselves suddenly responsible for the fugitives.

The Emancipation Proclamation turned the tide. It freed all slaves in the enemy states as of January 1, 1863. It declared that freed slaves "of suitable condition" would be "received into the armed service of the United States, to garrison forts, positions, stations, and other places, and to man vessels of all sorts."

Lincoln also agreed to enlist free African Americans. Secretary of War Edwin M. Stanton authorized Governor John A. Andrew of Massachusetts to recruit and organize African American soldiers into a regiment.

There was no question but that a European American officer would command the first African American regiment.

Governor Andrew had just the officer in mind: Captain Robert Gould Shaw, Virginia-born son of abolitionists who had commanded the Second Massachusetts Infantry Regiment. Although Shaw expected ridicule for commanding an African American regiment, he accepted Andrew's offer and a promotion to colonel.

Abolitionists rushed to recruit for the new regiment. Frederick Douglass recruited his own sons—Charles, nineteen, and Lewis, twenty-two. Robert Gould Shaw's father recruited Peter Vogelsang. The one thousand men who eventually comprised the regiment came from twenty-two states, the District of Columbia, and the West Indies. The majority were in their twenties.

When the Fifty-fourth was mustered into service in March 1863, all twenty-nine officers were European Americans. Colonel Robert Gould Shaw reported to General David Hunter in Hilton Head, South Carolina. Barely had the Fifty-fourth made camp when Colonel James Montgomery ordered Company H and seven others to travel further south to Darien, Georgia.

They watched as Union gunboats fired on the town. Then Montgomery ordered them to plunder and torch the houses. It was more like piracy than warfare. Shaw protested, but Montgomery was determined to destroy the town. The men of the Fifty-fourth reluctantly followed their orders.

Shaw promoted Peter Vogelsang almost as soon as the Fifty-fourth Massachusetts reached the South. He rose to sergeant first, and then, on April 17, to quartermaster sergeant, both non-commissioned ranks. Ordinarily, that would have meant a raise in pay. But the Fifty-fourth Massachusetts did not operate under ordinary circumstances.

In early July, the Fifty-fourth Massachusetts joined other Union regiments in a campaign against Charleston, South Carolina. The regiment sailed north on the steamer null. On July 11, Vogelsang and his comrades debarked on James Island, off the coast of South Carolina, where several Confederate regiments waited. It was there that the Fifty-fourth Massachusetts came under fire for the first time.

On June 30, the Fifty-fourth was mustered for pay for the first time. Instead of a soldier's $13 plus a clothing allowance, they got $10, the rate for laborers, minus $3 for clothing. Furious at this insult, they refused payment. Governor Andrew offered to make up the difference with money from the state treasury. But the men of the Fifty-fourth refused again. It was not the money but the principle involved.

They believed that their federal government should pay them as much as European American soldiers. Out of pride, they continued to refuse any pay at all for eighteen months, in spite of the hardships that decision imposed on their families. But they did not refuse to serve, although Shaw felt they should be released from duty if they were not to be treated equally with European American troops.

On July 16, 1863, the men of the Fifty-fourth were ordered to begin a forced march that lasted a day and a half. Their destination was Charleston, South Carolina, and their mission was to capture Fort Wagner, a Confederate stronghold guarding the entrance to Charleston

Harbor. They had rested from their long march only about thirty minutes when Brigadier General George C. Strong, who had replaced Colonel Montgomery, gave the order for the charge. The column advanced. Immediately, the fort's big guns and muskets fired on them. Colonel Robert Gould Shaw was killed, but his men fought on.

It seemed to Sergeant Peter Vogelsang that all at once "one hundred Rebels were swarming about me." He not only stood fast but advanced, taking with him his whole company. Although he was wounded, he still managed to accompany the Fifty-fourth to the battle that made it famous, the assault on Fort Wagner.

Although the Fifty-fourth failed to capture the fort, it proved its bravery. Northern newspapers made much of the battle and of the courage of the African American troops. Union General Ulysses S. Grant, commander of all army forces, wrote to President Lincoln, "By arming the African American we have added a powerful ally. They will make good soldiers and taking them from the enemy weakens him in the same proportion they strengthen us. I am therefore most decidedly in favor of pushing this policy to the enlistment of a force sufficient to hold all the South falling into our hands and to aid in capturing more."

Congress awarded fourteen members of the Fifty-fourth Massachusetts the Medal of Honor, established during the Civil War as the highest military award for bravery, for their courageous assault on Fort Wagner. That battle changed the attitude of many Northerners toward the African American volunteers.

The fifty-fourth Massachusetts continued to see action until the war ended in April 1865. Peter Vogelsang rose to second lieutenant and then first lieutenant—one of only three men in the Fifty-fourth to be commissioned as officers. On August 20, 1865, his term of service expired, Lieutenant Vogelsang returned to New York City and lived another twenty years. He died on April 4, 1887.

Chapter Eleven
Harriet Tubman

(1820 - 1913)

Harriet Tubman, a fearless scout, spy, and nurse, was born on the plantation of Edward Brodas in Dorchester County, Maryland. Her parents, Harriet Greene and Benjamin Ross, were enslaved. When she was born, she was named Araminta; but later she was called Harriet, after her mother. When Harriet was six, her master hired her out to work for local people, who treated her cruelly. On the Brodas plantation, she received an injury that would cause her to suddenly lose consciousness at random times for the rest of her life. She had attempted to block the way of an overseer chasing after a slave who was trying to escape. A brick intended for the runaway hit her instead.

In 1848, Harriet married John Tubman, a free man. When she confided in him that she wanted to escape, he threatened to report her. But when Harriet learned that she had been sold to a Georgia slave trader, she escaped and made her way to Philadelphia. After two years in Philadelphia, Harriet learned that her sister and children were about to be sold. She returned to Maryland to assist her sister's husband in rescuing his family from a slave pen in Cambridge, Maryland. Not long after that daring rescue, she returned to the

Brodas plantation. She wanted to persuade her husband to join her in the North. Instead, she found that he had remarried. Undaunted, Harriet brought out eleven slaves, including one of her brothers and his wife.

By 1851, she had become a legend as a conductor on the Underground Railroad, the network of people, African American and European American, who aided slaves escaping from the South to the North and freedom. She established a pattern that she kept to for six years, until 1857. Each year she made two trips to the South, one in the spring and one in the fall. She spent the winters in St. Catherine's, Ontario, where many fugitive slaves had settled, and the summers working in hotels in places such as Cape May, New Jersey, to earn money for her trips. In the spring of 1857, she managed to rescue her aged parents.

By the fall of 1858, Tubman had helped more than 300 slaves reach the North and freedom. She had come to be called Moses for leading her people to the promised land. By 1860, the reward for her capture was $40,000—a huge sum in those days. In December 1860, she made her last trip as a conductor on the Underground Railroad. By early 1861, the North and South were at war, and it was no longer possible to continue her trips south.

During the Civil War, Tubman served the Union cause in several ways. In May 1862, months before the first Northern African American regiments were authorized, Tubman arrived in Beaufort, South Carolina. She had joined a group of missionary-teachers to aid the hundreds of escaped slaves who had made their way to Union lines after the Union fleet had captured the South Carolina sea island. Tubman showed the women that by doing the soldiers' laundry, they could earn money and become self-supporting. Tubman personally built and financed a washhouse to get them started. She also nursed both soldiers and freedmen at the army hospital on the islands.

Harriet Tubman aided numerous expeditions, the most famous in 1863. She accompanied guerrilla fighter Colonel James Montgomery and about 800 African American soldiers of the Second South Carolina Volunteers on a gunboat raid along the Combahee River in South Carolina. She and her scouts surveyed the area and identified places where Confederate soldiers had placed explosives along the river. With this crucial information, the Union gunboats zigzagged up the river, avoiding the explosives and picking off small bands of Confederate soldiers. Meanwhile, Union troops made their way along both riverbanks, setting fire to plantation fields, dwellings, and stores of cotton.

Confederate troops retreated, and plantation families fled with them, taking as many slaves as they could. Some plantation slaves saw their chance for freedom. They ran to the river from all directions, waving and shouting to the Union gunboats. The seamen took them aboard and back to Union camps. That expedition rescued more than 750 African Americans.

An army officer asked her to go to Fernandina, Florida, to treat soldiers suffering from dysentery. She cured many with a medicine she prepared from roots dug out of the marshes. Tubman also recruited a group of former slaves as Union scouts. They hunted for Confederate camps. They reported on enemy troop movements and on the locations of cotton warehouses, ammunition depots, and slaves waiting to be liberated. Her years as an Underground Railroad conductor had taught her the back roads and forest paths of the upper South. She knew how to move around without being detected. She also knew how to play the role of the old harmless freedwoman when it suited her.

After about two years of serving the Union, Tubman received word that her parents, old and in poor health, needed her attention. She traveled to Auburn, New York, where she had bought a home for them, and cared for them until she herself became ill. But Harriet was strong. Soon enough, she was back on her feet, working as matron of the African American Hospital at Fortress Monroe.

After the war, Tubman tried, but failed, to secure a government pension for her service to the Union forces. So she started selling eggs and vegetables door-to-door. A neighbor helped her write her story, *Scenes from the Life of Harriet Tubman*. The book brought in a small income. In March 1869, she married Nelson Davis, more than twenty years her junior. He suffered from tuberculosis contracted during the war. Selfless as always, she cared for him until he died in 1888, at age forty-four. As his widow, she finally collected a military pension of $20 per month. She died on March 10, 1913.

Another African American woman who devoted herself to helping win the war was Susie King Taylor (1848-1912). Born a slave on a plantation near Savannah, Georgia, she joined the First South Carolina Volunteers. Starting out as a laundress, she accepted other tasks with enthusiasm.

In her memoirs, *Reminiscences of My Life in Camp (1902),* she wrote: "I learned to handle a musket very well and could shoot straight and often hit the target, I assisted in cleaning the guns and used to fire them off, to see if the cartridges were dry, before cleaning and reloading…[After a battle] I hastened down to the landing when the wounded began to arrive, some with their legs off, arm gone, foot off, and wounds of all kinds imaginable." "There are many people who do not know what African American women did during the war. Hundreds of them assisted Union soldiers by hiding them and helping them to escape. Many were punished for taking food to the prison stockades for the union prisoners…although they knew what the penalty would be should they be caught."

Chapter Twelve
Governor Pinckney Benton Stewart Pinchback

(1837-1921)

Pinckney Benton Stewart Pinchback was born free on May 10,1837, in Macon, Georgia. He was the eighth child of Eliza Stewart and Major William Pinchback, a European American Mississippi planter. Eliza Stewart had been enslaved when her seven other children were born, but by the time of Pinckney's birth, she had been freed.

When Pinckney and his older brother, Napoleon, were nine and sixteen respectively, their father sent them to Gilmore's School in Cincinnati. After eighteen months, they were called home. Major Pinchback was dying. On his death, his relatives back east seized his estate. Fearing that they might attempt to re-enslave her and her children, Eliza Stewart fled. She went to Cincinnati with her five youngest children—Napoleon, Mary, Pinckney, Adeline, and a baby girl.

Napoleon soon proved mentally unfit to work, so at the age of twelve, Pinckney became the major support of his family. He signed on as a cabin boy on the canal boats running between Cincinnati and Miami, Toledo and Fort Wayne, at a salary of $8 a month. Hardworking and smart, he was eventually promoted to steward. In 1860, he married Nina Emily Hawthorne, whom he had met in Memphis.

After the Confederates fired on Fort Sumter in 1861, Pinchback started looking for a way to get into the fight on the side of the Union. He found it in New Orleans, a cosmopolitan city with a large population of free African Americans. Union navy admiral David Farragut had captured New Orleans in 1862. Soon after, Major General Benjamin J. Butler put out a call for a regiment of African American soldiers, the Corps d'Afrique, for the Louisiana National Guard. Pinchback jumped at the chance to get into the military. He traveled to New Orleans, where he set about recruiting a company.

The enthusiastic twenty-four-year-old managed to raise an entire company in just over a week. The Second Louisiana Native Guards entered into service for the Union on October 12, 1862, under the command of Captain P.B.S. Pinchback.

What a contrast this was to the Union army in the North. For the first time, African American troops could serve under their African American officers. All three of the African American regiments—the First, Second, and Third Louisiana Native Guards (unlike the other regiments, the later was composed of former slaves)—had African American officers.

The African American units saw their first combat during May and June of 1863. The long battle of Port Hudson, Louisiana, included two Louisiana Native Guard regiments and six Corps d'Afrique regiments. Officers, European American and African American, had stories to tell of the brave African American soldiers.

Captain Pinchback's men incurred severe injuries, but rejoined the fray rather than go to a field hospital. With exceptional determination, they kept advancing when certain to be assaulted by enemy fire. Major General Banks reported on the African American troops; "The severe test to which they were subjected, and the determined manner in which they encountered the enemy, leaves upon my mind no doubt of their ultimate success."

The African American regiments distinguished themselves in battle, but that did not affect the opinion of Major General Nathaniel Banks. Ironically, even after witnessing the valor of the African American soldiers, Banks still disapproved of African American officers in general. Pinchback and the other African American officers learned that their commissions were merely temporary, pending qualification examinations. In the next few months, one by one they were disqualified and mustered out. Their places were taken by European American officers. Of all the original African American officers of the Corps d'Afrique, only Pinchback qualified.

Pinchback was determined to have the respect he deserved as a Union officer. He refused to ride on the New Orleans streetcars marked with a large star for "African American" passengers. Whenever he rode a streetcar, he rode along—the car blocked off by streetcar personnel so that no European American passenger could board. No direct action was taken against Pinchback. Instead, he was denied the opportunity to rise in the ranks of the corps d'Afrique. Twice he was passed over for promotion.

By September 1863, Pinchback had had enough. He was much too proud to allow the situation to continue. He submitted his letter of resignation:

Port Pike, Louisiana, September 10, 1863

General:

In the organization of the regiment I am attached to [Twentieth Corps d'Afrique] I find nearly all the officers inimical to me, and I can foresee nothing but dissatisfaction and discontent, which will make my position very disagreeable indeed. I would therefore, respectfully tender my resignation, and I am confident by so doing I best serve the interest of the regiment.

I have the honor to be, sir, very respectfully, your obedient servant.

P.B.S. Pinchback
Captain Second Class
Louisiana National Guard 2

After the war, Pinchback entered politics in Louisiana. He was an able leader. A delegate to the state constitutional convention, his major achievement was the successful introduction of the Thirteenth Amendment to the state's constitution, guaranteeing civil rights to all people of the state. He was elected first to the state senate, then as its president *pro tem*.

When the lieutenant governor died in 1871, Pinchback succeeded to that office. In early December 1872, Louisiana governor Henry Clay Warmoth was impeached, and Lieutenant Governor Pinchback succeeded him, serving as acting governor from December 9, 1872, to January 13, 1873. Those forty-two days made him the first African American governor of a state—and the only African American to hold such a position until the election of L. Douglas Wilder as governor of Virginia in 1990.

In 1872, Pinchback was elected to the U. S. House of Representatives from Louisiana; but his Democratic opponent protested the election and won the seat. The following year, Pinchback was elected to the U.S. Senate, but again he was refused the seat. When Reconstruction ended in 1877, Pinchback's career in elective office ended, too. He earned a law degree from Straight University, New Orleans, and was admitted to the bar of federal and state courts in Louisiana in 1886. He moved with his family to Washington, D.C., and in 1890 organized an American Citizens' Equal Rights Association. Traveling throughout the South and Midwest, he formed local branches of the association.

Governor Pinchback died on December 21, 1921. Two of his and Nina's sons had died, as had their one daughter. Of the two sons who survived, the younger, Walter A, also had a military career. A graduate of Andover Academy and Howard University Law School, Walter Pinchback, a lieutenant in the U.S. Army, served in the infantry in the Spanish-American War.

Chapter Thirteen
Captain Michael A. Healy

(1839-1904)

Michael A. Healy was born near Clinton, Georgia, on September 22, 1839. His father was Michael Morris Healy, an Irishman, who had come to Georgia from Canada in 1812. His mother was an enslaved African America. She was born on the cotton plantation owned by Sam Griswald, who was probably her father.

The Healys had ten children. Three became Catholic priests—one, the first African American Catholic bishop; another, the first and only African American president of Georgetown University in Washington, D.C.

As enterprising as his brothers, young Michael had little interest in a religious career or in going to college. Instead, on March 7, 1865, shortly before the Civil War ended, he enlisted in the United States Revenue Cutter Service, the forerunner of the United States Coast Guard.

Intelligent and able, Healy rose to second lieutenant by June 1866. He was named first lieutenant in 1870 and captain in 1883. He sailed mostly out of San Francisco to Alaska and the Arctic.

Among the ships Healy commanded were the *Chandler*, the *Bear*, and the *Corwin*. The *Bear* was particularly famous. In 1884, while part of the U.S. Navy fleet, she had rescued an expedition of explorers off the uncharted coast of Greenland. When the navy assigned the Bear to the U.S. Revenue Cutter Service, Captain Michael Healy was its first skipper.

Healy cared for the daily needs of the people of Alaska. It was his idea to import reindeer from Russia across the Bering Strait to provide food for the native Alaskans and hide for their clothing. He imported the first dozen reindeer in 1879. Over the next ten years, he helped bring in some 1,100 more.

When Captain Healy retired on September 22, 1903, he was the third-ranking captain in the U.S. Revenue Cutter Service. He died on August 30, 1904.

In the mid-1990s, the U.S. Coast Guard commissioned a new diesel electric ice-breaking ship able to carry a crew of seventy-five plus thirty-five science personnel. It was christened the USCGC (United States Coast Guard Cutter) *Healy*, a fitting honor.

The United States purchased Alaska from Russia in 1867 for a total of $7.2 million. The huge territory was the last earthly frontier of the United States. Its small population depended on the U.S. Revenue Cutter Service for mail and supplies and for legal authority.

For many years, Captain Healy protected the federal law in Alaska as a deputy marshal. One of the single most important people in the territory, he tracked down seal poachers and murderers. His unpredictable temper earned him the nickname Hell Roarin' Mike Healy.

Chapter Fourteen
Congressman Robert Smalls

(1839 - 1915)

The majority of African Americans who fought in the Civil War served in the Union army. Robert Smalls had the distinction of serving both the Confederacy and the Union at sea. But he did not voluntarily aid the Confederate cause.

Born in Beaufort County, South Carolina, Smalls had a Jewish father and an African American mother. He learned sail-making and rigging from his father. After the Civil War broke out, Smalls was pressed into the Confederate service on the ship *Planter*. As pilot, Smalls ferried supplies and munitions from Charleston Harbor out to Fort Ripley and Fort Sumter, avoiding the Union blockade.

In the spring of 1862, Robert Smalls had a daring idea. He made up his mind to hijack the *Planter*. He planned to make a run for the Union blockade even though two Confederate officers guarded the African American crew. Smalls and his brother John, the assistant pilot on the *Planter*, enlisted the support of the other African American crew members.

One night when the officers went ashore, the African American crew cast off from the dock at Charleston and slowly steamed down the harbor. As the *Planter* passed Fort Sumter, she fired her guns in salute. Since it was not unusual to see the ship traveling about in the early morning hours, she aroused no suspicion. The *Planter* managed to get by all the Confederate fortifications without any problem. The crew then raised a white flag signaling surrender and made their way at full steam toward the Union ships blockading the harbor entrance.

Fortunately for Smalls, the Union sailors saw the white flag just before they started to fire on *Planter*. Holding their fire, they were surprised to see only African Americans aboard. Nearing the stern of the Union ship *Onward*, Robert Smalls stepped forward, took off his hat, and said, "Good morning, sir! I've brought you some of the old United States guns, sir!"

The U.S. government offered prize money for any Confederate ship. Smalls and his crew received half the prize money for capturing the *Planter* and remained on the ship.

The navy had accepted African American enlistees even before the Civil War, but there is no evidence that either Smalls or any of his crew actually saw service in the United States Navy. U.S. Government records show that Smalls signed a contract to be master of the *Planter* for the Union from February to July 1865. There was always at least one European American Union officer on board. It was against navy policy to place African Americans in command. Smalls and his crew served for the remainder of the Civil War, once narrowly escaping recapture by the Confederates.

After the war, Smalls enlisted in the South Carolina National Guard, where he achieved the rank of major general. He was a delegate to the 1868 South Carolina Constitutional Convention. He then served two terms in the state legislature and two terms in the state senate. Smalls was among the sixteen African Americans who were elected to Congress during Reconstruction. He was elected to Congress in 1876, 1878, 1880, and 1882, serving longer than any other African American congressman of the period. Congressman Smalls died in 1915.

Chapter Fifteen

Sergeant Major Christian A. Fleetwood

(c. 1840 - ?)

Christian A. Fleetwood was born in Baltimore, Maryland, about 1840. Whether he was born free is not known, but he attended private schools. He went to Ashmund Institute, a new secondary school in Lincoln, Pennsylvania. The school later became Lincoln University, and Fleetwood was in the first graduating class of 1858. He seemed comfortably settled in free African American society. As he wrote later, "I had already some reputation as a singer of some note for the sweetness and purity of tone."

When the Civil War broke out, Fleetwood eagerly joined the Union army. "A double purpose induced me and most others to enlist, to assist in abolishing slavery and to save the country from ruin. "2 On August 11, 1863, he was assigned to army headquarters in Baltimore. Given the rank of sergeant major, he did bookkeeping. He kept the soldier's rosters and wrote reports.

Barely a month passed before Fleetwood's regiment headed out for Yorktown, Virginia. In less than a week, they were ordered on a raid. From then on, Fleetwood was in the thick of the war. There were raids once or twice a month. After April 1864, he was in Point Lookout, Maryland, guarding Confederate prisoners. Then the army formed the United States African American Troops.

Fleetwood's new, African American regiment was the Third Division, Eighteenth Army Troops. They built defenses, fought to hold them, and made reconnaissances. On June 15, some 250 men in the Third Division died in battle at Petersburg, Virginia.

They again faced heavy fire from enemy guns on September 29, 1864. At Chapin's Farm in New Market Heights, Virginia, under Major General William Birney, Fleetwood and his fellow soldiers lost two-thirds of their remaining force. Fleetwood saw the two color bearers shot down. He seized the colors and carried them for the rest of the battle. For his valor, he received the Medal of Honor on April 6, 1865.

Fleetwood performed garrison duty at Fort Slocum until May 1866. Then, like the vast majority of other African American soldiers, he was discharged from the army.

Dr. James Hall, Fleetwood's former employer, recognized his abilities and urged him to re-enlist. Writing to Hall on June 8, 1865, Fleetwood explained his reluctance: "Upon all our record there is not a single blot, and yet no member of this regiment is considered deserving of a commission or, if so cannot receive one. I trust you will understand that I speak not of and for myself individually or that the lack of the pay or honor of a commission induces me to quit the service. Not so by any means, but I see no good that will result to our people by continuing to serve. On the contrary, it seems to me that our continuing to act in a subordinate capacity with no hope of advancement or promotion is an absolute injury to our cause."

Soon after, Fleetwood helped found the Soldiers' and Sailors' League in Philadelphia, Pennsylvania. He settled in Washington, D.C. and became a respected citizen. For a time, he taught school. Then he worked with the Freedman's Bank. In 1881, he went to work in the War Department.

Using War Department records, he wrote about African American soldiers during the Revolutionary War. Fleetwood joined the District of Columbia National Guard, serving as captain in the Independent Company from 1880 to 1887 and as major from 1887 to 1892. In his old age, Fleetwood was deaf in the left ear from "gunshot concussion" and also in the right, a result of "disease contracted in the army." But he died of heart trouble.

When Sergeant Major Fleetwood died, the prominent reconstruction politicians P.B.S. Pinchback and Henry Johnson were honorary pallbearers. So was Major Charles R. Douglass, one of Frederick Douglass's sons. Fleetwood had been a member of the Frederick Douglass Post, G.A.R. After the funeral at St. Thomas Episcopal Church, he was laid to rest in Harmony Cemetery near Washington, D.C.

Chapter Sixteen

Sergeant William H. Carney

(c. 1840 - 1908)

T he first African American to win the Congressional Medal of Honor, William H. Carney was born to an enslaved African American woman and her free husband, a seaman, in Norfolk, Virginia. Carney and his mother were freed from slavery when he was fourteen years old.

When Carney was growing up, it was illegal to teach African Americans to read in Virginia, as elsewhere in the South. Carney studied for a time at a school secretly operated by a minister. He also worked at sea with his father.

In 1856, Carney's family moved to New Bedford, Massachusetts, a whaling seaport. There, he joined a church and studied for the ministry. But when the Civil War broke out, and the Union army began to accept African American enlistees, Carney signed up.

In February 1863, Carney joined the Fifty-fourth Massachusetts Volunteer Regiment, the first African American regiment recruited by the United States Army, raised by Massachusetts Governor John A. Andrew.

The Fifty-fourth Massachusetts headed to South Carolina. On July 18, 1863, after a forced march that had lasted a day and a half, the men of the Fifty-fourth faced Fort Wagner, a Confederate stronghold guarding the entrance to Charleston Harbor. They had rested from their long march only about thirty minutes when they got the order to begin the assault on the fort.

Their column advanced. Immediately, they felt the fire from the fort's big guns as well as from muskets. Colonel Robert Gould Shaw, their commander, fell dead at the head of his regiment. His men fought on. Many of them reached the fort's walls and clambered over them, aiming to disable the big guns. But the musket fire increased. European regiments in the vicinity could have helped the Fifty-fourth, but for various reasons none were able to do so. Without support, the regiment finally had to retreat, having lost a third of its men.

The Fifty-fourth did not capture the fort. But they proved their bravery and their willingness to die for the Union cause. The survivors knew this truth. It took nearly thirty years for the government to acknowledge it.

For his valor on June 18, 1863, during the Battle of Fort Wagner, Carney was cited for the Congressional Medal of Honor. He did not receive the actual medal until May 23, 1900.

In the thick of the fighting at Fort Wagner, Sergeant William H. Carney saw the bearer of the American flag fall. He grabbed the flag before it touched the ground. He planted it on the fort, taking Confederate bullets in each leg, one in the chest, and one in his right arm in the process. Just then the order came to retreat. Carney picked up the flag again and carried it safely back to the Union lines. "The old flag never touched the ground, boys, "he proudly said later.

After the war, the colors Carney carried were enshrined in the Massachusetts statehouse. Sergeant Carney was discharged from the army in 1864. He lived for two years in California, then returned to New Bedford, where he worked as a mail carrier until 1901. He retired that year and moved to Boston, where he worked as a messenger in the statehouse. He died on December 9, 1901.

Chapter Seventeen
Sergeant George Washington Williams

(1849 - 1891)

George Washington Williams fought not only in the Civil War but also in the Mexican War. Born on October 16, 1849, at Bedford Springs, Pennsylvania, Williams was the second child and firstborn son in his family. His mother, Ellen Rouse Williams, was of African and German heritage. His father, Thomas Williams, was of African and Welsh descent.

Thomas Williams was a minister and a barber. By 1860, he owned real estate valued at $500. He traveled a lot, and Ellen Rouse Williams went out to work, leaving young George pretty much on his own. George's education was scanty, but he knew that change was in the air. The Civil War was brewing.

In 1860, when he was only eleven, Williams wrote a letter to Union General O. Howard. In it, Williams said his "Heart Burned with Eager Joy to meet the Planter on the Field of Battle to prove our Human character."

This was in its fourth year in the summer of 1864, when, at the age of fifteen, Williams attempted to enlist. He was found to be too young. He tried again—this time traveling to Meadville in northwestern Pennsylvania to do so. He lied about his age and registered as William Seward—or Charles Steward.

According to Williams's own account, he served for a while with the Tenth Army Corps, commanded by Major General D. B. Birney. Wounded in September 1864 in an assault on Fort Harrison, near Richmond, Virginia, Williams recovered quickly and returned to the fight. When all the African American troops became the U.S. Troops, Williams was assigned to the Second Division of the Twenty-fifth Army Corps. He saw action at Hatcher's Run, Five Forks, and along the 16-mile battle line to Petersburg, Virginia. When Petersburg fell on April 2, 1865, Williams was there. Soon after, the Confederates surrendered.

Back home in Pennsylvania, Williams probably realized that a young African American man with no formal education and few skills had few opportunities. Most of the African American soldiers who had fought in the Civil War had been mustered out, and the United States army had taken few steps toward making a permanent place for African Americans.

After the war, the Twenty-fifth Army Corps went to Texas, and shortly thereafter, George Washington Williams left the army. He may have been discharged because of his age or mustered out as expected. He may have deserted. The real reason is not known.

The adventurous teenager crossed the Texas border into Mexico. Mexican general Espinosa was fighting to overthrow Emperor Maximilian, an Austrian archduke who was ruling Mexico for France. The United States was on General Espinosa's side. Williams joined Espinosa's army against the French. But it is unlikely that Williams or any of the other American soldiers of fortune who fought against Maximilian really understood the politics. He received a commission as lieutenant and served until the spring of 1867. Just before the final march to victory over Maximilian, Williams returned to the United States.

Regardless, Williams went to Pittsburgh and enlisted for five more years in the Twenty-seventh Infantry, under the command of Captain H. Haymond. As a drill sergeant, Williams helped get 100 recruits and then delivered them to Fort Riley, Kansas. Assigned to the Indian Territory with the Tenth Calvary, Williams assisted in the rebuilding of Fort Arbuckle and in providing protection for settlers on the frontier. The Tenth Calvary also campaigned against the Comanches, but it is not known whether Williams actively participated. He received a gunshot wound to his lung on May 19, 1868, but not in the line of duty. Whatever the circumstances, he was hospitalized for the rest of his time in the army.

On September 4, 1868, Williams received a Certificate of Disability for Discharge. His military career was over, and he had not yet reached his nineteenth birthday.

Following his discharge, Williams began to study for the ministry, first in St. Louis, Missouri, then at Howard University in Washington, D.C. Finally, he enrolled at Newton Theological Institution (now Seminary), in Newton, Massachusetts. In 1874, he was the first African American to graduate. That same year, he also married Sarah Sterrett of Chicago and was ordained a minister at Watertown, Massachusetts. For some years, he served as pastor of Twelfth Street Baptist Church in Boston. He and Sarah had one child before their divorce in 1886.

Ever restless, Williams moved to Washington, D.C., where he started a newspaper, *The Commoner.* He then moved to Cincinnati, Ohio, where he was named minister of Union Baptist Church and wrote for local publications. He started to read law, and he was admitted to the Ohio bar in 1879. That same year, he campaigned for and won election to the Ohio Legislature from Hamilton County, becoming the first African American state legislator in Ohio.

While in Ohio, Williams developed a strong interest in African American history and became a voracious reader. In 1883, he published a two-volume 1,000-page *History of the African American Race in America from 1619 to 1880*. Five years later, he published his *History of African American Troops in the War of Rebellion, 1861 - 1865*, making him the first major African American historian.

In a brief eight years after his first book was published, Williams visited the Congo in Africa, wrote a landmark article against colonialism, and served as a U.S. diplomat in Haiti from 1885-1886. Later, he moved to England, where he did research. Sadly, he died from a mysterious illness in 1891.

Part Four

Pioneers in Protest— The Early Years

Lerone Bennett Jr.

Chapter Eighteen

Crispus Attucks

1723-1770

Rouse the Dawn

The day dawned cold and cloudy. There was a film of ice on the narrow cobblestone streets and a tang of tension in the Boston air.

Boston, by now, was used to tension. As the center of the burgeoning resistance movement to British colonial rule, the city was virtually controlled by fiery revolutionaries who roamed the streets smashing windows, setting fires and pelting officials with snowballs and stones. Rioting and looting were common in the city, and there was constant skirmishing between bold young men and the red-coated British troops.

The day dawning now promised to be no better and no worse than the preceding days of this riotous season. Nobody knew then that the day would end in the blood and steel of the Boston Massacre. The good burghers of the city rose early, ate well and went to the shops and offices on Washington Street. Longshoremen and laborers moved by ones and twos to the docks and factories. Indentured servants—African American and European American—roused themselves for another day's work in the service of their Puritan masters.

During the day, a few inches of snow fell. The sky cleared late in the afternoon; and at sunset a new moon appeared in the cloudless skies over Beacon Hill. On Beacon Hill and in Roxbury and in the ghetto of New Guinea, men —African American and European American —clung to the routines of a lifetime. But beneath the surface moved explosive forces that would make this day—Monday, March 5, 1770—a day to remember.

Somewhere in Boston on this day, wily old Sam Adams and the Sons of Liberty were studying revolution and setting traps and snares.

Somewhere in Boston, an African American man named Crispus Attucks was moving toward a critical crossroad of history.

Somewhere in the city, Private Hugh Montgomery of the British Army was eyeing the building tension with apprehension.

Tension had been building in Boston now for eighteen months. Puritan revolutionaries were in open revolt against the government; and there was rising antagonism between well to-do Boston Loyalists, who sided with Great Britain, and angry Patriots, who contended that taxation without representation was tyranny. When, in the winter of 1770, the colonial masses pushed their way onto the stage, the struggle reached explosive proportions.

Throughout this long cold winter, the masses, who were exploited by the British and the colonists, rioted, stoned the houses of Loyalists and voiced open demands for a social as well as a political revolution. In this winter, as in the long hot summers of the American Revolution, riots became a political weapon. Behind the scenes, talented agitators like Samuel Adams fanned the fires of discontent by organizing demonstrations, boycotts, and riots.

African American people and other low-income Bostonians, who had nothing to lose and everything to gain, were in the front ranks of this struggle. Although there were only one thousand African Americans in the Boston population of twelve to fifteen thousand, patriots of color were vociferously visible in the street demonstrations and riots.

African American people, for example, were among the most creative and defiant of the Stamp Act rioters. Many years later, author John Miller described one of these riots. "For a fortnight," he wrote, "the tension in Boston continued to increase, until, on the night of August 28 [1765], boys and African Americans began to build bonfires in King Street and blow the dreaded whistle that sent the Boston mob swarming out of taverns, houses, and garrets. A large crowd immediately gathered around the bonfires, bawling for 'Liberty and Property."

These riots led to the germinal decision to send troops to Boston. And this decision led, bullet by bullet, to the Declaration of Independence. The quartering of troops in Boston gave Sam Adams and other revolutionaries an opportunity to create a revolutionary situation. The Puritan revolutionaries made good use of this opportunity, and within a short time the position of the troops was untenable. There were provocations on both sides and a series of bloody incidents.

A few months before the Boston Massacre, the Redcoats and the African Americans clashed on Boston Common. A Boston newspaper commented: "In the morning nine or ten soldiers of Colonel Carr's regiment were severely whipped on the Common. To behold Britons scourged by African American drummers was a new and very disagreeable spectacle."

Unquestionably; and yet the spectacle continued. There were repeated incidents in February. And on Friday, March 2, there was a brawl between the soldiers and the ropemakers. Ripples from this incident spread across the city, and by nightfall on Monday, March 5, Boston was boiling.

As soon as the new moon appeared over Boston Hill, the soldiers and civilians began jockeying for position. By eight o'clock, the streets were clogged with defiant men, spoiling for a fight.

Witnesses said later that a tall man, "almost a giant," dominated one segment of this wandering crowd. This man, who answered to the name Crispus Attucks, has caused traditional historians no end of trouble. In the first place, he was not a proper Bostonian. In fact, he was not even European American. By singular circumstance, the hero of the Boston Massacre and the first martyr of the Revolution was an African American man and a former slave.

It was Attucks who rallied the wandering crowd and focused its fury.

It was Attucks who carried the battle to the enemy. It was Attucks, an obscure African American man, who was "the first to defy, and the first to die."

Some writers have suggested that Attucks and his colleagues were maneuvered into action by behind-the-scenes agitators who wanted to create a revolutionary point of departure. To be sure, there is some evidence to indicate that the Sons of Liberty set the stage for the disturbance. But there is no convincing evidence to indicate that Attucks acted for anyone other than himself. The record indicates, moreover, that Attucks had a deep and unquenchable love of liberty.

Six feet two, with a fierce countenance and a volatile disposition, Attucks had been born in slavery some forty-seven years before this night in Framingham, Massachusetts. In September, 1750, he struck his first blow for freedom by running away from his master. On October 2, 1750, William Brown of Framingham entered the following description of the runaway in the Boston Gazette: "Short, curly hair, his knees nearer together than common; had on a light colored bearskin coat, plain brown fustian jacket, or a brown wool one, new buckskin breeches, blue yarn stockings and a checked woolen shirt. Whoever shall take up said runaway, convey him to above said master, shall receive ten pounds, old tenor reward, and all necessary charges paid. And all masters of vessels, or others, are hereby cautioned against concealing or carrying off said servant on penalty of the law."

Attucks eluded his pursuers and apparently went to sea as a sailor. There is some evidence to indicate that he spent a great deal of time around the docks in lower Boston. But his movements prior to the night of the Boston Massacre are a matter of conjecture. It was said later that he was in Boston on March 5th awaiting a ship for North Carolina. However that might be, the fact remains that Attucks —bold, defiant, and adventurous—was at center stage on the night of the first momentous act of America's birth.

This drama entered a new phase shortly after eight o'clock on the night in question when the British soldiers sallied out of Murray's Barracks and went for a stroll. This maneuver was designed apparently to prove that the soldiers were not afraid. If so, it was ill-timed and ill-considered. For the soldiers were soon embroiled in a free-for-all with the inflamed citizenry. Someone ran to the Old Brick Meeting House and rang the fire bell. Men poured out of the garrets and houses, and Boston vibrated with the sounds of incipient rebellion —the beating of drums, the ringing of bells, cries, screams, imprecations.

At about the same moment, not too far away, a sentry and a barber's apprentice exchanged insults. The sentry clubbed the youth with the butt of his musket. The youth ran screaming through the streets, embellishing the story, no doubt, as he went. In the wake of this event, wild rumors circulated through the crowd. Some men said the sentry had stabbed the youth. Some men said they had it on good authority that the youth was already dead.

Reports of the altercation reached Crispus Attucks in Dock Square. According to one report, he exploded, saying: "The way to get rid of these soldiers is to attack the main guard. Strike at the nest!"

The Dock Square crowd, with Attucks in the forefront surged toward King Street shouting: "Let us drive out these ribalds. They have no business here." Part of the crowd went up Royal Exchange into King Street. But the largest group followed Crispus Attucks through Boylston's Alley. Attucks was armed with a large cordwood stick.

According to an eyewitness, Attucks and his men were hazing and whistling and then holding sticks upright over their heads.

Before long, there was a crowd of perhaps a hundred whooping, hollering, cursing Bostonians in the little square near the Custom House. The barber's apprentice pointed to the sentry and said, "This is the _ _ _ who hit me." The crowd shouted, "Knock him down! Kill him!"

The sentry backed up the steps of the Custom House, shoved the rammer down his musket and primed it. By this time, reinforcements—seven subalterns and Captain Thomas Preston—were pushing through the crowd.

Crispus Attucks, who was standing in the rear of the crowd, sized up the situation and seized command.

"Do not be afraid," he said. "They dare not fire." The crowd echoed Attucks' words.

"Damn them! They dare not fire. Fire! and be damned."

Attucks and his party gave three cheers and pushed to the front of the crowd, advancing to the tips of the soldiers' bayonets. It was about nine-thirty now, and the bayonets of the beleaguered soldiers glistened in the light of the clear moon. For several seconds, Attucks and the soldiers stood face to face. Then, without warning, someone threw a stick. The stick hit Private Hugh Montgomery, who fell backwards, raised his musket and fired. Attucks, who was standing near the gutter, pitched forward, blood gushing from wounds in his chest. The crowd surged forward and other soldiers fired. When the smoke cleared, five men lay sprawled in the snow —three dead, two mortally wounded.

Like other seminal chapters in history, the events of this night pushed men across the borders of themselves. "From that moment," Daniel Webster said later, "we may date the severance of the British Empire."

John Adams, America's second President, said: "On that night, the foundation of American independence was laid." He added: "Not the Battle of Lexington or Bunker Hill, not the surrender of Burgoyne or Cornwallis, none more important events in American history than the Battle of King Street on the 5th of March, 1770."

Three days later, on Thursday, March 8, there was a public funeral for Attucks and three other martyrs. All the shops in Boston closed in their honor, and all the bells of the city and neighboring towns pealed in remembrance. Contemporaries reported that "a greater number of persons assembled on this occasion, than ever before gathered on this continent for a similar purpose."

The public outcry following the funeral forced withdrawal of the British regiment to Castle Island. Seven of the soldiers were tried for murder and acquitted. Two were found guilty of manslaughter and received minimal sentences.

At the trial, John Adams, the defense attorney, was critical of the Boston crowd which he called "a motley rabble of saucy boys, African Americans and mulattoes, Irish Teagues and outlandish Jack Tars." Adams said that Attucks appeared "to have undertaken to be the hero of the night; and to lead this army with banners, to form them in the first place in Dock Square, and march them up to King Street with their clubs."

Although most of the soldiers were exonerated, Attucks and his comrades were speedily transformed into exemplar myths. The date of their death was celebrated as the national holiday until the adoption of the Declaration of Independence.

One hundred and eighteen years after their death, a monument was erected to the martyrs on Boston Common. John Boyle O'Reilly wrote a special poem for the occasion.

And honor to Crispus Attucks, who was leader and voice that day:

> The first to defy, and the first to die, with Maverick, Carr,
> and Gray.
> Call it riot or revolution, or mob or crowd as you may,
> Such deaths have been seeds of nations, such lives shall be
> honored
> for ay...

Chapter Nineteen
Benjamin Banneker

1731-1806

The Stargazer

Every night as soon as the moon appeared over the hills on the Patapsco River, the African American farmer stole from his cabin with a cloak and pencil and paper. Spreading the cloak on the ground, oblivious of the startled gaze of prying neighbors, the man took up his favorite position: flat on his back, hands under his head, eyes fixed on the fireflies of stars and suns hundreds of light years away. Until dawn, until the stars melted away in light, the stargazer maintained his vigil. Then, brushing himself off, he retreated, absentmindedly, into the cabin where neighbors, in search of salt or information, found him asleep at midday.

The good dull farmers of Ellicott's Lower Mills (now Ellicott City), near Baltimore, were shocked. Good farmers didn't act that way. A farmer, it was said, should be up and doing in the morning and early to bed at night. What kind of behavior was this? What kind of house was the man operating?

People who understood such things tried to explain. They said the man was studying the motions of the heavenly bodies or something of the kind —an explanation, under the circumstances, that did more harm than good. The stolid, unimaginative farmers listened to the explanations with the mounting anger the normal mind throws up to fend off the unusual. In an age when few European American men read books, and even fewer considered scientific careers, it was worse than useless to tell people that an African American man was studying the stars. One can almost hear the peals of laughter as the stories made the rounds. An African American man studying the motions of the heavenly bodies! Who ever heard of such goings-on?

Before too many years had passed, the whole world had heard of Benjamin Banneker, the first African American scholar and the first African American man of national stature to give vent to the African American protest. As an advocate, and as an example, Banneker made a fundamental contribution during the formative years of the American people.

In the years of the Revolution, and after, when Thomas Jefferson and others expressed doubts about the mental endowment of African American people, Banneker stood out, like a rock in a raging stream, as a center of safety and truth for African Americans and European Americans who lost their footing and surrendered to the deception of appearances. He preached eloquently in letters and in private conversation against "the long-established illiberal prejudice against the African Americans." Of even more importance was the propaganda of his deeds. As a mathematician, as an astronomer, surveyor, poet, mechanic, philosopher, clock-maker, and zoologist, Banneker startled men and made them question their assumptions.

All over the world, at this juncture, reason followed profit; and men, as usual, found it easy to believe what served their pocketbooks. They believed, in other words, that African American men were phylogenetically incapable of absorbing "the wonders and mysteries" of Western civilization. Wherever this doctrine was preached, men had to overcome the hurdle of Banneker, who not only beat European American men at their own games but also devised new games for European American men to play.

In Paris, the founders of the Societe des Amis des Noirs discussed the phenomenon of "America's African American Astronomer." So did Pitt and Wilberforce and Buxton in the House of Commons in London. After 1791, when Banneker participated in the survey of Washington, D.C., Americans admitted his weight, though some, characteristically, looked upon him as a biological sport who proved only that it was dangerous to mix African American people and alphabets.

The Banneker years and the Banneker protests were one with the founding of America. Banneker's grandfather came to America on a slave ship. But so, in a manner of speaking, did his European American grandmother.

The grandmother, an extraordinary personage named Molly Welsh, was a poor English worker who ran afoul of the harsh laws regulating employers and employees. For a minor offense, she was shipped to America and sold to a planter for seven years to pay the cost of her passage. Molly Welsh, in short, was an indentured servant —as were many, perhaps most, of the first settlers.

Most European American indentured servants were singularly free of racial prejudice. They worked in the fields with African American slaves and African American indentured servants; they shared huts and tankards of rum with African Americans —and they married them, even in the South.

The relationship between African American and European American indentured servants was close in Maryland, where Molly Welsh worked out her term of servitude and acquired, by stringent econo- mies, a small nest egg. After completing her term of service, she bought a small farm and acquired, as another token of upward mobility, two slaves from a ship in Chesapeake Bay.

One of the slaves was an African of some importance who continued to worship African gods. According to tradition, he was the son of an African king. However that may be, the African in question, one Bannaky, certainly had the airs of a royal person. Or so it seemed to Molly Welsh, who worked the two slaves for a spell and then freed them. Immediately thereafter she married Bannaky and took his name, which was subsequently Anglicized to Bannaker or Banneker.

To Banneker and his English wife were born four children, only one of whom concerns us here. Mary, the oldest, followed her mother's example and married a native African, Robert, who took her name. Among their children was Benjamin Banneker, who was born on November 9, 1731. Six years later, Robert Banneker bought 102 acres in a thinly populated region near Baltimore and built a family home on the brow of a hill overlooking the Patapsco Valley.

Young Benjamin Banneker grew up in a world of ambiguity and change. The status of free African Americans at that time was relatively high. They could vote, marry anyone who wanted to marry them, hold property and dispose of it. Although free African Americans had a place, the place was not well-defined; it depended on a multiplicity of variables and an ingenious African American man could rise by exploiting fissures in the wall.

Banneker, like his famous contemporary Phillis Wheatley, exploited and eventually transcended the wall that hemmed African American people in. Like Wheatley, he was a bookworm. His grandmother taught him letters and he was soon reading the Bible. The family arranged for the precocious youngster to attend an integrated neighborhood school. With his African American and European American schoolmates, Banneker learned the rudiments of arithmetic, writing, and reading.

Then he dropped out of school to help his father with the farm. But he was no longer the same boy. Farm work irked him now, for he had caught a vision of a larger world. He wanted books, pencil, and paper. But the little farming community near Baltimore provided few opportunities for scholars—African American or European American. Most of Banneker's European American neighbors were illiterate, books were hard to come by, and learning was considered a luxury. Here and there, provisions were made for bright and well-to-do European American boys. But an African American scholar and scientist! Everyone —or almost everyone—knew that African Americans could not learn —a "fact" that was related in some way to the color of their skin.

Perceiving the drift of the age, probing into the web of relationships that bound and separated African American and European American folk, Banneker retreated within himself and made his own world. While tending cows or tilling the ground, he chewed over the basic problems he had learned in school. Within a few years, he had thoroughly digested the basic principles of mathematics. Retreating further inward, the farm boy concentrated on his senses and sensations.

The whole world —the sky, the ground, the rain, the seasons— became a school to him. By the time he reached twenty, Banneker had a photographic memory and the eye and instincts of a man of science. Although he had never seen a clock, he made one, using as a model a borrowed watch. All parts of the clock, which was probably the first homemade clock in America, were chipped laboriously out of wood. Banneker's clock, which was completed about 1761, worked perfectly for more than twenty years and people came from miles around to hear it sound the hours.

By 1770, Banneker was a community celebrity. It was the fashion in this age for men of leisure to exchange difficult mathematical problems. In this game, Banneker had few peers. He often returned the answers in rhyme. His fame, as a result, leaped the bounds of Maryland. From all over Colonial America came problems and questions for the African mathematician.

But Banneker's primary problem —a vocation—remained unsolved. On the death of his father and mother, he became the sole proprietor of the farm. There are indications that the idealistic young man considered this windfall a calamity. He was appalled by the time he would have to spend away from his musings and meditations.

A stroke of fate saved the scholar from the pig pen. On the eve of the Revolutionary War, the Ellicotts, a talented and humane Quaker family, settled in the community and erected a flour mill. Three sons of this distinguished family were mathematicians and astronomers of note. They immediately perceived what their duller peers missed: that Banneker was a man of unusual talents. George Ellicott gave Banneker three books, Mayer's Tables, Ferguson's Astronomy, Leadbetter's Lunar Tables, and some astronomical instruments. The Ellicotts also solved Banneker's domestic problems. In return for an annuity of twelve pounds, and a life interest in the farm, Banneker conveyed his property to his European American friends.

Freed now from cows and corn, with leisure for contemplation and books for study, Banneker gave himself up to scholarly pursuits. Astronomy became the burning passion of his life. Within a few years, he could predict eclipses. In 1791, he completed calculations for his first almanac, which was published in 1792.

James McHenry, a prominent Baltimore politician who later served as secretary of war, helped Banneker find a publisher for the almanac. In a letter to Goddard & Angel, the Baltimore publishers, he underlined Banneker's importance as an advocate in the flesh. "I consider this African American as fresh proof that the powers of the mind are disconnected with the color of the skin, or, in other words, a striking contrast to Mr. Hume's doctrine, that the African Americans are naturally inferior to the European Americans, and unsusceptible of attainments in arts and sciences.' In every civilized country, we shall find thousands of European Americans liberally educated and who have enjoyed greater opportunities for instruction than this African American, his inferiors in those intellectual acquirements and capacities that form the most characteristic features in the human race."

McHenry was one of several powerful European Americans who came within the orbit of Banneker's influence. In his dealings with men of substance, Banneker was artful in his advocacy of the African American's cause. He always urged upon his friends the emancipation of African American slaves and the elevation of free African Americans. To deprive African Americans of ambition and hope, he said, was to rob them of the credentials of manhood.

Another influential friend, Major Andrew Ellicott, succeeded in getting Banneker appointed to the commission that laid out the city of Washington, D.C. With the approval of George Washington, Banneker and Ellicott were named to assist Pierre Charles L'Enfant, the brilliant and temperamental French engineer who conceived and drew up the original plan for the ten-mile-square area set aside for the nation's Capital. The naming of Banneker to the Capital commission marked the first presidential appointment received by an African American.

The African American astronomer accompanied Ellicott and L'Enfant to Washington and shared in the deliberations and computations of the commission. The Georgetown Weekly Ledger of March 12, 1791, noted the arrival of L'Enfant and Ellicott, who were "attended by Benjamin Banneker, an Ethiopian, whose abilities as surveyor and astronomer already prove that Mr. Jefferson's concluding that that race of men were void of mental endowment, was without foundation."

L'Enfant was the moving spirit behind the Washington plan. With Ellicott and Banneker assisting, he laid out a show city with great avenues and vistas and open spaces. When a major property owner and political power erected a mansion that obstructed one of his vistas, L'Enfant, the temperamental .artist, immediately tore it down. Washington reluctantly dismissed him, and L'Enfant departed in a huff, leaving the Calculations to Ellicott and Banneker.

In the middle of 1791, Banneker returned to his home near Baltimore. He was now fifty-five, and he was the best known African

American man in America. Invitations were pressed upon him from all quarters and strangers beat a path to his farm. On a favorite horse, Banneker made the rounds and related his experiences in Washington. People who had ridiculed him for wasting his time now gathered close to hear words from his lips. Sitting in the middle of a group in the combination post office and store, leaning on his staff, Banneker told his neighbors of the currents at work in the outside world. Of medium stature, running to fat around the middle, white-haired, pleasant-minded, with dreamy, otherworldly eyes, the county celebrity made a noble appearance. He dressed in "superfine broadcloth" cut in the current mode: a plain coat with straight collar and long waistcoat topped by a broad-brimmed hat.

By all standards, Banneker should have been the happiest of men. His work was going well. Scholars had acclaimed his dissertation on bees and a study which proved that the locust plague recurred in seventeen-year cycles. Now, in the middle of 1791, publishers were bringing out his first almanac.

It is true that he had no family. But he seemed to prefer it that way. With no wife, with no responsibilities, he was free to study stars at night and sleep during the day. In his spare time, he washed his own clothes, cooked his own food and corresponded with scholars. For relaxation, he sat under a huge chestnut tree in his orchard and played the flute or the violin. He was famous, free, and comparatively well-to-do. What else could he want?

There was something. Banneker had returned from Washington with a sense of impending doom. The winds of change were blowing in the new nation called America, and they were blowing the African American no good.

Banneker concluded that the wave of revolutionary idealism in America had reached its peak. The great tide of interracial amity that followed the Revolutionary War was receding, leaving in its wake fear and hate and anxiety. All about him were signs. Free

African American men were being hemmed in by restrictions and oppressive rules: they were insulted on the streets, barred from employment, and proscribed in the church. Laws were being devised that stripped slaves of every vestige of human personality. Walls —walls of hate and fear and guilt—were closing off every avenue of African American advancement. In Banneker's youth, it had been possible for African Americans and European Americans to marry. He himself had attended an integrated school.

Now, a scant fifty years later, these things were no longer possible. There were 757,000 African American people in America, two out of every ten persons. Of this number, 59,000 were free. But the differences between African American slaves and free African Americans were being flattened out and obscured. It seemed almost that men feared free African Americans more than they feared African American slaves. Something, Banneker told himself—something must be done.

Why, he wondered, didn't the African-American's friends speak out? A word now could make a great deal of difference. Banneker's mind turned to Thomas Jefferson, who was the threat and brooding symbol of the age. Jefferson had, when his mood was hot, championed emancipation and manumission of slaves. In a burst of revolutionary idealism, he had written: "All men are created equal." But Jefferson was not the first, nor the last, to set down words that frightened him.

As the years wore on, as the African American population increased, Jefferson hedged his bet with polysyllabic rationalizations. He had not disowned the Declaration of Independence. But he seemed to be saying now that European American men were created more equal than African American people. And worse, he had not manumitted the hundred or more slaves he held at Monticello.

Thinking about these things, following the eddies and currents of the age, Banneker decided that the time was ripe for an act. There had been individual acts of protest in Boston and Philadelphia, but these protests were muted. Free African Americans claimed, with good cause, that their lifelines were too exposed to make an open protest. Banneker proposed to abandon caution and speak openly —as a man. To whom? To Thomas Jefferson, of course. Banneker gathered the manuscript pages of his first almanac and sat down at the oval table in his living room. Dipping pen in ink, he put down these words:

MARYLAND, BALTIMORE COUNTY, August 19, 1791

SIR,

I am fully sensible of the greatness of the freedom I take with you on the present occasion; a liberty which seemed to me scarcely allowable, when I reflected on that distinguished and dignified station in which you stand, and the almost general prejudice and prepossession, which is so prevalent in the world against those of my complexion.

I suppose it is a truth too well attested to you, to need a proof here, that we are a race of beings, who have long laboured under the abuse and censure of the world; that we have long been looked upon with an eye of contempt; and that we have long been considered rather as brutish than human, and scarcely capable of mental endowments.

Sir, I hope I may safely admit, in consequence of the report which has reached me, that you are a man less inflexible in sentiments of this nature, than many others; that you are measurably friendly, and well disposed towards us; and that you are willing and ready to lend your aid and assistance to our relief, from those many distresses, and numerous calamities, to which we are reduced.

Now Sir, if this is founded in truth, I apprehend you will embrace every opportunity, to eradicate that train of absurd and false ideas and opinions, which so generally prevail with respect to us; and that your sentiments are concurrent with mine, which are, that one universal Father hath given being to us all; and that He hath not only made us all of one flesh, but that He hath also, without partiality, afforded us all the same sensations, and endowed us all with the same faculties; and that however variable we may be in society or religion, however diversified in situation or colour, we are all of the same family, and stand in the same relation to Him.

Sir, if these are sentiments of which you are fully persuaded, I hope you cannot but acknowledge, that it is the indispensable duty of those, who maintain for themselves the rights of human nature, and who profess the obligations of Christianity, to extend their power and influence to the relief of every part of the human race, from whatever burden of oppression they may unjustly labour under....

Sir, I freely and cheerfully acknowledge, that I am of the African race, and in that colour which is natural to them, of the deepest dye; and it is under a sense of the most profound gratitude to the Supreme Ruler of the Universe, that I now confess to you, that I am not under that state of tyrannical thralldom, and inhuman captivity, to which too many of my brethren are doomed, but that I have abundantly tasted of the fruition of those blessings, which proceeded from that free and unequalled liberty with which you are favoured; and which, I hope, you will willingly allow you have mercifully received, from the immediate hand of that Being from whom proceedeth every good and perfect gift.

Sir suffer me to recall to your mind the time, in which the arms and tyranny of the British crown were exerted, with every powerful effort, in order to reduce you to a state of servitude; look back, I entreat you, on the variety of dangers to which you were exposed; reflect on that time, in which every human aid appeared unavailable...and you cannot but be led to a serious and grateful sense of your miraculous and providential preservation…

This, Sir, was a time when you clearly saw into the injustice of a state of slavery, and in which you had just apprehensions of the horrors of its condition. It was then that your abhorrence thereof was so excited that you publicly held forth this true and invaluable doctrine, which is worthy to be recorded and remembered in all succeeding ages: "We hold these truths to l« self-evident, that all men are created equal; that they are endowed by their Creator with certain inalienable rights, and that among these are life, liberty, and the pursuit of happiness."

Here was a time, in which your tender feelings for yourselves had engaged you on thus to declare; you were then impressed with proper ideas of the great violation of liberty, and the free possession of those blessings, to which you were entitled by nature; but, sir, how pitiable it is to reflect, that although you were so fully convinced of the benevolence of the Father of Mankind, and of His equal and impartial distribution of these rights and privileges, which He hath conferred upon them, that you should at the same time counteract His mercies, in detaining by fraud and violence, so numerous a part of my brethren under groaning captivity, and cruel oppression, that you should at the same time be found guilty of that most criminal act, which you professedly detested in others, with respect to yourselves.

I suppose that your knowledge of the situation of my brethren is too extensive to need a recital here; neither shall I presume to prescribe methods by which they may be relieved, otherwise than by recommending to you and all others, to wean yourself from those narrow prejudices which you have imbibed with respect to them, and as Job proposed to his friends, "put your soul in their soul's stead"; thus shall your hearts be enlarged with kindness and benevolence towards them; and thus shall you need neither the direction of myself or others, in what manners to proceed herein.

Banneker stopped and reread his lines. Perhaps he had been too bold. After all, it was not the custom for African American people to speak thus to European American people. It was certainly not customary for African American people to speak frankly to a man of Jefferson's stature. Banneker thought for a moment and then added a modest and clever disclaimer.

And now, Sir, although my sympathy and affection for my brethren has caused my enlargement thus far, I ardently hope that your candour and generosity will plead with you in my behalf, when I make known to you that it was not originally my design; but having taken up my pen in order to direct to you, as a present, a copy of an Almanac which I have calculated for the succeeding year, I was unexpectedly and unavoidably led thereto.

This calculation is the product of my arduous study, in this my advanced stage of life.... I have taken the liberty to direct a copy to you which I humbly request you will favourably receive and although you may have the opportunity of perusing it after its publication, yet I desire to send it to you in manuscript previous thereto, thereby you might not only have an earlier inspection, but that you might also view it in my own handwriting.

And now, Sir, I shall conclude, and subscribe myself, with the most profound respect.

Your most obedient humble servant,

BENJAMIN BANNEKER

The letter reached Jefferson, who was then secretary of state in George Washington's cabinet, at Philadelphia. Jefferson's immediate impressions are not a matter of record. Over the next decade, he said various things about Benjamin Banneker, some of them quite harsh. But to Banneker himself he presented his best face in reply.

PHILADELPHIA, Aug. 30, 1791

SIR,

I thank you most sincerely, for your letter of the 19th instant, and for the Almanac it contained. Nobody wishes more than I do, to see such proofs as you exhibit, that nature has given to our African American brethren talents equal to those of the other color of men; and that the appearance of the want of them is owing merely to the degraded condition of their existence, both in Africa and America. I can add with truth, that nobody wishes more ardently to see a good system commenced, for raising the condition, both of their body and mind, to what it ought to be, as far as the imbecility of their present existence, and other circumstances, which cannot be neglected, will admit.

I have taken the liberty of sending your Almanac to Monsieur de Condorcet, Secretary of the Academy of Sciences, at Paris, and Member of the Philanthropic Society, because I considered it as a document to which your whole colour have a right for their justification against the doubts which have been entertained of them.

I am, with great esteem, Sir, Your most obedient humble servant,

THO. JEFFERSON

MR. BENJAMIN BANNEKER, near
ELLICOT'S LOWER MILLS, BALTIMORE COUNTY

Banneker's letter and Jefferson's answer made a big ripple in tin-events of the day. The correspondence was discussed in France, England, and the South. But nothing happened. Slavery continued its ominous march across the soul of America. Frightened by the successful Haitian Revolution and abortive slave revolts in Virginia and other states, masters elaborated increasingly severe rules for the control of African American slaves and free African Americans.

In dwindling hope, then, and with foreboding for the country he loved, Banneker lived out his measured days.

A gentle, Christian man who never joined a church, he turned in his winter days to the advocacy of peace. His plan for a Lasting Peace anticipated many of the principles of the League of Nations and the United Nations. But neither in peace nor in tolerance did he overcome. The whole drift of the age was against him.

Wars and rumors of wars and the clanking of slave chains: these things were in the wind in October, 1806. Banneker was resting in his home one day in that month when he seemed to hear voices beckoning him to another world. On an impulse, he rose and started down the path leading from his house. He had not gone far when his strength gave out and he sank helplessly to the ground. He died later that day and was buried in an unmarked grave.

But the idea the gentle scholar and advocate symbolized could not be disposed of so easily. Within twenty years, Banneker was disturbing the peace of racists from the grave. His name and his letter ("Look back, I entreat you") were cited repeatedly by abolitionists in their successful assault on the intellectual props of the slave South. Banneker has been no less persuasive in our own times. For men who dare and dream, for men who appeal from the gutters to the stars, for men who stand up and protest, no matter what the odds, the stargazer remains a persuasive and articulate example.

Chapter Twenty
Prince Hall

1748-1807

Colonial Catalyst

Colonies were ablaze with indignation. In Virginia, Patrick Henry was speaking of liberty or death. In New York and South Carolina, in Rhode Island and Maryland, Sons of Liberty were demonstrating and boycotting. Boston, the center of colonial discontent, was a festering boil of boycotts, processions, and bonfires. An unruly crowd of African American laborers, European American artisans, seamen and mechanics virtually controlled Boston streets. Business was at a standstill. Stores, offices, even courts, were closed. Night after night, men poured from garrets and taverns, screaming, "No taxation without representation."

Moving along the edge of the tumultuous Boston crowds was a thin, delicate-looking teenager. His name was Prince Hall and he had just arrived from Barbados, where he had been born about 1748, the son of an Englishman and a free African American woman. He was, in theory, free; but he was also an African American man and he knew that neither in Boston nor in Barbados were African American men free in fact. As the revolutionary drama swirled in the streets before him, Prince Hall wondered what it all meant to Puritan slaveholders. He wondered if they were sincere and if it had occurred to them that every principle from which they acted was "stronger than a thousand arguments in favor" of African American people and slaves.

The audacity, the sheer effrontery, of American patriots fascinated Hall. The colonists held in servitude more than a half million human beings, some of them European American; yet they proposed to go to war in support of the theory that all men were created equal. In 1765, when Hall worked his way to Boston on a ship, there were almost sixteen thousand African American people in New England—almost all of them slaves and social pariahs.

Prince Hall moved around Boston with his eyes open and he was appalled by the social and economic conditions of slaves and free African Americans. Even more appalling to the sensitive youth was the indifference of colonial patriots. Boston, at that time, was a center of the American slave trade. In one way or another, most men of substance benefited from the trade in men and the ancillary businesses that grew up around it. Most of the major leaders of the revolutionary movement, in fact, were slaveholders or investors in slave-supported businesses. What did these men mean by freedom?

Not only Hall but thousands of other Americans were disturbed by this question. Tom Paine, James Otis, Abigail Adams and other revolutionary leaders told the colonists that their pretensions were inconsistent with their practices. Patrick Henry, an honest slaveholder, admitted that slavery was wrong but said he was "drawn along by the general inconvenience of living without them [slaves]."

What of the African American slaves and the free African Americans? What did the revolutionary agitation mean to them?

Prince Hall investigated the wharves and alleys where unattached African Americans lived. He listened to their discussions and their arguments and noted, with approval, the rapid growth of political and social consciousness. There had been individual protests and collective revolts, as Prince Hall knew. But free African Americans had been strangely silent. Now, as Hall watched, the ghetto came alive. For the first time in America, for the first time anywhere, city African Americans found a voice and a technique. Slave revolts and underground resistance had taken place outside the system.

African Americans proposed now to use the ideology and instruments of the system to smash the system. They proposed to bore from within and destroy legal forms with legal forms. Their first technique, one that would reach full flower 194 years later, was legal contention.

In the 1760's, Prince Hall watched with burning interest as the African American soul expanded and made its first tentative probes in enemy territory. As early as 1766, one year after Hall's arrival, Boston African Americans filed a test case against slavery. The movement spread to Connecticut and other states. Under the leadership of men whose names were not recorded, slaves and free men collected money, hired lawyers, and filed suits, asking for freedom and damages for unlawful detention. In Connecticut and Massachusetts, slave-instigated suits were appealed to the highest courts. In some courts, judges granted the pleas of slave petitioners.

African Americans, in this period, also experimented with mass pressure. Meetings were held, petitions for freedom were circulated and signed. Courts and legislatures were bombarded with petitions from Americans protesting tyranny and oppression in America.

Ingenious men found other ways to turn the revolutionary turmoil to their advantage. Some African American men, like Crispus Attucks, the leader of the crowd in the Boston Massacre, appropriated American slogans and assumed leadership in the street riots in Boston and other cities. Still others, more cynical or more realistic, sided with the British. As the agitation intensified, slaves and free men became bolder. The number of slave escapes increased sharply, the number of incidents multiplied.

The first wave of agitation unfolded without conscious planning or direction. In the 1770's, however, self-conscious men who considered themselves leaders and were so considered by others stepped from the anonymity of the crowd and assumed of men and events.

Among the most talented of these leaders was Prince Hall, who had moved for six or seven years on the edge of events, studying men and organizations. Hall spent his first years in Boston in study and hard work. Working as a laborer in the day and studying at night, he saved enough money to buy property. He also became a Methodist minister and a talented organizer and advocate of freedom. Within ten years of his arrival in Boston, the young man from Barbados was one of the leading lights of the first Freedom movement.

As one of America's first abolitionists, Hall made a big contribution to the movement that led to the erosion of slavery in the North. As organizer and leader of the first African American organization outside the African American church, Hall also made an important contribution to the development of African American morale and solidarity. Hall excelled in the areas of organization and technique.

During the first wave of agitation, he learned the value of an organizational base. And he was soon preaching the virtues of solidarity and collective action to the scattered and largely demoralized African American population of Boston. Though free, Hall made a point of signing slave petitions, an act that dramatized the unity of fate of free African Americans and slaves.

His major contribution, however, was the organization of the first African American Masonic lodge. He attempted first to enter a lodge of the European American Masons. Rebuffed, he applied to a lodge attached to a British regiment stationed near Boston. On March 6, 1775, Prince Hall and fourteen other African American men were initiated into Masonry in the British Army lodge. When the British regiment withdrew, the African American Masons formed, under a limited permit, African Lodge No. 1, one of the first African American organizations in America.

After the war, Hall was granted a charter from the Grand Lodge of England. On May 6, 1787, African Lodge No. 459 was formally organized in Boston with Hall as master. This event, coming less than a month after the founding of the Free African Society of Philadelphia, was an epochal leap forward in African American consciousness. In 1797, Hall helped organize African American lodges in Philadelphia and Providence, Rhode Island, thereby becoming a pioneer in the development of an African American interstate organization.

Throughout this period, Hall protested bigotry and discrimination. Like most African Americans, he fought on two fronts in the Revolutionary War. As an American patriot and a soldier in George Washington's army, Hall opposed British tyranny. As an African American man, he opposed American bigots with their own weapons: the lofty words of the Declaration of Independence.

With many other African Americans, Hall saw service on Bunker Hill. When George Washington arrived to take command of the Army of Cambridge, he found scores of African American men in the ranks. Although these veterans had fought with distinction at Lexington, Concord, and Bunker Hill, Washington immediately barred them from the Continental Army. The African Americans of New England refused to accept this blow without protest. Hall, according to tradition, led a delegation of free African Americans who took their complaints to Washington's headquarters. Washington was impressed by the delegation's plea. Hall and his group were too diplomatic and clever to show all their cards, but they managed somehow to convey a subtle threat.

The colonists, at that moment, were pressed on all sides. They lacked manpower and weapons. To make matters worse, an uncomfortably large number of Americans were siding with Great Britain. In this volatile situation, America could ill afford additional enemies. Lord Dunmore made this abundantly clear when he issued a proclamation welcoming African American slaves and free African Americans to the British Army. Thousands of slaves, including some who belonged to Thomas Jefferson and George Washington, abandoned the plantations to fight for their own freedom.

Apprised of these developments, George Washington overruled himself and countenanced the enlistment of free African Americans who had served in the army at Cambridge. In a letter to the president of Congress, Washington explained his decision. Said he: "It has been presented to me, that the free Negroes, who have served in this army, are very much dissatisfied at being discarded. As it is to be apprehended, that they may seek employ in the ministerial [British] army, I have presumed to depart from the resolution respecting them, and have given license for their being enlisted…" After the disastrous winter of Valley Forge, Washington scrapped all resolutions and accepted free African Americans and African American slaves.

Prince Hall and other African American leaders continued to trouble the soul of America during the war years. In pamphlets and petitions, they stressed the close connection between American freedom and African American freedom. Hall was the moving force behind a "slave petition" that openly questioned the sincerity and the good sense of American patriots. This petition, which was filed on January 13, 1777, with the General Court of Massachusetts, is reproduced, in part, below:

> The petition of a great number of African Americans, who are detained in a state of slavery in the very bowels of a free and Christian country, humbly showing,—
>
> That your petitioners apprehend that they have, in common with all other men, a natural and inalienable right to that freedom, which the great Parent of the universe hath bestowed equally on all mankind, and which they have never forfeited by any compact or agreement whatever.

But they were unjustly dragged by the cruel hand of power from their dearest friends, and some of them even torn from the embraces of their tender parents, —from a populous, pleasant and plentiful country, and in violation of the laws of nature and of nations, and in defiance of all the tender feelings of humanity, brought hither to be sold like beasts of burthen, and like them, condemned to slavery for life —among a people possessing the mild religion of Jesus —a people not insensible of the sweets of national freedom, nor without a spirit to resent the unjust endeavors of others to reduce them to a state of bondage and subjection...

[The petitioners] cannot but express astonishment that it has never been considered, that every principle from which America has acted, in the course- of her unhappy difficulties with (Great Britain, bears stronger than a thousand arguments in favor of your humble petitioners.

They therefore humbly beseech Your Honors to give their petition its due weight and consideration, and cause an act of the legislature to be passed, whereby they may be restored to the enjoyment of that freedom, which is the natural right of all men, and their children (who were born in the land of liberty) may not be held as slaves after they arrive at the age of twenty-one years.

So may the inhabitants of this State (no longer chargeable with the inconsistency of acting themselves the part which they condemn and oppose in others) be prospered in their glorious struggles for liberty, and have those blessings secured to them by Heaven, of which benevolent minds cannot wish to deprive their fellowmen.

And your petitioners, as in duty bound, shall ever pray:

LANCASTER HILL,
PETER BESS,
BRISTEN SLENFEN,
PRINCE HALL,
JACK PIERPONT, [his X mark]
NERO FUNELO, [his X mark]
NEWPORT SUMNER, [his X mark]

Also active during this period were Hall's contemporaries, Phillis Wheatley and Paul Cuffe. Wheatley, the second American woman to publish a book, did not voice open protests; but she struck blows for the cause with her poems. Cuffe, a wealthy captain who sailed his own ships to Europe and Africa, was outspoken and inventive. Barred from the ballot box in Dartmouth, Massachusetts, he refused to pay taxes and filed a defiant petition of protest. After a long controversy it was decided that taxation without representation in America was tyranny.

The case was widely regarded as establishing a precedent for African American suffrage.

After the war, the Freedom movement continued with assaults on the slave trade and the African American's perennial issue, equal education. By this time, Hall was known throughout New England as a skillful user of the public petition. In 1787, He filed one of the first public petitions for equal education. He later asked the selectmen of Boston to establish a school house for African American children. Education, to Hall, was a key to power. "We...must fear for our rising offspring," he said, "to see them in ignorance in a land of gospel light, when there is provision made for them as well as others and yet [they] can't enjoy them, and [no other reason] can be given [than that] they are African American..."

Hall also took the lead in antislavery agitation. When three African American men were kidnapped and sold into slavery in the West Indies,

Hall sprang into action. Under his leadership, African American people filed an antislavery petition with the Massachusetts legislature. Spurred on by the petition, Governor John Hancock filed an official protest. The three men were located and returned to Boston, where a huge celebration was held.

This incident and the protest of African Americans and European Americans led to the passage of a state law against the slave trade.

Despite isolated gains, this was a difficult period for the African Americans. In the first flush of victory, there was a rash of manumissions. Other African Americans received freedom as a result of war service, court suits or legislative action. By 1790, slavery was a dying institution in the North.

Not all men rejoiced.

To poor European Americans, the recently emancipated slaves were an economic threat. To aristocrats and businessmen, free African Americans were social dynamite, an anomalous group in a social system designed for two: African American slaves and free European American men. With one eye on the Haitian Revolution, which began in 1791, and another on the sharp upswing in the free African American population in towns and cities, men of power began enacting discriminatory legislation. The freedom of African American people was severely restricted.

They could not walk on the streets of Boston after 9 P.M. without a pass; they could not go outside the bounds of their community without a pass. They could not own certain types of property. Worse, they were barred from the best jobs. In Boston, in the turbulent years after the Revolution, free African American men were insulted, threatened, and beaten by mobs of poor European Americans. On public occasions, they were barred from Boston Common.

Prince Hall watched the darkening clouds with deepening despair. The old patriot was especially horrified by the desecration of the

symbols of the Revolution. On July 4th, public-spirited crowds celebrated the birth of the Republic by whipping African Americans and
driving them from the streets of Boston.

Particularly shocking was an incident involving one Colonel Middleton, a hard-swearing, hard-fighting African American man who had
commanded an African American company in the Revolutionary
War. Prince Hall was doubtless aware of the Boston riot described by
Lydia Maria Childs, who witnessed it as a child. "About three o'clock
in the afternoon," she wrote, "shouts of a beginning fray reached us.
Soon, terrified children and women ran down Belknap street, pursued by European American boys, who enjoyed their fright."

"The sounds of battle approached; clubs and brickbats were flying in
all directions. At this crisis, Col. Middleton opened his door, armed
with a loaded musket, and, in a loud voice, shrieked death in the first
European American men who should approach."

Hundreds of human beings, European American and African American, were pouring down the streets, the African Americans making
but a feeble resistance, the odds in numbers and spirit being against
them. Col. Middleton's voice could be heard above every other,
urging his party to turn and resist to the last. His appearance was ter-
rific, his musket was leveled, ready to sacrifice the first European
American man that came within its range. The African American
party, shamed by his reproaches, and fired by his example, rallied,
and made a short show of resistance."

Lydia Maria Child's father approached Colonel Middleton and asked
him to put away his gun. The colonel stood for a while in defiance,
then said: "I will do it for you, for you have always been kind to me."
So saying, the old African American soldier retired from the scene,
weeping and cursing as he went.

That men who had risked life and limb should be treated so grieved
Prince Hall. To be sure, Hall himself was not personally affected by
the climate of creeping bigotry. He and his second wife (his first wife

died in 1769) had a comfortable and well-appointed home. They had no children, but they had a wide circle of friends; and their home in Lendell's Lane was a windbreak against the gathering storm.

As a soap manufacturer and artisan, Hall had accumulated money and property. As a minister and grand master in the Masonic order, he was a man of weight and substance in the community. European American men of power considered him something of an exception, a patronizing attitude that Hall neither encouraged nor accepted.

A slight man of small stature with brooding good looks, fair skin and commanding eyes, Hall was reasonably happy and content. Still, he feared for the future of his people. And he raised his voice in rebuke and remonstrance. It seemed to some, and it must have seemed sometimes to Hall himself, that he was tilting at windmills. But he continued to speak out, demanding for African American men not only freedom but the full credentials of citizenship: social, political, and economic equality. Hall's hope, faith, and forbearance did not find an echo in the hearts of "stand-and-shoot" men like Colonel Middleton. But his insistence on full equality raised the consciousness of many of his contemporaries.

Until his death on Friday, November 4, 1807, Hall championed the twin interests of his life: organizational effectiveness and human brotherhood. His charge to the African Lodge, delivered at Menotomy (now West Cambridge) on June 24, 1797, was a requiem to the death of a dream stillborn. But it was also an extraordinary leap of faith in one of the African American's worst hours. Hall began with a doleful recitation of woes and tribulations.

> "...let us see our friends and brethren; and first let us see them dragged from their native country, by the iron hand of tyranny and oppression, from their dear friends and connections, with weeping eyes and aching hearts, to a strange land, and among a strange people, whose tender mercies are cruel,— and there to bear the iron yoke of slavery and cruelty, till death, as a friend, shall relieve

them. And must not the unhappy condition of these, our fellowmen, draw forth our hearty prayers and wishes for their deliverance from those merchants and traders...."

"Now, my brethren, as we see and experience, that all things here are frail and changeable and nothing here to be depended upon: Let us seek those things which are above, and at the same time let us pray to Almighty God, while we remain in the tabernacle, that he would give us the grace of patience and strength to bear up under all our troubles, which at this day God knows we have our share."

"Patience, I say, for were we not possessed of a great measure of it, you could not bear up under the daily insults you meet with in the streets of Boston; much more on public days of recreation, how are you shamefully abused, and that at such a degree, that you may truly be said to carry your lives in your hands; and the arrows of death are flying about your heads; helpless old women have their clothes torn off their backs, even to the exposing of their nakedness..."

What then was to be done?

Hall was honest; he had no easy answers. The tentacles of slavery were penetrating the private places of every man's soul and it seemed, in this white hour, that slavery would never die. But this, Hall said, was the deception of appearances "for the darkest hour is just before the break of day." Hall urged his listeners to persevere. He reminded them of the unexpected successes of the Haitian Revolution and concluded with a Jubilee for the day when men would receive men as friends and treat them as brothers.

Even as Hall spoke, storm clouds were gathering that would give meaning to his years of pioneering protest and his ringing affirmation of hope: "Thus does Ethiopia stretch forth her hand I turn slavery to freedom and equality."

Chapter Twenty-One

Samuel E. Cornish and John B. Russwurm

Cornish 1795-1858/Russwurm 1791-1851

Founders of the African American Press

Day in and day out, the African American people of New York City were mercilessly lampooned in the European American press. In the dying days of 1826, the campaign of vilification and slander reached nauseous heights. The integrity and courage of African American men were openly questioned. Worse, editors invaded homes and impugned the chastity of African American women.

The leader of this campaign was Mordecai M. Noah, an eccentric dramatist and entrepreneur who controlled several newspapers at various times. Obsessed by what he considered African American degradation, he pushed a bitterly personal one-man crusade. And his crusade was the proximate or immediate cause of the founding of what became the largest and most powerful minority press in America. For it was to devise a defense against the scurrilous attacks of this editor that New York leaders came together in the early weeks of 1827.

Meeting in the home of Boston Crummell, the patriarch of the African American community, the leaders decided that African American people could not depend on either their friends or their enemies for a complete articulation of their ideals and aspirations. After a long and heated discussion, the African American leaders decided to organize a newspaper to answer not only the charges of individual editors, but also the collective assault of European Americans on the African American psyche.

This was a time of acute crisis for all African Americans and the leaders were agonizingly conscious of the forces arrayed against them. Bread was dear in every ghetto, and anti-African American riots were common. More ominous was the creeping power of the American Colonization Society. Not only the African American's enemies, notably the New York editor, but also his friends, notably Benjamin Lundy, Gerrit Smith, and, before 1830, William Lloyd Garrison, were saying that African Americans would probably be better off in a hotter climate—Africa, one wit put it, or either hell.

Samuel E. Cornish and John B. Russwurm, two of the youngest and most promising of the New York leaders, were assigned the task of inventing a journal that could speak forcibly to both the enemy and faint friend without and the "brethren" within, the veil. Cornish and Russwurm were eminently fitted for the task. Both were of free stock, and both were articulate exponents of persistent protest. Cornish, who is virtually unknown today, was born about 1795 in Delaware and raised in the relatively free environments of Philadelphia and New York City. After graduating from the Free African schools, he became a minister and organized the first African American Presbyterian Church on New Demeter Street in Manhattan.

Russwurm, who is generally credited with being the first African American graduate of an American college, was a Jamaican, the son of a European American man and an African Jamaican woman. His father, motivated perhaps by a sense of guilt, sent him secretly to a Canadian school where he was registered under the name of John

Brown. The father neglected to inform his European American wife of the sins of his youth; but after his death, the widow learned of the existence of the son and insisted that "John Brown" assume his rightful name of John B. Russwurm. She also financed Russwurm's education at Bowdoin, where he was graduated in 1826.

Despite the difference in their backgrounds, Russwurm and Cornish made an excellent team. Cornish, the idealist and uncompromising fighter, complemented Russwurm, who was a pragmatist dedicated to "the art of the possible."

With the idealistic Cornish at the helm as senior editor and the practical Russwurm in second place as junior editor, the African American-owned and African American-operated publishing company confounded the skeptics by making tangible steps toward what many considered an impossible goal, the publishing of an African American newspaper.

The prospectus for the proposed paper was a masterly blend of idealism and practicality. "We shall ever regard the constitution of the United States as our polar star," Cornish and Russwurm wrote. "Pledged to no party, we shall endeavor to urge our brethren to use their rights to the elective franchise as free citizens. It shall never be our object to court controversy though we must at all times consider ourselves as champions in defense of oppressed humanity. Daily slandered, we think that there ought to be some channel of communication between us and the public, through which a single voice may be heard, in defense of five hundred thousand free people of colour. Too often has injustice been heaped upon us, when our only defense was an appeal to the Almighty, but we believe that the time has now arrived, when the calumnies of our enemies should be refuted by forcible arguments...."

On Friday, March 16, 1827, the first issue of Freedom's Journal, the first African American newspaper in the Western world, appeared on the streets of New York City. In the first editorial, Cornish and Russwurm struck a note that is as modern as today's headlines.

We wish to plead our own cause. Too long have others spoken for us. Too long has the publick been deceived by misrepresentations, in things which concern us dearly, though in the estimation of some mere trifles; for though there are many in society who exercise towards us benevolent feelings; still (with sorrow we confess it) there are others who make it their business to enlarge upon the least trifle, which tends to the discredit of any person of colour! and pronounce anathemas and denounce our whole body for the misconduct of this guilty one….

Our vices and our degradation are ever arrayed against us, but our virtues are passed by unnoticed. And what is still more lamentable, our friends, to whom we concede all the principles of humanity and religion, from these very causes seem to have fallen into the current of popular feeling and are imperceptibly floating on the stream—actually living in the practice of prejudice, while they abjure it in theory, and feel it not in their hearts. Is it not very desirable that such should know more of our actual conditions; and of our efforts and feelings, that in forming or advocating plans for our amelioration, they may do it more understandingly?

Having stated succinctly the immediate causes of the founding of the African American press —the calumnies of enemies and the timidity of avowed friends—Cornish and Russwurm went on to take their stands on the great rocks of the African American press—civil rights in general and the ballot in particular. "The civil rights of a people being of the greatest value, it shall ever be our duty to vindicate our brethren, when oppressed; and to lay the case before the publick. We shall also urge upon our brethren…the expediency of using their elective franchise; and of making an independent use of the same. We wish them not to become the tools of the party."

As for policy, the editors pledged themselves to print "everything that relates to Africa" and to hold up always the banner of the downtrodden, especially the slaves "[who] are our kindred by all the ties of nature."

"It is our earnest wish," the first editorial of the first African American newspaper said, "to make our Journal a medium of intercourse between our brethren in the different states of this great confederacy; that through its columns an expression of our sentiments, on many interesting subjects which concern us, may be offered to the publick; that plans which apparently are beneficial may be candidly discussed and properly weighed; if worthy, receive our cordial approbation; if not, our marked disapprobation."

In these historic words, Cornish and Russwurm stated the mission and purpose of the African American press which some students believe to be the most powerful institution in the African American community. Indeed, Myrdal and others have asserted that the African American press created the African American as a social and political being.

Back then only a few men recognized the power and potential of the paper with the prophetic title, Freedom's Journal.

The paper, in truth, was a modest thing. In structure and conception, it was more a magazine than a newspaper. Not more than two of the sixteen columns were devoted in foreign and domestic news. The remaining columns were filled with material not unlike the stories and features in Ebony and other African American-oriented magazines. The first issue, for example, contained the first installment of the "Memoirs" of Paul Cuffee, the African American captain, a report on the illegal imprisonment of a poet, articles on the "Common Schools of New York," and "The Church and the Auction Block," "A True Story," an essay on "The Effect of Sight Upon a Person Born Blind," antislavery material, entertainment and variety departments. There was even an article with disguised sex appeal, "On Choosing a Wife By Proxy."

Also included in the paper were notices of marriages, deaths, and court trials. Commercial advertisements were printed on the last page.

The paper was published every Friday at No. 5 Varick Street in Manhattan. Free African Americans in all sections of the country, and in Canada, Haiti, and England, rallied to the support of the Journal, organizing local societies. Among the prominent African Americans who served as correspondents were James Forten, David Walker, and Richard Allen.

Like John H. Johnson of Ebony, Jet, and Negro Digest, like John Sengstacke of the Chicago Defender, Carl Murphy of the African American, Melvin B. Miller of the Bay State Banner, Clovis Campbell of the Arizona Informant, Cornish and Russwurm stressed those facets of the Afro-American personality which are ignored in European American media. African American achievement, as expressed in the careers of Phillis Wheatley, Toussaint Louverture, and Richard Allen, was prominently featured in Freedom's Journal. Race/Culture pride, another value of the modern African American press, was also emphasized.

Freedom's Journal played an extremely important role not only as a protest journal, but also as an instrument for revealing the human dimension of the African American personality. European American men of that day scoffed at the idea of love and family ties among African Americans. By featuring the Afro-American as a parent, a bride, a mother or a father, the paper exposed the one-dimensional treatment of the African American in the European American press.

Since the paper was founded, at least in part, as a reaction to the slurs on African American women, Cornish and Russwurm played up the trials and triumphs of African American mothers and wives, noting:

> Black I am, oh daughter fair
> But my beauty is most rare.

Cornish and Russwurm were African American editors, but they were also editors who published a great deal of literary and scientific material which had no immediate bearing on race/culture. "Only a strong necessity," they said, forced them to stress race/culture. And it would be necessary, they said, to stress race/culture as long as the "strong necessity" existed, as long, in fact, as the European American press refused to present African American people in the totality of their being.

As shapers and reflectors of African American opinion and sentiment, the two pioneer editors prepared public opinion for the antislavery crusade. Long before William Lloyd Garrison, they advocated immediate emancipation and unconditional freedom with full civil rights. In fact, Freedom's Journal and Samuel E. Cornish were largely responsible for the conversion of the early European American abolitionists, who were, as one leader put it, being "swept away by the waves of expatriation."

For two years, Freedom's Journal served as a beacon for both African American and European American protestants. Cornish retained an interest in the Journal throughout this period, but he resigned the senior editorship in September, 1827, and became an agent for the Free African schools. Russwurm succeeded him as editor. But Russwurm, as it turned out, was undergoing a crisis of conscience.

As the flames of fear and phobia leaped higher and higher, Russwurm became convinced that the American Colonization Society was right. In February, 1829, he announced his support of "the return to Africa movement." Enraged African American leaders forced him to resign and accused him of "selling out" to the enemies of African American people. Russwurm maintained that he was sincere; but this was no comfort to African American leaders, who burned him in effigy.

By this time, Russwurm had moved to a position that would be called African American nationalism today. Believing that the "man of color would never find a place in the Western Hemisphere to lay his head," he called for a return to Africa and a revival of the great empires of the Middle Ages. What angered other African American leaders was his acceptance of a liberal offer from the conservative Maryland Colonization Society and his defense of the African American exclusion laws of Ohio because "our rightful place is in Africa."

After receiving an M.A. degree from Bowdoin College Russwurm sailed for Liberia, where he founded the Liberia Herald and served as superintendent of schools. He later became famous as governor of the Maryland Colony at Cape Palmas. The pioneer editor died in Liberia in 1851.

African American leaders of the nineteenth century never forgave Russwurm for his alleged defection. Until the latter part of the century, they were almost unanimous in deprecation of Russwurm and praise of Cornish. Today, in one of history's strange little jests Russwurm is universally praised and Cornish is forgotten.

After Russwurm's forced resignation, Cornish resumed editorial control of Freedom's Journal. In May, 1829, two months after the temporary suspension of the Journal, Cornish started a new paper, The Rights of All. Thereafter, he was associated with a number of periodicals. He was also a member of the executive committee of the board of the American Antislavery Society and was probably the first African American to champion Tuskegee- type trade schools.

Cornish, unlike Russwurm, called for a fight to the finish in America. "Let there be no compromise," he said, "but as though born free and equal, let us contend for all the rights guaranteed by the constitution of our native country."

As for the designation "American," Cornish contended that African American people had a better right to the word than most European American men. "Many," he said, "would rob us of the endeared name, 'American,' a description more emphatically belonging to us, than to five-sixths of this nation, and one that we will never yield." Cornish's lonely and uncompromising fight unnerved weaker men.

And he was, in part, responsible for the survival of the African American press as an effective instrument of protest.

Before the Civil War, some twenty-four newspapers sprang up to champion the cause of men Cornish called "Colored Americans." During this same period, the pioneer African American magazines appeared: the National Reformer in 1833, the Mirror of Liberty in 1837, and the African Methodist Episcopal Review in 1841.

Men made in the image of Cornish and other pioneers of the African American press carried the fight into the enemy camp and validated the African American man's right to soil fertilized by the blood and tears of African American men and women. By 1841, it was clear to almost everyone that the African American was here to stay and that room would have to be made for him.

Today, more than a century after the founding of Freedom Journal, the same message leaps from the pages of hundreds of newspapers and magazines that are lengthened shadows of Cornish and Russwurm who, as Bella Gross said, delivered "the first authentic messages of the New African American to the World."

Chapter Twenty-Two

David Walker

1785-1830

The Fanon of the Nineteenth Century

He was a firebell which wouldn't stop ringing. He came out of the South, vibrating with the indignities of slavery, and he rang with such force and clarity that some men couldn't rest until the bell of his life had been stilled.

His name was David Walker. He was a free African American man. His mission was the liberation of the colored peoples of the world—by whatever means necessary.

Walker's theater of action was the printed page. He was a propagandist, a theorist, a man of words. But words to Walker were acts, not ways of avoiding acts. And he used words to act upon slavery and the supporters of slavery.

Nothing indicates this more strikingly than the main act of his life, the publication, in 1829, of a slim, seventy-six-page book with the imposing title: *David Walker's Appeal To The COLOURED CITIZENS OF THE WORLD, but in particular and very expressly, to those of THE*

UNITED STATES OF AMERICA. In this work, which caused consternation in European American America, Walker sounded the doom of the slave system and told the slaves it was their Christian duty to slit their oppressors' throats from ear to ear. "O Americans! Americans!!!" he wrote. "I call God—I call angels—I call men, to witness, that your DESTRUCTION is at hand, and will be speedily consummated unless you REPENT."

So writing and so believing, Walker anticipated the twentieth century's Frantz Fanon and inaugurated the militant movement for African American liberation in America.

The appearance of David Walker marked a transition in the liberation movement from the quiet protest of the colonial leaders to the revolutionary posture of the militant abolitionists. Even more importantly, Walker recalled and refocused the militant tradition of direct and open defiance which characterized the first generation of African Americans.

It was this tradition, flowing out of the ethos of Africa, which animated the African American colonial rebels who stood toe to toe with the colonial slavemasters, hacking, maiming, and burning. It was this tradition which prompted a lieutenant governor of Virginia in 1730 to order European American men to take their pistols to church with them. It was this tradition and the fear that it spawned that seared the spirit of America and made the slave in the south a prisoner.

When, in 1785, David Walker was born, the tradition of defiance was still a burning presence in the breasts of the slaves, Fifteen years after his birth, Gabriel Prosser led an unsuccessful slave revolt in Virginia. Twenty-two years later, Denmark Vesey planned and almost executed a revolutionary uprising in Charleston, South Carolina.

David Walker came to maturity within the compass of these events. He was born free on September 28, 1785, in Wilmington, North Carolina. His father, a slave, died before he was born; and he was raised by his mother, a free African American woman. He apparently learned to read and write. He tells us in his book that he traveled widely and that he loathed oppression. So embittered was he by the barbarism of slavery that he resolved to seek a freer climate.

"If I remain in this bloody land," he told himself, "I will not live long. As true as God reigns, I will be avenged for the sorrow which my people have suffered. This is not the place for me —no, no. I must leave this part of the country. It will be a great trial for me to live on the same soil where so many men are in slavery; certainly I cannot remain where I must hear their chains continually, and where I must encounter the insults of their hypocritical enslavers. Go, I must."

And so, feeling thus, Walker went, settling some time in the 1820's in Boston, where he applied himself with diligence to study and work. For some four years, a contemporary said, he was "hurtfully indefatigable" in his studies. He was also active in I the economic field, accumulating enough money to open a second-hand clothing store on Brattle Street near the docks.

But it quickly became apparent that Walker's business was revolution, not business. During and after business hours, he shuttled from group to group, preaching solidarity and manly assertion. He also plugged into the currents of the developing national movement by serving as the Boston correspondent of Freedom's Journal.

As a writer and speaker, Walker became known for his revolutionary tone and his radical appraisals. Then and later, he rallied against the artificial distinctions within the African American group and urged support of African American leaders and African American institutions. He was vocal on the virtues of revolutionary education. It was the duty of every African American man, he said, to disseminate education and truth. Speaking to the free African American elite of his day, he said: "I call upon you therefore to cast your eyes upon the wretchedness of your brethren, and to do your utmost to enlighten them—go to work and enlighten your brethren!"

Walker practiced what he preached. Wherever he went, he raised inconvenient questions and pointed to the hard road of duty. "I promiscuously fell in conversation once," he later wrote, "with an elderly coloured man on the topics of education, and of the great prevalency of ignorance among us: Said he, 'I know that our people are very ignorant, but my son has a good education: I spent a great deal of money on his education: He can write as well as any man, and I assure you that no one can fool him...'

"Walker questioned the man closely and brought out that the son's education had little relevance to his needs and the needs of his people. Walker heaped scorn on that kind of education and said: "I pray that the Lord may undeceive my ignorant brethren, and permit them to throw away pretensions, and seek after the substance of learning."

As for himself, Walker said: "I would crawl on my hands and knees through mud and mire, to the feet of a learned man, where I would sit and humbly supplicate him to instill into me, that which neither devils nor tyrants could remove, only with my life —for coloured people to acquire learning in this country, makes tyrants quake and tremble on their sandy foundation." An educated man, in Walker's view, was a revolutionary man, particularly in a situation of oppression. "

"Do you suppose," he asked, "that one man of good sense and learning would submit himself, his father, mother, wife and children, to be slaves to a wretched man like himself, who, instead of compensating him for his labours, chains, hand-cuffs and beats him and his family almost to death, leaving life enough in them, however, to work for, and call him master. No! No! he would cut his devilish throat from ear to ear, and well do slave-holders know it. The bare name of educating the coloured people, scares our cruel oppressors almost to death..."

On another occasion, Walker met an African American man with a string of boots on his shoulders. "We fell into conversation," Walker reported, "and in the course of which, I said to him, what a miserable set of people we are! He asked, why? —Said I, we are so subjected under the European Americans, that we cannot obtain tin-comforts of life, but by cleaning their boots and shoes, selling old clothes, waiting on them, shaving them. Said he, (with the boots on his shoulders) 'I am completely happy!!! I never want to live any better or happier than when I can get plenty of boots and shoes to clean!!!'"

"Oh! How can those who are actuated by avarice only, but think, that our Creator made us to be an inheritance to them forever, when they see that our greatest glory is centered in such mean and low objects? Understand me, brethren, I do not mean to speak against the occupations by which we acquire enough and sometimes scarcely that, to render ourselves and families comfortable through life. I am subjected in the same inconvenience, as you all. —My objections are, to our glorying and being happy in such low employments; for if we are men, we ought to be thankful to the Lord for the past, and for the future."

Walker was scornful of the efforts of African American and European American colonizationists who wanted to return Afro-Americans to Africa. "America," he said, "is more our country, than it is the European Americans—we have enriched it with our blood and tears. The greatest riches in all America have arisen from our blood and tears:— and will they drive us from our property and homes, which we have earned with our blood? They must look sharp or this very thing will bring swift destruction upon them."

Thus David Walker, a teacher without a classroom, a revolutionary in search of a cadre, a man obsessed, always imitating, always pointing, always signifying.

As Walker moved among his contemporaries, studying their condition and their aspirations, instructing and scolding, he conceived the idea of confronting the future with a book. By the middle of 1827, this idea had become the all-consuming passion of his life, blotting out all other considerations. One can imagine him in this period walking dazedly through the narrow Boston streets. One can picture him in his rooms, summoning words of horror. He tells us that he wrote the book in a passion of indignation "with eyes streaming with tears," and with his ears ringing "with the cries, tears and groans of his oppressed people."

Walker's book startled.

It was, in fact, more than a book—it was an event, a happening.

Men who saw it in that light were not deceived. For, Fanon apart, there has never been another book quite like it in the history of African American-European American relations in America.

First of all and most importantly of all, Walker's Appeal was addressed to the revolutionary consciousness of the oppressed, not to the Christian conscience of the oppressor. Like Fanon, more than a hundred years later, Walker bypassed the missionary and the do-gooder and spoke directly to the disinherited. And he spoke in tones of revolutionary indignation. In his imagery, in his rhetoric, Walker made clear what he was about. He was not writing another Christian appeal to European American men; he was writing a revolutionary manual for the African American men of the world; for it was, he said, an "unshaken and for ever immovable fact, that your full glory and happiness as well as all other coloured people under Heaven, shall never be fully consummated, but with the entire emancipation of your enslaved brethren all over the world."

Camus said once that the only philosophical question is the question of suicide. Concerning which, one might reply that, for the oppressed, the only philosophical question is homicide.

Walker confronted that question. More than any other American writer, before or afterwards, Walker grappled with the question of violence. And he began his disquisition by charging that oppression was in and of itself violence. Therefore, the question of the counter-violence of the oppressed was at best academic and at worst mystification. In a situation maintained by the violence of the oppressor, the only solution, he said, was violence by the oppressed.

170

More than one hundred years before Fanon, Walker said that violence was cathartic and necessary for the oppressed.

Unlike Sorel and Engels, Walker did not offer a long theoretical argument in defense of counterviolence. To him, it was self-evident. It was as natural, he said, as taking a drink of water. "Now," he wrote, "I ask you, had you not rather be killed than to be a slave to a tyrant, who takes the life of your mother, wife, and dear little children, and answer God Almighty: and believe this, that it is no more harm for you to kill a man, who is trying to kill you, than it is for you to take a drink of water when thirsty; in fact, the man who will stand still and let another murder him, is worse than infidel, and, if he has common sense, ought not to be pitied."

Walker did not pity the oppressed; he prodded them, saying it was their Christian duty to rise up and wage a war to the knife on the enemies of man.

Walker reached this melancholy conclusion by a rigorous examination of the obstacles and the options. He asked himself, first of all, the cause of the wretchedness of his people. And he answered: slavery. And what was the cause of slavery? Greed, Walker answered—that and the historic miscarriage of European American civilization.

Although Walker wrote out of a religious framework, he identified the primary problem as economic exploitation. European American people, he said, were determined to live out of the blood and sweat of African American people. They wanted African American people "to dig their mines and work their farms; and thus go on enriching them, from one generation to another with our blood and our tears!!!"

Some European Americans were so corrupted by greed for gold that they believed, Walker charged, that God made them "to sit in the shade, and make the African Americans work without remuneration for their services." As a matter of fact, Walker added, "the labour of slaves comes so cheap to the avaricious usurpers, and is (as they think) of such great utility to the countries where it exists, that those who are actuated by sordid avarice only, overlook the evils, which will sure as the Lord lives, follow after the good."

In Walker's view, Euro-Americans had corrupted themselves- perhaps beyond redemption. "The European Americans," he wrote, "have always been an unjust, jealous, unmerciful, avaricious and blood-thirsty set of beings, always seeking after power and authority."

"We view them all over the confederacy of Greece, where they were first known to be anything, (in consequence of education) we see them there, cutting each other's throats—trying to subject each other to wretchedness and misery —to effect which, they used all kinds of deceitful, unfair, and unmerciful means."

"We view them next in Rome, where the spirit of tyranny and deceit raged still higher. We view them in Gaul, Spain, and in Britain.—"

"In fine, we view them all over Europe, together with what were scattered about in Asia and Africa, as heathens, and we see them acting more like devils than accountable men. But some may ask, did not the African Americans of Africa, and the mulattoes of Asia, go on in the same way as did the European Americans of Europe. I answer, no —they never were half so avaricious, deceitful and unmerciful as the European Americans, according to their knowledge."

Walker said that the conversion of the Europeans to Christianity had not improved their morals. "In fact, take them as a body, they are ten times more cruel, avaricious and unmerciful than ever they were." Walker went on to question whether European Americans were "as good by nature" as the African Americans and he suggested "that if ever the world becomes Christianized, (which must certainly take place before long) it will be through the means, under God, of the African Americans."

Walker said European American people had made themselves "the natural enemies" of African American people.

"I say," Walker wrote, "from the beginning, I do not think that we were natural enemies to each other. But the European Americans having made us so wretched, by subjecting us to slavery, and having murdered so many millions of us, in order to make us work for them, and out of devilishness—and they taking our wives, whom we love as we do ourselves—our mothers, who bore the pains of death to give us birth —our fathers and dear little children, and ourselves, and strip and beat us one before the other —chain, hand-cuff, and drag us about like rattlesnakes—shoot us down like wild bears, before each other's faces, to make us submissive to, and work to support them and their families.... They (the European Americans) know well, if we are men...and see them treating us in the manner they do, that there can be nothing in our hearts but death alone, for them...Man, in all ages and all nations of the earth, is the same..."

European American oppression, Walker said, had had an unfortunate effect on African Americans who were ignorant, divided and permeated by a mean and servile spirit. Like Fanon, Walker hid nothing. Like Fanon, he was pitiless in his exposure of the weaknesses of the colonized. He saw African American men "groveling in submission," "protecting devils and fighting each other." All of this, he said, was a result of ignorance which he called "the mother of treachery and deceit." In a prophetic insight, he charged that ignorance was not only the product of oppression but the aim and the intent of the system of oppression.

European American people, he said, were promoting ignorance in the African American population. Worse, missionaries and "preachers of Jesus Christ" were conditioning the African Americans to a state of servility by a pervasive campaign of brainwashing. "O! save us, we pray thee, thou God of Heaven and of earth, from the devouring hands of the European American Christians!!!"

Reviewing this catalogue of social evils, Walker was overcome ("Oh Heaven! I am full!!!! I can hardly move my pen!!!") by a thirst for vengeance and he asked: "Can the Americans escape God Almighty?" He said he hoped European American people would see the errors of their ways and repent, but he was not hopeful. At any rate, he said, some European Americans were beyond the pale of redemption.

A curse, he said, hung over the land. The cup of America was "nearly full." The day was "fast approaching, when (unless there is a universal repentance on the part of the European Americans, which will scarcely take place, they have got to be so hardened in consequence of our blood, and so wise in their own conceit.)" European American people, moreover, had degraded African American people and taught them "the art of throat-cutting." And "some of them," he said, "would curse the day they ever saw us."

Walker issued a clarion call for African American men to stand up like men and stop submitting —whatever the cost. "I ask you, oh my brethren!" he wrote, "are we MEN? Did our Creator make us to be slaves to dust and ashes like ourselves? Are they not dying worms as well as we?" And he added: "If ever we become men (I mean respectable men, such as other people are) we must exert ourselves to the full...." What did this mean?

It meant, Walker said, a holy war against the usurpers.

Walker commended African American men to the care of "the God of the armies," the God of Abraham and Jacob and Isaac. That God, Walker said, "will give you a Hannibal." He urged African American men to watch for "...the day of our redemption from the abject wretchedness draweth near, when we shall be enabled, in the most extended sense of the word, to stretch forth our hands to the LORD our God, but there must be a willingness on our part, for God to do these things for us, for we may be assured that he will not take us by the hairs of our head against our will and desire, and drag us from our very mean, low and abject condition."

African American people, he said, had been misrepresented. There "is an unconquerable disposition in the breasts of the African Americans, which, when it is fully awakened and put in motion, will be subdued, only with the destruction of the animal existence. Get the African Americans started, and if you do not have a gang of tigers and lions to deal with, I am a deceiver of the African Americans and of the European Americans."

Walker was horrified by the destruction he foresaw. "But," he said, "when I reflect that God is just, and that millions of my wretched brethren would meet death with glory, yea, more, would plunge into the very mouths of cannons and be torn into particles as minute as the atoms which compose the elements of the earth, in preference to a mean submission to the lash of tyrants, I am with streaming eyes, compelled to shrink back into nothingness before my Maker, and exclaim again, thy will be done, O Lord God Almighty."

The harvest was at hand, and Walker called for strong and steady laborers. He recommended careful planning and deliberate action. "Never make an attempt to gain our freedom or natural right" he said, "from under our cruel oppressors and murderers, until you see your way clear —when that hour arrives and you move, be not afraid or dismayed; for be you assured that Jesus Christ the King of heaven and of earth who is the God of justice and of armies, will surely go before you." He added: "…if you commence, make sure work —do not trifle, for they will not trifle with you —they want us for their slaves, and think nothing of murdering us in order to subject us to that wretched condition—therefore, if there is an attempt made by us, kill or be killed."

There was no need, Walker said, for fear or doubt. "Can our condition be any worse?" he asked. "If there are any changes, will they not be for the better, though they may appear for the worse at first? Can they get us any lower? Where can they get us? They are afraid to treat us worse, for they know well, the day they do it they are gone."

Walker concluded with a solemn word of warning to Americans. "I speak, Americans," he said, "for your good. We must and shall be free I say, in spite of you. You may do your best to keep us in wretchedness and misery, to enrich you and your children; but God will deliver us from under you. And woe, woe will be to you if we have to obtain our freedom by fighting."

Walker flung his completed book like a spear at the hearts of his contemporaries and they fled precipitately from the sharp tips of his words. Within a year, the book went through three editions and copies turned up in several Southern states. European American abolitionists like William Lloyd Garrison and Benjamin Lundy immediately disowned the book, deprecating its violent tone. Said Lundy: "A more bold, daring, inflammatory publication, perhaps, never issued from the press of any country. I can do no less than set the broadest seal of condemnation on it. Such things have no earthly effect than to injure our cause."

In the South, the reviews were more hysterical. The Greensborough Patriot said: "If Perkins' steam-gun had been charged with rattlesnakes, and shot into the midst of a flock of wild pigeons, the fluttering could not have been greater than has recently been felt in the eastern part of this state by a few copies of this perishable production...When an old African American from Boston writes a book and sends it among us, the whole country is thrown into commotion."

The commotion reached unprecedented proportions. The legislatures of several Southern states went into secret sessions to consider Walker's Appeal, and the mayor of Savannah, Georgia, asked the mayor of Boston to arrest Walker and suppress his book.

More sinister yet were reports of rewards for Walker's death. Friends, fearing for his safety, urged him to flee to Canada. But Walker refused, saying: "If any are anxious to ascertain who I am, know the world, that I am one of the oppressed, degraded and wretched sons of Africa, rendered so by the avaricious and unmerciful, among the European Americans.—If any wish to plunge me into the wretched incapacity of a slave, or murder me for the truth, know ye, that I am in the hands of God, and at your disposal. I count my life not dear unto me, but I am ready to be offered at any moment. For what is the use of living, when in fact I am dead."

A few months later, on June 28, 1830, Walker was found dead near the doorway of his store. His supporters said he had been poisoned by racists or agents of racists.

In this way or some other way, the pen of the gifted and impassioned prophet was stilled. But the bell of his words continued to ring, and the echo was heard in distant places.

Chapter Twenty-Three
Harriet Tubman

1820-1913

Guerrilla in the Cottonfields

Black as the night and as bold, she slipped across the Mason-Dixon line and headed for a rendezvous point in the old slave South. With revolver cocked, she moved unerringly across the fields and through the forests, flitting from tree to tree and from ditch to ditch.

From time to time, she froze in her tracks, forewarned by a personal radar that never failed. A broken twig, the neigh of a horse, a cough, a sneeze: these said danger ahead. And so she halted, listening, waiting, her body tensed for attack. She was a gentle woman; but she was African American and she could ill afford sentimentality.

There was a price on her head, some forty thousand dollars, and the slightest mistake would mean death. Slave patrols, guards, planters—eyes—were everywhere, and all were on the lookout for fugitive slaves in general and one woman in particular. No matter. The short African American woman was without nerves and she had no peer, male or female, in her chosen trade: organizing and managing slave escapes. She had been this way many times before and she had brought out hundreds of slaves. Now she was at it again, slipping through Pennsylvania, Delaware, and Maryland.

On and on she went, deeper and deeper into the slave South, traveling by night and hiding by day, moving closer and closer to a rendezvous point on the Eastern Shore of Maryland near Cambridge. There, a group of slaves forewarned by a code letter to a sympathetic free African American, waited with terror and with hope. Harriet Tubman materialized from nowhere, rapping her code on a chosen door in the slave quarters or standing deep in the woods and singing, for a tantalizing moment, a few bars of a Spiritual code:

> I'll meet you in the morning
> Safe in the Promised Land, On the other side of Jordan,
> Bound for the Promised Land.

Waiting ears, hearing the code knock or the code song, perked up and word raced through the cabins of the initiated: "Moses is here." After certain preparations, "the woman," as she was called, led a group of slaves through Maryland, Delaware, Pennsylvania, and New York into the Promised Land of Canada. Nineteen times she made this dangerous round trip; nineteen times, single-handed, she baited the collective might of the slave power —and nineteen times she won.

What she did, Thomas Wentworth Higginson said, was "beyond anything in fiction." Sarah Bradford, her first biographer, said "her name deserves to be handed down to posterity, side by side with the names of Jeanne D'Arc, Grace Darling, and Florence Nightingale…" In truth, her name should stand higher for, as Mrs. Bradford added, "not one of these women, noble and brave as they were, [showed] more courage, and power of endurance, in facing danger and death than the woman known to posterity as Harriet Tubman, 'the Moses of her people.'"

The great slave rebel, whose name struck terror in the hearts of Eastern Shore planters, was born a slave and lived the life of a slave.

She was born in 1820 or 1821 in Bucktown near Cambridge on the Eastern Shore, one of the eleven children of Harriet Green and Benjamin Ross. As a child, she was called both Harriet and Araminta. But she was never really a child. For at the age of five, she was working full-time, cleaning European American people's houses during the day and tending their babies at night. When she fell asleep, she was whipped mercilessly.

"I grew up," she said later, "like a neglected weed—ignorant of liberty, having no experience of it. I was not happy or contented: every time I saw a European American man I was afraid of being carried away. I had two sisters carried away in a chain gang —one of them left two children. We were always uneasy...I think slavery is the next thing to hell. If a person would send another into bondage lie would, it appears to me, be bad enough to send him to hell if he could."

Harriet was a rebellious child. It would not be too much of an exaggeration to say that she was born a rebel. Fighting back with whatever she could lay hands on, she survived; and, having survived, she set her sights higher. By the time Harriet reached her teens, her master, despairing of ever making her a house servant, put her out to field where she plowed, drove oxen, .and cut wood. She remembered later with pride that she "could lift huge barrels of produce and draw a loaded stone boat like an ox."

All this time, young Harriet was gathering fury against the slave system. She was, by all accounts, the despair of European American over-seers, who could not break her rebellious will. On one occasion, a male slave abandoned his post and went to town. The slave was closely followed by the overseer, who was closely followed by Harriet. The overseer cornered the slave in a store and called on Harriet for aid. The young slave girl, who was only thirteen, ignored the order and went to the aid of the slave. When the slave dashed through the door, Harriet stepped between him and the overseer. The overseer, enraged, picked up a two-pound weight and flung it at the escaping slave. The weight struck Harriet, tearing a hole in her skull.

For several weeks, Harriet hovered between life and death. Then, slowly, she began to recover. It was discovered later that the blow had pushed a portion of her skull against her brain. Ever afterwards, she suffered from what was called a "stupor" or "sleeping sickness." Four or five times a day, she would suddenly fall asleep. After a short spell, she would regain consciousness and continue the conversation or her work at the precise point where she left off. Because of this ailment, European American people in the neighborhood, and some slaves, assumed that Harriet was "half-witted"—an assumption the wily Harriet encouraged.

During her lengthy convalescence, Harriet developed a deep and intensely personal religious faith. She had always been a dreamy, indrawn child. But now she gave herself over wholly to God, "praying," she said, "without ceasing." She prayed first for her master, asking God to soften his heart and make him mindful of the sacred ties between human beings. But the master did not change. Word reached Harriet one day that he was planning to sell her and other members of the family to the deep South. "Then," said Harriet, "I changed my prayer. I began to pray, 'Oh, Lord, if you aren't ever going to change that man's heart, kill him, Lord, and take him out of the way, so he won't do no more mischief.'"

Later, on the death of her master, Harriet was smitten with a sense of contrition. "He died, just as he had lived," she said, "a wicked, bad man. Oh, then, it 'peared like I would give the world full of silver and gold if I had it, to bring that poor soul back. I would give myself; I would give everything! But he was gone, I couldn't pray for him no more."

Putting her master behind her, Harriet began now to consider seriously the possibilities of escape. The constantly recurring idea of escape struck such deep roots in her mind that she dreamed repeatedly of a "line" across which there was freedom and human dignity. After her marriage to John Tubman, a free African American man, the dreams increased in frequency and intensity. When Harriet learned that her new master planned to sell her and two of her brothers, she decided to run away. She tried to persuade her brothers to accompany her, but they refused.

So she set out alone in the summer of 1849, traveling at night through Maryland and Delaware and finally reaching Philadelphia. She went with a threat in her heart. "For," said she, "I had reasoned this out in my mind; there was one of two things I had a right to, liberty or death; if I could not have one, I would have the other, for no man should take me alive…"

When she crossed the "line" between slavery and freedom, she was overwhelmed by a sense of fulfillment. "I looked at my hands," she said, "to see if I was the same person now I was free. There was such a glory over everything, the sun came like gold through the trees, and over the fields…."

But there was a shadow in Harriet's Eden. She perceived suddenly with startling clarity that she could never be free until her people were free. "I knew of a man," she said, "who was sent to State Prison for twenty-five years. All these years he was always thinking of his home, and counting by years, months, and days, the time till he should be free, and see his family and friends once more."

"The years roll on, the time of imprisonment is over, the man is free. He leaves the prison gates, he makes his way to his old home, but his old home is not there. The house in which he had dwelt in his childhood had been torn down, and a new one had been put up in its place; his family were gone, their very name was forgotten, there was no one to take him by the hand to welcome him back to life."

"So it was with me," Harriet added. "I had crossed the line of which I had so long been dreaming. I was free; but there was no one to welcome me to the land of freedom. I was a stranger in a strange land,

and my home after all was down in the old cabin quarter, with the old folks, and my brothers and sisters. But to this solemn resolution I came; I was free, and they should be live also; I would make a home for them in the North, and the Lord helping me, I would bring them all here..."

So resolving, Harriet Tubman dedicated herself to work unceasingly for the complete emancipation of her people. In Philadelphia and other Northern cities, she worked day and night as a domestic. When she had accumulated enough money to finance a slave escape, she would return to the South and lead out a group of slaves.

The first trip occurred shortly after her escape. In December, 1850, she returned to Maryland and spirited out her sister and two children. Four months later, she returned and guided her brother and two other slaves to freedom. Returning to the South in the fall of 1851 for her husband, she discovered he had married again. This was a shattering blow, but Harriet had no time to grieve over personal problems. Abandoning her original plan, putting John Tubman behind her, she organized a group of slaves and carried them to Canada. Thereafter, she made a series of forays into the South, bringing out relatives, friends, and anyone else who wanted to go.

To understand what Harriet was about, to understand the magnitude of her accomplishments, it is necessary to understand the system she was challenging. The slave South was a totalitarian system. Every instrument of power in the South was bent to the detection and destruction of slaves like Harriet Tubman. To penetrate the defenses of this system, to guide hundreds of slaves of all ages and physical conditions through thousands of miles of closely guarded territory required tactical ability approaching genius.

Harriet approached her task with thoroughness and dispatch. Between trips, she accumulated money by working as a cook, maid, laborer. Since she could neither read nor write, she employed Northern confederates to write coded letters to free African Americans or sympathetic European Americans in the area she planned to visit.

A free African American in Cambridge, for example, received the following letter before a Harriet Tubman strike. "Read my letter to the old folks, and give my love to them, and tell my brothers to be always watching unto prayer, and when the good old ship of Zion comes along, to be ready to step aboard." [Emphasis supplied.]

After contacting the slaves, Harriet accumulated the tools of her trade: a revolver and fresh ammunition, fake passes for slaves of varying description, and paregoric to drug babies. With these and other "tools" hidden on her person, she slipped across the Mason-Dixon line and made her way to selected plantations where slaves were informed of her presence by code songs, prayers, or some other stratagem. Selected slaves were then apprised of the rendezvous area and the time of departure. General Tubman, as she was called, was very strict about time. She waited for no one —not even a brother who was delayed on one trip by the imminent arrival of a new baby in his family.

Once the slaves were assembled, Harriet sized them up, searching them closely with her eyes. Satisfied, she placed the group under strict military discipline. During the trip, she was in absolute and total control and no one could question her orders. William Still, the African American rebel who operated the key Philadelphia station of the Underground Railroad, said she "had a very short and pointed rule of law of her own which implied death to anyone who talked of giving out and going back."

Once a slave committed himself to a Tubman escape, he was committed to freedom or death. On several occasions, slaves collapsed and said they were tired, sick, scared. Harriet always cocked her revolver and said: "You go on or die. Dead niggers tell no tales." Faced with a determined Harriet Tubman, slaves always found new strength and determination. During ten years of guerilla action, the great commando leader never lost a slave through capture or return.

Of the tricks of her trade, Harriet was a past mistress. She almost always began her escapes on Saturday night. Since it was impossible to advertise for runaway slaves on Sunday, this gave her a twenty-four-hour start on pursuers. She also made a practice of escaping in the carriages of masters, covering the slaves with vegetables or baggage and driving all night Saturday and all day Sunday before abandoning the appropriated vehicle. This stratagem served two purposes. It rapidly moved escapees from the immediate neighborhood, and it befuddled guards and planters who assumed usually that a slave boldly driving a carriage was on an errand for his master.

After abandoning the carriage, Harriet and her charges made their way north by following the North Star or feeling the moss on the sides of trees. Harriet tried usually to keep her groups together, but she sometimes dispersed them, sending twos or threes through hostile towns. On occasions, she dressed men in women's clothes and vice versa.

In an emergency, the guerrilla leader acted swiftly, even ruthlessly. On one night, she escaped capture by hiding her charge in a manure pile and sticking straws in their mouths so they could breathe. On another trip, she eluded pursuers by buying tickets and putting the slaves on a train heading south. No one, of course, expected fugitive slaves to be on a southbound train.

The great slave rebel was helped enormously in her extraordinary career by a natural talent for acting. Indeed, Thomas Wentworth Higginson, the antislavery preacher, believed she was one of the greatest actresses and comediennes of the age. "One of her most masterly accomplishments," he said, "was the impression of a decrepit old woman."

"On one of her expeditions…she had the incredible nerve to enter a village where lived one of her former masters. This was necessary for the carrying out of her plans for the trip. Her only disguise was a bodily assumption of age. To reinforce this, her subtle foresight prompted her to buy some live chickens, which she carried suspended by the legs from a cord. As she turned a corner she saw coming toward her none other than her old master. Lest he might see through her impersonation and to make an excuse for flight, she loosed the cord that held the fowls and, amid the laughter of the bystanders, gave chase to them as they flew squawking over a nearby fence."

No less effective was the use Harriet made of melody. She was proud of her singing voice and she used it repeatedly in managing slave escapes. Alice Stone Blackwell, the feminist leader, said: "If I remember correctly, Harriet Tubman told me I hat when she was convoying parties of fugitives, she used to guide them by the songs that she sang as she walked along the roads.... It was when her parties of fugitives were in hiding, that she directed them by her songs as to whether they might show themselves, or must continue to lie low.... No one would notice what was sung by an old African American woman, as she trudged along the road."

What made the Tubman exploits so extraordinary was the fact that she could not read or write. This led, on occasion, to hair- raising encounters. The story is told of the time she fell asleep on a train beneath a "wanted" poster bearing her likeness. Awakening and hearing several European American men discussing her and the poster, Harriet grabbed a book and began to "read," praying fervently that she was not holding the book upside down. The European American men lost interest for the poster said clearly that the "dangerous" wanted woman could neither read nor write.

A cool customer, Harriet Tubman—cool, determined and bold, never wanting for the right gesture or the right retort. Her steadiness stemmed from a total and absolute faith in God. She talked to God every day, believed He was always with her and would never let her down.

On one expedition, Harriet's personal radar told her there was danger, great danger, ahead. She discussed the matter with God, saying: "You been wid me in six troubles, Lord, be wid me in the seventh." What happened next was related by Thomas Garret, who heard it from Harriet Tubman's lips. "She said that God told her to stop, which she did; and then asked him what she must do. He told her to leave the road, and turn to the left; she obeyed, and soon came to a small stream of tidewater; there was no boat; no bridge; she again inquired of her Guide what she was to do."

"She was told to go through. It was cold, in the month of March; but having confidence in her Guide, she went in; the water came up to her armpits; the men refused to follow till they saw her safe on the opposite shore. They then followed, and, if I mistake not, she had soon to wade a second stream, soon after which she came to a cabin of African American people, who took them all in, put them to bed, and dried their clothes, ready to proceed next night on the journey…The strange part of the story we found to be, that the masters of these men had put up the previous day, at the railroad station near where she left, an advertisement offering a large reward for their apprehension."

From 1850 to December, 1860, the month of her last expedition, Harriet guided some three hundred slaves out of the South. Perhaps her most famous expedition occurred in 1857 when she returned for her father and mother. Learning that her father faced arrest and trial on a charge of aiding slaves to escape, she rushed to Maryland and "moved his case," she said, to "a higher court." At this point, Harriet's mother and father were old and decrepit. Neither could walk very fast. How then did Harriet Tubman succeed in moving them from Maryland to Canada?

Thomas Garrett, who managed the Wilmington Underground Railroad station, said: "They started with an old horse, fitted out in primitive style with a straw collar, a pair of old chaise wheels, with a board on the axle to sit on, another board swung with ropes, fastened to the axle, to rest their feet on."

"She got her parents, who were both slaves belonging to different masters, on this rude vehicle to the railroad, put them in the cars, turned Jehu herself, and drove to town in a style that no human being ever did before or since." Harriet later moved her parents to Auburn, New York, where William H. Seward, one of her admirers, sold her a plot of land at a very reasonable price.

As a result of her underground work, the former slave became a heroine of the abolitionist crusade. During the late fifties, she began to appear on the platform as an antislavery and feminist advocate. "For eight or ten years previous to the breaking out of the Rebellion," William Wells Brown said, "all who frequented anti-slavery conventions, lectures, picnics, and fairs, could not fail to have seen an African American woman of medium size, upper front teeth gone, smiling countenance, attired in coarse, but neat apparel, with an old-fashioned reticule or bag suspended by her side...."

It was during this period that Harriet Tubman met John Brown, who said she was the "most of a man, naturally, that I ever met." Both John Brown and Harriet Tubman were rebels, if not revolutionaries, who were somewhat contemptuous of abolitionists who fought mainly with their voices and their pens. Because they shared the same vision of battle, the two rebels became close friends, and Harriet helped John Brown to plan his famous attack on Harpers Ferry.

In fact, the evidence indicates that Harriet Tubman intended to accompany John Brown. But she became ill in October of 1859 and missed the celebrated raid. Thereafter, Harriet Tubman venerated John Brown over all other Americans, insisting that he was more responsible for the destruction of slavery than Abraham Lincoln. "It was not John Brown that died at Charlestown," she said. "It was Christ; —it was the Saviour of our people."

From the start, the slave rebel was cool toward Abraham Lincoln. She was critical of Lincoln's initial attempt to wage war without disturbing the institution of slavery. Recalling the old proverb, "Never wound a snake but kill it," she said the war could not be won until men addressed themselves to the root cause of the war —slavery. "God is ahead of Lincoln," she said. "God won't let Mister Lincoln beat the South till he does the right thing. Mister Lincoln, he is a great man, and I'm a poor Negro; but this Negro can tell Mister Lincoln how to save the money and the young men. He can do it by setting the Negroes free."

"Suppose there was an awfully big snake down there on the floor. He bites you. You send for the doctor to cut the bite; but the snake, he rolls up there, and while the doctor is doing it, he bites you again. The doctor cuts down that bite, but while he's doing it the snake springs up and bites you again, and so he keeps doing till you kill him. That's what Mister Lincoln ought to know."

During the first phase of the Civil War, Harriet Tubman continued her guerrilla strikes, leading slaves to federal lines in Maryland and other states. In May, 1862, she was sent by Governor Andrew of Massachusetts to Port Royal, South Carolina, which was then under the control of federal troops. She served in the Port Royal area as a liaison person between federal troops and freedmen and as a nurse in camp hospitals.

Even more important perhaps was her work as a Union Army spy, scout, and commando. At the request of Union officers, she organized an intelligence service, recruiting several former slaves from surrounding areas. She later accompanied Colonel James Montgomery on several raids in South Carolina and Georgia. Indeed, there is a great deal of evidence which indicates that Harriet, not Montgomery, was the commander of Montgomery's most famous exploit, the June 2, 1863, raid up South Carolina's Combahee River. Harriet's role in this raid was clearly indicated by a dispatch which appeared on the front page of the Commonwealth, a Boston newspaper, on July 10, 1863.

Col. Montgomery and his gallant band of 300 African American soldiers, under the guidance of an African American woman, dashed into the enemy's country, struck a bold and effective blow, destroying millions of dollars worth of commissary stores, cotton and lordly dwellings, and striking terror into the heart of rebeldom, brought off near 800 slaves and thousands of dollars worth of property, without losing a man or receiving a scratch. It was a glorious consummation

After they were all fairly well disposed of in the Beaufort charge, they were addressed in strains of thrilling eloquence by their gallant deliverer, to which they responded in a song, "There is a white robe for thee," a song so appropriate and so heartfelt and cordial as to bring unbidden tears.

The Colonel was followed by a speech from the African American woman, who led the raid, and under whose inspiration it was originated and conducted. For sound sense and real native eloquence, her address would do honor to any man, and it created a great sensation....

Since the rebellion she has devoted herself to her great work of delivering the bondman, with an energy and sagacity that cannot be exceeded. Many times she has penetrated the enemy's lines and discovered their situation and condition, and escaped without injury, but not without extreme hazard.

A few months later, Harriet helped to bury the dead and to nurse the wounded after the famous charge of the 54th Massachusetts Volunteers, an all-African American regiment, on Fort Wagner in the Charleston, South Carolina, harbor. Her incisive description of the war, quoted later by Albert Bushnell Hart, probably referred to that battle. "And then we saw the lightning," she said, "and that was the guns; and then we heard the thunder, and that was the big guns; and then we heard the rain falling, and that was the drops of blood falling; and when we came to get in the crops, it was dead men that we reaped."

At war's end, Harriet returned to her home in Auburn and began a thirty-seven-year effort to get government compensation for three years of war services. She wanted the money not for herself but to found schools and rest homes for the freedmen and their children. Although high-ranking officers and officials furnished depositions and affidavits on her war services, the federal government never fully paid the claim.

It was, in part, to buttress Harriet's claims that Sarah H. Bradford wrote a book on her life in 1886. Harriet and the, author requested commendations from several prominent Americans, including Frederick Douglass, who answered:

> "You ask for what you do not need when you call upon me for a word of commendation. I need such words from you more than you can need them from me, especially where your superior labors and devotions to the cause of the lately enslaved of our land are known as I know them. The difference between us is very marked. Most that I have done and suffered in the service of our cause has been in public, and I have received encouragement at every step of the way.
>
> You, on the other hand, have labored in a private way. I have wrought in the day—you in the night. I have had the applause of the crowd and the satisfaction that comes of being approved by the multitude, while the most that you have done has been witnessed by a few trembling, scared, and foot-sore bondsmen and women, whom you have led out of the house of bondage, and whose heartfelt 'God bless you has been your only reward. The midnight sky and the silent stars have been the witnesses of your devotion to freedom and of your heroism. Excepting John Brown —of sacred memory—I know of no one who has willingly encountered more perils and hardships to serve our enslaved people than you have. Much that you have done would seem improbable to those who do not know you as I know you...."

The book Douglass commended brought Harriet Tubman a thousand dollars which she contributed to African American schools in the South. Harriet also maintained open house in her home in Auburn, giving all she had to the poor, the needy, and the infirm.

During this period, she married a young Union Army veteran she had met in the Port Royal area. Her new husband, Nelson Davis, was in poor health and he soon died. After his death, the government gave Harriet a widow's pension of eight dollars a month. The pension was later increased to twenty dollars a month.

By this time, Harriet Tubman was something of a legend to Americans. She was good copy for most newspapers, and reporters from all over the country came to Auburn to interview her. To Frank C. Drake of the *New York Herald*, she told a story that reflected rather accurately the vicissitudes of her life:

> "You wouldn't think that after I served the flag so faithfully I should come to want its folds."
>
> She looked musingly toward a nearby orchard, and she asked suddenly: "Do you like apples?" On being assured that I did, she said: "Did you ever plant an apple tree?" With shame I confessed I had not.
>
> "No," she said, "but somebody else planted them. I liked apples when I was young, and I said, 'Some day I'll plant apples myself for other young folks to eat,' and I guess I did it."

Frank C. Drake noted in his dispatch that Harriet Tubman told this story "not plaintively, but rather with a flash of scorn in her eyes." At the time of this interview, Harriet was in need. But she was referring here to a deeper, trans-personal need. It grieved her that the government for which she fought had turned its back on her. And she was deeply concerned about the atrocities in the South. More than once, in this period, the tough old woman wept for the ingratitude of man.

As the years passed, turning the fork of the fateful twentieth century, Harriet Tubman girded herself for one last effort on behalf of her life-long dream, a "John Brown Home" for indigent African American people. By peddling fruit and by begging, she accumulated enough money to buy land and lay the foundations for the home. She later deeded the property and her home to the African Methodist Episcopal Zion Church.

As 1913 approached, Harriet turned her face toward the other world. She went to her favorite AME Zion Church for the last time and told the parishioners that the end was near. "I am in nearing the end of my journey," she said. "I can hear them bells a-ringing, I can hear the angels singing, I can see the hosts a-marching. I hear somebody say: 'There is one crown left and that is for Old Aunt Harriet and she shall not lose her reward.'"

On March 10, 1913, in the fiftieth year of Emancipation, Harriet Tubman claimed her crown. She was buried with military rites and the next year the city of Auburn closed down in an unprecedented one-day memorial to the rebel and Union spy. The Auburn Citizen, as Earl Conrad noted, caught the spirit and meaning of this occasion in an editorial.

The meeting at the Auditorium last night may be said to rank among the most unique in the history of this state, if not the nation. Every thoughtful person in the audience carried away the thought —what a remarkable women Harriet Tubman must have been to deserve this tribute, an enduring monument from the European American race to one of the lowliest and most humble of the African Americans! Where has anything like it been recorded!...

How many of the European American race/culture exist today who will ever merit equal recognition with Harriet Tubman?

Chapter Twenty-Four
Charles Sumner and Thaddeus Stevens

Sumner 1811-1874/Stevens 1792-1868

European American Architects of African American Liberation

C harles Sumner and Thaddeus Stevens were some of the best friends African American Americans have had in public power.

More than any past or present politician, more even than the celebrated Lincoln, Sumner and Stevens were consumed by the cause of African American liberation. As the dominant figures in Civil War and post-Civil War Congresses, Sumner and Stevens were primarily responsible for the legal scaffolding that undergirds equal rights in America.

In the turbulent Reconstruction era, Stevens was the virtual dictator of the House of Representatives and Sumner was, in Emerson's words, "the conscience of the Senate." Together and separately, alone and with like-minded colleagues, they made the U. S. Congress and the American people take the longest stride of soul in the history of the Commonwealth.

The Thirteenth, Fourteenth, and Fifteenth amendments arc permanent testimonials to the courage and devotion of Sumner and Stevens; and the most daring proposals of contemporary legislators are only pale reflections of the civil rights bills they offered in the 1860's and 1870's.

It was Stevens who captured the imagination of freedmen with a proposal for allocating "forty acres and a mule" to each freedman. It was Sumner who proposed a civil rights bill that would have banned segregation in schools, churches, cemeteries, public conveyances, and places of public accommodation. It was Sumner and Stevens who insisted that there could be no just and lasting racial peace except on the basis of equal rights for all men.

Both Sumner and Stevens were European American, but both repudiated in principle and in practice the claims of white supremacy. Both were politicians, but both rose above the petty machinations of the typical politician. Both were lawyers, but both believed that laws were made for men and not men for laws. "…anything for human rights," Charles Sumner said, "is constitutional…There can be no states rights against human rights."

Because they believed African American men and women were human beings, they acted on that belief in their public and private lives, Sumner and Stevens have been systematically vilified by a whole generation of historians.

They have been denounced as "fanatics" who forced African American suffrage and equal rights on the South, thereby precipitating "the horrors" of Reconstruction. The truth of the matter is that the failure of Reconstruction and America's current racial crisis are direct results of the failure to adopt and carry through the comprehensive Reconstruction plan articulated by Sumner and Stevens.

This program included not only African American suffrage and equal rights but also land reform and a complete revamping of the social system of the South. It was no accident that Sumner and Stevens became the most articulate political advocates of the African American cause.

Both men were reared on the verities of the Declaration of Independence; and both men were, in a sense, products of the crisis they transcended. Stevens, the older of the two, was born on April 4, 1792, in Danville, Vermont, to Jacob Stevens, a poor surveyor, and his wife, Sarah.

He was born with a clubfoot and this deformity colored his whole life. Shy, sensitive, embarrassed by his deformity, Stevens developed a passion for the poor, the disinherited, and the driven-against-the-wall. He was not a happy boy. A friend who knew him in those days remembered him as "still and quiet-like, different from the rest of the boys," who would "laugh at him, boy-like, and mimic his limping walk." As a defense mechanism, Stevens secreted a hard shell of cynicism which encased and protected his inner core of compassion and sensitivity. Ever afterwards, his sharp tongue and his brusque forbidding exterior would hold the world at arm's length.

Like many other sensitive and disturbed youths, Stevens hid his hurt in books. He was a good, if not spectacular, student at the grade schools of Peacham, Vermont, and at Dartmouth College, where he was graduated in 1814. Moving on to Pennsylvania after graduation, he taught school for a year and then opened a law office in Gettysburg.

Aloof, withdrawn, his energy focused almost entirely on the problem of making a living, Stevens soon moved to the forefront of the professional community in Gettysburg. Within nine years after settling in Gettysburg, he was the largest real estate owner in the county. Stevens later became the principal owner of an iron business and moved his base of operations to the larger city of Lancaster. With his base secure, the young lawyer entered politics and won election to the Pennsylvania General Assembly. Opposed to all special privileges, he distinguished himself in a bitter fight against secret societies. Standing alone in one session, he repulsed foes of public education and won the title of father of the common school system in Pennsylvania.

As a legislator and private citizen, Stevens was an early champion of the free African American man and the African American fugitive slave. He waged an unsuccessful fight for universal suffrage, and he assisted individual African American men and women financially and spiritually. Despite his heavy schedule, Stevens always had time to take the cases of fugitive slaves. When courts ruled against him, Stevens usually purchased the freedom of his clients.

During this same period, Charles Sumner was moving toward his encounter with reality. Sumner was born into comfortable circumstances in Boston, on January 6, 1811. Like Stevens, Sumner was a bookworm; unlike Stevens, however, he used books as a crutch. It would be said later, with some justification, that his speeches were overloaded with quotations and classical allusions.

Something of a dandy, Sumner made his mark in Boston social circles and went on to Harvard University and the Harvard University Law School. He then made an extended tour of European cities before settling down to law practice in Boston. Finding the traditional fare of the lawyer somewhat restrictive, Sumner was soon engaged in unpopular causes as an advocate and agitator. He distinguished himself in the late 1840's in one of the first separate-but-equal school suits, arguing unsuccessfully for a group of African American Boston parents.

Sumner, like Stevens, would have been an extraordinary man in any era. But it seems likely that he and Stevens would have been lost to posterity had it not been for the issue of slavery, which began to exert a persuasive influence on the lives of men in the 1830's and 1840's. In these years, the South inaugurated an ominous policy of external expansion. The net result was that a variety of issues—the Mexican War, the annexation of Texas, the fugitive slave bill—stretched the fabric of the Union to the breaking point and forced a realignment of parties. It was in this climate that both Sumner and Stevens found the consuming passion of their lives.

Stevens, who was already a political power in Pennsylvania, came to the fore first, winning election in 1849 to the national House of Representatives. In his maiden speech, he announced a new policy of open Northern resistance to the steady advance of the slave power. "How often," he wondered, "had these walls been profaned and the North insulted by insolent threats that if Congress legislated against the Southern will it would be disregarded, resisted to extremity and the Union destroyed? During the present session, we have been more than once told amid raving excitement that if we dared to legislate in a certain way the South would teach the North a lesson."

With cool defiance, Stevens told the South: "You have too often intimidated Congress. You have more than once frightened the tame North for its propriety and found dough-faces enough to be your tools." That day, Stevens said, had passed. Hereafter, he concluded, the South would have to contend with men.

With this speech, Stevens became the acknowledged leader of anti-slavery forces in the House. For the rest of the term, he fought a brilliant campaign against compromise and timidity in Northern ranks. But the tide of Northern appeasement was too strong for Stevens to hold back. After passage of the Compromise of 1850, which was designed, in part, to shut off debate on the question of slavery, Stevens retired from the House and returned to Lancaster.

Far from shutting off debate, the Compromise of 1850 widened the controversy, particularly in Massachusetts, where Charles Sumner waded out into the depths as a leader of men. Sumner, who had won some fame as an orator, announced that he would not obey the Fugitive Slave law, which was an integral part of the Compromise of

1850. "We are told," he said, "that the slavery question is settled…Nothing, sir, can be settled which is not right. Nothing can be settled which is against freedom." Sumner went on to say that "the friends of freedom cannot lightly bestow their confidence."

He added:

> "They can put trust only in men of tried character and inflexible will. Three things at least they must require; the first is backbone; the second is backbone; and the third is backbone. When I see a person of upright character and pure soul yielding to a temporizing policy, I cannot but say, he wants backbone.

> When I see a person talking loudly against slavery in private, but hesitating in public and failing in the time of trial, I say, He wants backbone. When I see a person leaning upon the action of a political party and never venturing to think for himself, I say, He wants backbone. Wanting this they all want the courage, constancy, firmness, which are essential to the support of principle. Let no such man be trusted."

Whatever Sumner lacked, he did not lack backbone. Taking a leading position in the gathering controversy, he was elected in 1851 to the Senate, which he made a forum for the anti-slavery cause. In a series of great speeches, he said that slavery presented a clear and present danger to the free institutions of the North.

Like Stevens, who returned to the House in 1858 as a member of the new Republican party, Sumner said that the Declaration of Independence argued against any artificial distinctions between man and man.

Angered by Sumner's speeches, the South struck back. On Thursday, May 22, 1856, while Sumner was writing letters at his desk on the Senate floor, a proslavery congressman, Preston Brooks of South Carolina, attacked him with a heavy cane. Brooks rained blows on Sumner's head until he collapsed on the Senate floor.

This incident, following hard on the heels of the bitter North-South struggle for Kansas, inflamed the political climate of the North. Sumner, who was seriously injured in the attack, remained away from the Senate for more than three years, and Massachusetts left his seat vacant as a reproach to the South.

During Sumner's absence, Stevens and other antislavery congressmen continued the fight for African American liberation. There was, at the same time, a widening of the circle of combatants, as evidenced by the steady growth of the Republican party. When, in 1859, Sumner returned to the Senate, the stage was set for the North-South rupture which occurred after the election of Abraham Lincoln.

Both Sumner and Stevens saw the Civil War as an opportunity to complete the Revolution of 1776. From the beginning of the conflict to their death, Sumner and Stevens waged an unceasing battle for the ending of slavery and the granting of equal rights to all men. Far in advance of Lincoln and the country, Sumner and Stevens educated Lincoln and the country to a policy of African American emancipation. To them, as much as to the more conservative Lincoln, African American people owe their freedom.

After issuance of the Emancipation Proclamation, the two legislators turned to the problems of Reconstruction. By this time, the center of initiative had passed to Congress, and Sumner and Stevens were among the most powerful men in the land. As chairman of the powerful Ways and Means (Committee of the House, Stevens was in undisputed control of that body.

He used his great powers to wrench control of Reconstruction from the executive and to focus the country's mind on the "radical" reconstruction of the South. Blunt and sarcastic in debate and brilliant in behind-the-scenes maneuvering, he won his way by sheer force of will. His favorite stratagem was to move suspension of the rules so the House could go into a Committee of the Whole to consider his bills. Before the vote, he would move that general debate on the bill lie closed in an hour or thirty minutes. On one occasion, he even limited debate on a major bill to thirty seconds.

Stevens was a political being, dedicated to the art of the possible. Sumner, on the other hand, was a moralist to whom nothing was impossible. "I am in morals," he was given to saying, "not politics." Unlike Stevens, who loved the give and take of politics, Sumner took the high road, lecturing his colleagues on history and morals. By constantly raising an issue and forcing his colleagues to go on record, he usually won his way. So insistent was Sumner that one of his colleagues asked him to give the Senate "one day without the nigger."

As long as Sumner lived, the Senate resounded with the cry of the African American man. By amending an act, he stopped discrimination on streetcars in Washington D.C. The next year he stopped exclusion of witnesses on account of color in the federal courts. He also introduced and carried a bill to amend the law which provided that "no one other than a European American person should be employed to carry the mail."

The Massachusetts senator also played a pivotal role in abolishing slavery in Washington D.C. and carried the recognition of Haiti and Liberia as independent states. In gratitude, Haiti voted him a medal and hung his portrait in its state house.

Sumner, like Stevens, was at the height of his power in the dying days of the Civil War. An English traveler described him in the following terms. "That great, sturdy, English-looking figure, with the broad, massive forehead, over which the rich mass of nut-brown hair, streaked here and there with a line of gray, hangs loosely; with the deep, blue eyes and the strangely winning smile, half bright, half full of sadness."

"He is a man whom you would notice amongst other men, and whom, not knowing, you would turn round and look at as he passed by you…A child would ask him the time in the streets, and a woman would come to him unbidden for protection." Though Sumner was favored by nature, he was essentially a lonely man who married late in life and was soon divorced.

Stevens never married. His homes in Lancaster and in Washington were presided over by an African American housekeeper, Lydia Hamilton Smith, an attractive widow. Because Stevens called his housekeeper "Mrs. Smith," gossips said there was more to their relationship than met the eye. Indifferent to and contemptuous of public opinion, Stevens disdainfully ignored the gossips and went his lonely way.

Cynical and tough-talking, Stevens was a man with few close friends. His chief form of relaxation was gambling. The story is told of the time he emerged from a gambling house after a profitable night and met a preacher who asked for a donation for his church. Without a word, Stevens handed the preacher a fistful of bills. As the preacher walked away, Stevens remarked to a friend: "The Lord moves in mysterious ways, His wonders to perform."

No respecter of idols and myths, tart-tongued, indifferent to both status and color, Stevens was the chief architect of the constitutional revolution which yielded the Fourteenth and Fifteenth amendments. Acting with the boldness that characterized his entire life, He wrested control of Reconstruction from President Andrew Johnson and vested it in the Joint Congressional Committee. From this committee, with Stevens leading the way, came the momentous Fourteenth and Fifteenth amendments.

Stevens also waged a long and unsuccessful fight for forty acres of land for each freedman. "The whole fabric of Southern society must be changed," he said, "and it never can be done if this opportunity is lost.... How can republican institutions, free schools, free churches, free social intercourse, exist in a mingled community of nabobs and serfs, of the owners of twenty thousand acre manors with lordly palaces and the occupants of narrow huts inhabited by 'low white trash'?"

"If the South is ever to be made a safe republic let her lands be cultivated by the toil of the owners or the free labor of intelligent citizens.

This must be done even though it drives her nobility into exile! If they go, all the better. It will be hard to persuade the owner of ten thousand acres of land, who drives a coach and tour, that he is not degraded by sitting at the same table or in the same pew, with the embrowned and hard-handed farmer who has himself cultivated his own thriving homestead of 150 acres. The country would be well rid of the proud, bloated and defiant rebels…. The foundations of their institutions…must be broken up and re-laid, or all of our blood and treasure have been spent in vain."

Stevens' Reconstruction plan was part of a comprehensive program for the reordering of the relations between African Americans and European Americans. He told the House: "We have turned, or are about to turn, loose four million slaves without a hut to shelter them or a cent in their pockets. The infernal laws of slavery have prevented them from acquiring an education, understanding the commonest laws of contract, or of managing the ordinary business life. This Congress is bound to provide for them until they can take care of themselves. If we do not furnish them with homesteads, and hedge them around with protective laws; if we leave them to the legislation of their late masters, we had better have left them in bondage."

Stevens went on to denounce the idea that this is a European American man's country. "Governor Perry of South Carolina and other provisional governors and orators proclaim that 'this is the European American man's government'…."

"Demagogues of all parties, even some high in authority, gravely shout, 'this is the European American man's government.' What is implied by this? That one race of men are-to have the exclusive rights forever to rule this nation, and to exercise all acts of sovereignty, while all other races and nations and colors are to be their subjects, and have no voice in making the laws and choosing the rulers by whom they are to be governed…."

"Our fathers repudiated the whole doctrine of the legal superiority of families or races, and proclaimed the equality of men before the law. Upon that they created a revolution and built the Republic.... It is our duty to complete their work. If this Republic is not now made to stand on their great principles, it has no honest foundation, and the Father of all men will still shake it to its center. If we have not been sufficiently scourged for our national sin to teach us to do justice to all God's creatures, without distinction of race or color, we must expect the still more heavy vengeance of an offended Father...."

Stevens' vision of a complete reconstruction of the South was too bold for most men, and the equalitarian legislator, who was known as "The Great Commoner," admitted defeat in a great House speech. "In my youth," he said, "in my manhood, in my old age, I had fondly dreamed that when any fortunate chance should have broken for a while the foundation of our institutions, and released us from obligations the most tyrannical that ever man imposed in the name of freedom, that the intelligent, pure and just men of the Republic, true to their professions and their consciences, would have so remodeled all our institutions as to have freed them from every vestige of human oppression, of inequality of rights, of the recognized degradation of the poor, and the superior caste of the rich. In short, that no distinction would be tolerated in this purified republic but what arose from merit and conduct."

"This bright dream has vanished 'like the baseless fabric of a vision.' I find that we shall be obliged to be content with patching up the worst portions of the ancient edifice, and leaving it, in many of its parts, to be swept through by the tempests, frosts and the storms of despotism."

In the patching up, Stevens was aided enormously by Sumner who had, single-handed, defeated every compromise that evaded the issue of African American suffrage. Said he: "Equality of rights is the standing promise of nature to man.... In harmony with the promise of Nature is the promise of our fathers recorded in the Declaration of Independence. It is the twofold promise; first, that all are equal in rights; and, secondly, that just government stands only on the consent of the governed,—being the two great political commandments on which hang all laws and constitutions. Keep these truly and you will keep all. Write them in your statutes; write them in your hearts. This is the great and only final settlement of all existing questions."

Sumner and Stevens went to their graves fighting for a final and just solution of the racial/cultural problem. Shortly before his death, Sumner inaugurated a fight for a civil rights bill which would have barred segregation in public accommodations. On his death bed, surrounded by Frederick Douglass and other African American friends, he whispered his last words: "Take care of my civil rights bill —take care of it —you must do it." Sumner died in March, 1874. His civil rights bill was enacted by Congress in March, 1875.

Thaddeus Stevens had said that he intended to "die hurrahing." And he did. After his death on August 11, 1868, he was buried in an African American cemetery.

The stone above the ground bears words that invoke the meaning of the great fight that he and his colleague, Charles Sumner, waged:

> I repose in this quiet and secluded spot
> not from any natural preference for solitude,
> but finding other cemeteries
> limited by charter rules as to race.
> I have chosen this that I might illustrate in my death
> the principles which I advocated through a long life.
> Equality of Man before his Creator.

Chapter Twenty-Five
Frederick Douglass

1817-1895

Father of the Protest Movement

On a hot day in August, 1864, a prominent politician entered the White House and paused in the President's outer office. "It was dark," Judge Joseph T. Mills wrote later, "and there in a corner I saw a man quietly reading who possessed a remarkable physiognomy."

The man awed Judge Mills. "I was riveted to the spot," he said, adding: "I stood and stared at him. He raised his flashing eyes and caught me in the act. 1 was compelled to speak. Said I, 'Are you the President?' 'No,' replied the stranger, 'I am Frederick Douglass.'"

It was an honest mistake.

Frederick Douglass was in Washington to see Abraham Lincoln. He was not the President, but, under different circum-stances, he could have been. He had all the gifts—presence, passion, bearing, brilliance—all the gifts save one: he was Non-European American. Color —an accident of birth —barred him from the highest prize, but it did not prevent him from becoming one of the noblest of all Americans.

Born in the lowest position of society, Douglass emancipated himself and became an orator, an abolitionist, an editor, a politician, a seer, and a prophet. Born African American and hungry in a society that forbade slaves to read, he lifted himself by his own efforts and became one of the great names in an age that abounds in greatness. For fifty years, from 1845 to 1895, he was in the forefront of the fight for human freedom. During this period, he laid the foundation for the African American protest movement.

Although he died in 1895, Frederick Douglass speaks with uncommon force to the problems of this age. One hundred and ten years ago, he was staging sit-ins on Massachusetts railroads. One hundred and six years ago, he was leading a fight for integrated schools in Rochester, New York. One hundred years ago, he was denouncing hypocrisy and fraud with pre-Baldwin fury:

> "The whole history of the progress of human liberty shows that all concessions yet made to her august claims, have been born of earnest struggle.... If there is no struggle, there is no progress. Those who profess to favor freedom and yet deprecate agitation, are men who want crops without plowing up the ground, they want rain without thunder and lightning. They want the ocean without the awful roar of its many waters.

> "This struggle may be a moral one, or it may be a physical one, or it may be both moral and physical, but it must be a struggle. Power concedes nothing without a demand. It never did and it never will.... Men may not get all they pay for in this world, but they must certainly pay for all they get. If we ever get free from the oppressions and wrongs heaped upon us, we must pay for their removal. We must do this by labor, by suffering, by sacrifice, and if needs be, by our lives and the lives of others."

More important than the eloquence of Douglass' words was the eloquence of his life. He was born Frederick Augustus Washington Bailey in February, 1817, on the eastern shore of Maryland. He never knew his father (who was rumored to be his master) and he only saw his mother five or six times. Slavery, he said once, abolished both fatherhood and motherhood. As a child, he knew the brutality and degradation of slavery. He knew hunger and pain, and he saw his aunt and other African American men and women whipped.

A stroke of luck sent Douglass to Baltimore, Maryland, where he learned at an early age that knowledge is power. His mistress wanted to teach him the alphabet, but his master forbade it. "Give a nigger an inch," he said, "and he will take a mile…Learning would spoil the best nigger in the world."

The slave boy, not yet ten years old, brooded over this message and concluded that words were weapons. He hid dirty pages in his pockets and when no one was looking, he extracted the pages and spelled out the magic words. Three years later, Douglass came across a book called The Columbian Orator, which gave him an insight into his own condition. The Columbian Orator told Douglass who he was and how he got that way and what he could do about it. "With that book," he said, "I penetrated to the secret of all slavery and all oppression and perceived my own human nature and the facts of my past and present experiences."

Later, while still a slave, Douglass learned that power has its limitations. This was an extraordinary discovery and it changed the whole course of his life. It happened this way. He refused to buckle down to his master and was sent to a professional African American-breaker, who specialized in destroying the spirit of slaves who would not submit to the slave regime. The African American-breaker's name was Edward Covey, and Covey was good at his trade. He worked Douglass until he was ready to drop from exhaustion and whipped him until he bowed and smiled. But worms—and slaves and Negroes—turn.

One day, Douglass tells us, he turned and made a desperate last stand. The two men grappled to an indecisive draw. Covey stalked off and never afterwards touched Douglass. Looking back on this incident many years later, Douglass said: "A man without force, is without the essential dignity of humanity. Human nature is so constituted, that it cannot honor a helpless man, although it can pity him; and even this it cannot do long if the signs of power do not arise. He only can understand the effect of this combat on my spirit who has himself incurred something, hazarded something, in repelling the unjust and cruel aggressions of a tyrant.... I had reached the point, at which I was not afraid to die."

"This spirit made me a free man in fact, while I remained a slave in form. When a slave cannot be flogged, he is more than half free." Douglass added: "Experience proves that those are oftenest abused who can be abused with the greatest impunity. Men are whipped oftenest who are whipped easiest."

Four years later, at the age of twenty-one, Douglass escaped from slavery. In 1838, he borrowed a sailor suit and an official-looking paper with a big American eagle on it. Grabbing a train, he traveled to New York, flashing his eagle-stamped paper as he went. In New York, he immediately married Anna Murray, a charming, free African American woman from Baltimore who had followed him to New York.

With the help of underground agents, the young couple settled in two rooms on "M" Street overlooking Buzzard's Bay in New Bedford, Massachusetts. One of Douglass' friends, Nathan Johnson, a literary fan of Sir Walter Scott, suggested that Douglass abandon his slave name and adopt the name of one of Scott's characters. Douglass agreed and Frederick Augustus Washington Bailey began his life as a free man under the name of Frederick Douglass.

For almost three years, Douglass lived and worked in New Bedford, where his first children were born. During this period, Douglass supported his family by sawing wood, waiting tables, working on the docks, and at a local brass foundry. He recalled later that he often nailed newspapers to the post near his bellows and studied while he was performing his work.

It did not take Douglass long to realize that he had escaped from the chattel slavery of the South into the caste slavery of the North. Outraged by the remembered wrongs of chattel slavery and the experienced wrongs of caste slavery, Douglass allied himself with the currents of the emerging abolitionist movement. He subscribed to Garrison's Liberator and attended meetings held by local African Americans.

By 1841 Douglass was a leader of the African American community of New Bedford. It was in August of that year that William Lloyd Garrison and other abolitionist leaders heard him speak at an abolitionist convention in Nantucket. Garrison was overwhelmed by Douglass' speech which he said "would have done honor to Patrick Henry."

Garrison and his aides offered Douglass $450 a year to become a lecturer for the Massachusetts Anti-Slavery Society. Douglass accepted and at the age of twenty-four joined the phalanx of African American and European American men who were waging an intensive cold war against slavery. European American abolitionists like William Lloyd Garrison and free African American men like Charles Lennox Remond were in the forefront of the movement, but they did not have the first-hand knowledge that Douglass had; and their speeches lacked his concreteness and fire.

Douglass on the platform was a sight to see. He was a good-looking man, tall, well-built, with olive skin and a halo of hair worn long in the African style. His physical presence moved people. So did the rolling thunder of his voice. By turns humorous, dolorous, and indignant, he transported his audience to slave row. A master mimic, he could make people laugh at a slave owner preaching the duties of Christian obedience, could make them see the humiliation of an

African American maiden ravished by a brutal slave-owner, could make them hear the sobs of a mother separated from her child. Through him, people could live slavery. "European American men and African American men," William Wells Brown said, "had talked against slavery, but none had ever spoken like Frederick Douglass."

Life in this age was not easy for a European American agitator: it was impossible for an African American man. Douglass was roughed up by pro-slavery thugs; his right hand was broken; he was thrown down steps. But he took his knocks and stood his ground. It was difficult in this age to find a hall that would let an African American abolitionist use its facilities. In Grafton, Massachusetts, he took a bell and made the rounds announcing his own meeting. In Dorchester, New York, Douglass took a stand under a tree and began addressing five people. By the time he warmed up, he-had an audience of five hundred.

Within a few years, Douglass was a household name. In 1845, on publication of his first book, *The Autobiography of Frederick Douglass*, Douglass was forced to flee the country to avoid recapture by his owner. During this enforced exile, Douglass traveled to England, Ireland, and Scotland, was feted by ladies, lords, and earls.

In a famous letter from Ireland, Douglass painted a harsh picture of America: "In thinking of America, I sometime find myself admiring her bright blue sky—her grand old woods—her fertile fields —her beautiful rivers—her mighty lakes, and star-crowned mountains. But my rapture is soon checked, my joy is soon turned to mourning. When I remember that all is cursed with the infernal spirit of slaveholding, robbery and wrong, —when I remember that with the waters of her noblest rivers, the tears of my brethren are borne to the ocean, disregarded and forgotten, and that her most fertile fields drink daily of the warm blood of my outraged sisters, I am filled with unutterable loathing, and led to reproach myself that any thing could fall from my lips in praise of such a land. America will not allow her children to love her. She seems bent on compelling those who would be her warmest friends, to be her worst enemies."

"May God give her repentance before it is too late, is the ardent prayer of my heart. I will continue to pray, labor and wait, believing that she cannot always be insensible to the dictates of justice, or deaf to the voice of humanity."

Douglass' reception was so warm in England, Ireland, and Scotland that he was tempted to remain abroad. But in an eloquent farewell speech at London Tavern, he said: "I choose rather to go home; to return to America. I glory in the conflict, that I may hereafter exalt in the victory. I know that victory is certain. I go, turning my back upon the ease, comfort, and respectability which I might maintain even here, ignorant as I am. Still, I will go back, for the sake of my brethren. I go to suffer with them; to toil with them; to endure insult with them; to lift up my voice in their behalf; to speak and write in their vindication; and struggle in their ranks for that emancipation which shall yet be achieved by the power of truth and of principle for that oppressed people."

So, turning his back on ease, comfort and respectability, Douglass returned to America. For almost six years, he had labored in the Garrison vineyard. Now he stepped out on his own. In 1847, he started publishing the North Star in Rochester, New York. From that year until the abolition of slavery, he was in the forefront of the abolitionist ranks.

Then and later, Douglass was a formidable advocate.

First of all and most important of all, Douglass was a man, in the deepest and truest sense of that much abused word. Douglass knew that to be a man is to be, precisely, responsible. He knew, too, that manhood is founded on self-respect and self-esteem. Frederick Douglass did not doubt himself, nor did he apologize for his place of birth or the color of his mother's skin.

He was involved. He did not isolate himself from the masses. Wherever he went, the African American man went with him. He bitterly criticized free African Americans—and there were many—who were indifferent to the antislavery cause. Free African Americans and African American slaves, he said, were chained together and would rise or fall together. His mission, he said, was "to stand up for the downtrodden, to speak for the dumb, and to remember those in bond as bound with me." He added: "It is more than a figure of speech to say, that African Americans are as a people chained together."

"We are one people—one in general complexion, one in common degradation, one in popular estimation. As one rises, all must rise; and as one falls, all must fall…. Every one of us should be ashamed to consider himself free, while his brother is a slave.— The wrongs of our brethren should be our constant theme. There should be no time too precious, no calling too holy, no place too sacred, to make room for the cause."

Douglass was consumed by the cause. Wherever he was, he sought out the struggle and involved himself in it. As superintendent of the Underground Railroad in Rochester, New York, he participated in the dangerous—and illegal—work of helping fugitive slaves escape into Canada.

He was militant. He not only told the truth, but he also lived it. He refused to accept segregation and discrimination; he assumed that every door open to a human being was open to him; and, if turned away, he made an issue of it. When asked to leave a Jim Crow car, he would refuse to move. The conductor usually called assistants who would drag Douglass out of the car along with several seats he always managed to hold onto.

He was independent. No man dictated to him, and no party or faction could silence his voice. Although he was ambitious, although he hungered and thirsted after political office, he never sold his principles. No dream of honors, no hope of office, could still his advocacy of freedom. "I am a Republican," he said once, "but I am not a Republican right or wrong."

And he was catholic. He was a universal man and he refused, he said, to allow himself "to be insensible to the wrongs and sufferings of any part of the great family of man." He fought for women's suffrage, free speech, "poor barefoot Ireland," and the Chinese; and he opposed flogging in the Navy, monopolies, and capital punishment. "I base no man's rights," he said, "upon his color, and plead no man's rights because of his color. My objection to slavery is not that it sinks a African American to the condition of a brute, but that it sinks a man to that condition." Douglass realized, however, that individuality is universality.

He realized that a man is most human when he is most himself. And he made no apologies for raising inconvenient questions. When he was rich in honors and money, he accepted an invitation to speak in Ohio; but he warned the sponsors that he did not intend to bite his tongue. African American people, he said, "still need the help of all who can say a word in their behalf. If I come to you in July, I shall bring the African American man with me."

Throughout this period, Douglass took the lead in militant, direct action against the chattel slavery of the South and the caste slavery of the North. In 1850, for example, he staged a school boycott in Rochester, New York. He explained later: "[My children] were not allowed in the public school in the district in which I lived, owned property, and paid taxes, but were compelled, if they went to a public school, to go over to the other side of the city to an inferior African American school. I hardly need say that I was not prepared to submit tamely to this proscription...so I had them taught at home for a while.... Meanwhile I went to the people with the question, and created a considerable agitation."

"I sought and obtained a hearing before the Board of Education, and after repeated efforts with voice and pen, the doors of the public schools were opened and African American children were permitted to attend them in common with others."

In an age of danger and doubt, Douglass and other African American abolitionists came to grips with dilemmas which lie deep in the African American heart. Douglass asked the old and insistent question: "How can I sing the Lord's song in a strange land?" The answers revolved around the traditional trilogy: ballots, bullets, or Bibles, and Iago's injunction: "Go, make money." The followers of William Lloyd Garrison condemned "complexional institutions" (African American churches, lodges, schools, newspapers and conventions). The Garrisonians also abandoned political action and advocated a campaign based on passive resistance and moral force.

After 1851, Douglass favored ballots, if possible, and bullets, if necessary. He was an opportunist on the issue of "complexional institutions." He demanded complete integration, but if circumstances made this impossible, he unhesitatingly recommended special institutions. At stake here was a bitter issue of power.

Douglass was an independent man who felt uncomfortable in a subsidiary role; he demanded a share in the "generalship" of the movement. In a statement which anticipated the contemporary African American power movement, he said: "If we are ever elevated, our elevation will have been accomplished through our own instrumentality. The history of other oppressed nations will confirm us in this assertion. No People that has solely depended upon foreign aid, or rather, upon the efforts of those in any way identified with the oppressor, to undo the heavy burdens, ever stood forth in the attitude of Freedom. Someone, imbued with the spirit of human freedom, from among themselves, has arisen to lead them on to victory. They have dashed their fetters to the ground."

When Garrison and other European American abolitionists refused to share the "generalship" of the movement, Douglass struck out on his own. He believed that he and other African American abolitionists could make a positive contribution by proving that African American people were active rather than passive cogs in the anti-slavery machinery. He said that "…the man who has suffered the wrong is the man to demand redress—that the man STRUCK is the man to CRY OUT—and that he who has endured the cruel pangs of Slavery is the man to advocate Liberty. It is evident that we must be our own representatives and advocates, not exclusively, but peculiarly—not distinct from, but in connection with our European American friends."

Douglass was scornful of the missionary mentality of some European American abolitionists. "The relation," he said, "subsisting between the European American and African American people of this country is the vital question of the age…Here, a man must be hot or be accounted cold, or, perchance, something worse than hot or cold. The lukewarm and the cowardly, will be rejected by earnest men on either side of the controversy. The cunning man who avoids it, to gain the favor of both parties, will be rewarded with scorn; and the timid man who shrinks from it, for fear of offending either party, will be despised. To the lawyer, the preacher, the politician, and to the man of letters, there is no neutral ground. He that is not for us, is against us."

As a theorist and advocate, Douglass stressed the structural roots of racism. He said it was libelous to call the race/cultural problem the African American problem. The real problem, he said, was the European American problem. The real problem, he said, was the determination of European Americans to live out of the blood and the labor of African Americans. The only solution, he told African Americans, was struggle.

He urged African Americans to pool their resources in a massive crusade against racism. Although he considered the ballot indispensable, he did not neglect economic power. Economic power and political power, he said, were linked, for political power could translate itself into economic power and vice versa. "Every blow of the sledgehammer, wielded by a sable arm, is a powerful blow in support of our cause," he said. "Every African American mechanic, is, by virtue of circumstances, an elevator of his race. Every house built by African American men is a strong tower against the allied hosts of prejudice…It is impossible for us to attach too much importance to this aspect of the subject…. Understand this, that independence is an essential condition of respectability. To be dependent, is to be degraded. Men may indeed pity us, but they cannot respect us."

In the midst of the terrible economic crisis of the 1850's, Douglass told African Americans that it was necessary to find new ways of making a living, adding:

> "The old avocations, by which African American men obtained a livelihood, are rapidly, unceasingly and inevitably passing into other hands; every hour sees the African American man elbowed out of employment...
>
> European American men are becoming house-servants, cooks, and stewards on vessels—at hotels. They are becoming porters, stevedores, wood-sawyers, hod-carriers, brickmakers, white-washers and barbers, so that African Americans can scarcely find the means of subsistence—a few years ago, and a European American barber would have been a curiosity—now their poles stand on every street.
>
> Formerly African Americans were almost the exclusive coachmen in wealthy families: this is so no longer, European American men are now employed, and for aught we see, they fill their servile station with obsequiousness as profound as that of the African Americans. The readiness and ease with which they adapt themselves to these conditions ought not to be lost sight of by the African American people. The meaning is very important, and we should learn it.
>
> We are taught our insecurity by it. Without the means of living, life is a curse, and leaves us at the mercy of the oppressor to become his debased slave. Now, African American men, what do you mean to do, for you must do something?...One thing is certain: we must find new methods of obtaining a livelihood, for the old ones are failing us very fast."

Despite the intensity of the crisis, Douglass was contemptuous of the back-to-Africa plan of Martin Delany, another pioneer African American nationalist. As he said later, "It is all nonsense to talk about the removal of eight millions of the American people from their homes in America to Africa. The expense and hardships, to say nothing of the cruelty attending such a measure, would make success impossible."

"The American people are wicked, but they are not fools; they will hardly be disposed to incur the expenses, to say nothing of the injustice which the measure demands.... The bad thing about it is, that it has, of late, owing to persecution, begun to be advocated by African American men of acknowledged ability and learning, and every little while some European American statesman becomes its advocate. These gentlemen will doubtless have their opinion of me; I certainly have mine of them. My opinion is, that if they are sensible, they are insincere; and if they are sincere, they are not sensible."

"They know, or they ought to know, that it would take more money than the cost of the late war, to transport even one half of the coloured people of the United States to Africa. Whether intentionally or not, they are, as I think, simply trifling with an afflicted people. They urge them to look for relief where they ought to know that relief is impossible."

Douglass believed that African Americans and European Americans were inseparably joined. "My friends, the destiny of the African Americans...is the destiny of America. We shall never leave you. The allotments of Providence seem to make the African American man of America the open book out of which the American people are to learn lessons of wisdom, power and goodness—more sublime and glorious than any yet attained by the nations of the old or the new world."

"Over the bleeding back of the American bondsman we shall learn mercy. In the extreme difference of color and features of the African American and the Anglo-Saxon, shall be learned the highest ideas of the sacredness of man, and the fullness and perfection of human brotherhood."

And again:

> "We are here, and here we are likely to be. To imagine that we should ever be eradicated is absurd and ridiculous. We can be modified, changed, assimilated, but never extinguished. We repeat, therefore, that we are here; and that this is our country; and the question for the philosophers and statesmen of the land ought to be, What principle should dictate the policy of the nation toward us? We shall neither die out, nor be driven out; but shall go with this people, either as a testimony against them, or as an evidence in their favor throughout their generation…."

America's failure to make a meaningful response to the abolitionist campaign infuriated Douglass and he lashed out with the fire and the eloquence of the Old Testament prophets. Speaking at Rochester, New York, on July 5, 1852, he indicted every structure of power in America. "What," he asked, "to the American slave is your Fourth of July? I answer; a day that reveals to him, more than all other days in the year, the gross injustice and cruelty to which he is the constant victim."

"To him, your celebration is a sham; your boasted liberty, an unholy license; your national greatness, swelling vanity; your sounds of rejoicing are empty and heartless; your denunciation of tyrants, brass-fronted impudence; your shouts of liberty and equality, hollow mockery; your prayers and hymns, your sermons and thanksgivings, with all your religious parade and solemnity, are, to him, more bombast, fraud, deception, impiety, and hypocrisy—a thin veil to cover up crimes which would disgrace a nation of savages…"

"You boast of your love of liberty, your superior civilization, and your pure Christianity…You hurl anathemas at the crowned headed tyrants of Russia and Austria and pride yourselves on your Democratic institutions, while you yourselves consent to be the mere tools and bodyguards of the tyrants of Virginia and Carolina."

"You invite to your shores fugitives of oppression from abroad, honor them with banquets, greet them with ovations, cheer them, toast them, salute them, protect them, and pour out your money to them like water; but the fugitives from your own land you advertise, hunt, arrest, shoot, and kill."

"You glory in your refinement and your universal education; yet you maintain a system as barbarous and dreadful as ever stained the character of a nation—a system begun in avarice, supported in pride, and perpetuated in cruelty. You shed tears over fallen Hungary, and make the sad story of her wrongs the theme of your poets, statesmen, and orators, till your gallant sons are ready to fly to arms to vindicate her cause against the oppressor; but, in regard to the ten thousand wrongs of the American slave, you would enforce the strictest silence, and would hail him as an enemy of the nation who dares to make these wrongs the subject of public discourse!"

Douglass dared to make "the ten thousand wrongs" the subject of public discourse. Week after week, year after year, in the crucial decades before the Civil War, he went up and down the North, warning, preaching, demanding. He and other African American abolitionists played a major role in shaping the crisis which led to the Civil War.

Like Denmark Vesey, like Martin Luther King, Douglass was a curious blend of idealism and practicality. Nothing indicates this more clearly than his confrontation with John Brown on the eve of the Harpers Ferry Raid. John Brown begged Douglass to accompany him, but Douglass refused, saying the raid was impractical and doomed to failure.

After long arguments, after weeping and much gnashing of teeth, the two men parted, never to meet again, Douglass going toward life, Brown toward death, both men serving in their different ways both life and man. By this, we must understand, as playwright Barry Stavis has said, that two men, both dedicated to the same cause at the same time, can take totally different courses and yet serve in their different ways both history and man.

During the Civil War, Douglass prodded the famous "Slow Coach at Washington"—Abraham Lincoln. Long before Lincoln perceived it, Douglass was saying that the war was a struggle to give America a new birth of freedom. Long before Lincoln saw it, Douglass was saying that the African American man was inextricably involved in the root cause of the war and that the war could not be fought or ended without coming to grips with the meaning of the African American man and the meaning of America.

Douglass saw the Civil War as a struggle to complete the American Revolution. Legal emancipation alone, he said, would not free the slaves. It would be necessary to train new leaders, reknit shattered African American family life, and instill in the hearts of Southerners respect for democratic processes.

The task before America, Douglass said, was "nothing less than radical revolution in all the modes of thought which had flourished under the blighted slave system." The great African American abolitionist was openly contemptuous of men like Lincoln who placed the Union above freedom. The old Union, he said, was dead, "We are fighting for something incomparably better than the old Union. We are fighting for unity. Unity of idea, unity of sentiment, unity of object, unity of institutions, in which there shall be no North, no South, no East, no West, no African American, no European American, but a solidarity of the nation, making every slave free, and every free man a voter."

There was poetry in this audacious conception and Douglass pushed it for all it was worth. With Wendell Phillips and Charles Sumner and Thaddeus Stevens, Douglass prepared the high ground of emancipation which Lincoln occupied so reluctantly and so grudgingly.

After the Emancipation Proclamation was issued, Douglass demanded ballots for the freedmen, and land —and said, with impeccable logic, that "as one learns to swim by swimming, the Negro must learn to vote by voting." Four things, he said, were necessary: "the right to the cartridge box, the ballot box, the jury box" —and "the knowledge box." When the North reneged on its promise and turned the freedmen over to the tender mercies of their former masters, Douglass was merciless in his denunciation.

In 1883, he denounced the African-Americans' "so-called emancipation as a stupendous fraud, a fraud upon him, a fraud upon the world." America had abandoned the African American, ignored his rights and left him "a deserted, a defrauded, a swindled, and an outcast man —in law, free; in fact, a slave.

In speech after speech Douglass told America that it was courting social disaster. It was impossible, he said, to degrade African American people without degrading the social fabric of America. The perversion of legal processes, he said, would eventually force African American people outside the community, for "where justice is denied, where poverty is enforced, where ignorance prevails, and where any one class is made to feel that society is an organized conspiracy to oppress, rob, and degrade...neither persons nor property will be safe..."

"Hungry men," he said, "will eat. Desperate men will commit crime. Outraged men will seek revenge."

Foreseeing the summers of 1968 and 1969, Douglass said in 1894 and 1895, that America, if it did not alter its course, would create an aggrieved class of African American revolutionaries.

All this was true and extremely enlightening. But what was to be done? Douglass said African American people should refurbish their weapons, dig trenches, expose, warn, appeal, exhort —and contest every inch of ground. Time, he said, would fight the African American man's battles—time and the African American man's birthrate.

"Every year adds to the African American man's numbers. Every year adds to his wealth and to his intelligence. These will speak for him."

In these years, Douglass was a magnet, a pole star and a lighthouse. Men said he was waging a hopeless battle, that African American people could not win by agitation, litigation, or any other tactic. Perhaps. But they are cowards who fight only when victory is sure. Men, though outnumbered, fight when they reach the wall, when to say no is to affirm one's humanity.

Consider, for example, the range and the depth of Douglass' utterances in this period:

> The African American is now discussed on every hand. The platform, the pulpit, the press, and the legislative hall regard him, and struggle with him, as a great and difficult problem, one that requires almost divine wisdom to solve. Men are praying over it. It is always a dangerous symptom when men pray to know what is their duty.
>
> — Speech, Washington, D.C., 1889

In whatever else the African American may have been a failure, he has, in one respect, been a marked and brilliant success. He has managed by one means or another to make himself one of the most prominent and interesting figures that now attract and hold the attention of the world. Go where you will, you will meet him.

He is alike present in the study of the learned and thoughtful, and in the play house of the gay and thoughtless. We see him pictured at our street corners, and hear him in the songs of our market places. I he low and the vulgar curse him, the snob and the flunky affect to despise him; the mean and the cowardly assault him, because they know that his friends are few, and that they can abuse him with impunity, and with the applause of the coarse and brutal crowd. But, despite it all, the African American remains like iron or granite, cool, strong, imperturbable and cheerful.

— Speech, Washington, 1883

My friends, the present is a critical moment for the African American people of this country; our fate for weal or for woe...trembles now in the balance. No man can tell which way the scales will turn. There is not a breeze that sweeps us from the South, but comes laden with the wail of our suffering people [This is an hour] when the American people are once more being urged to do from necessity what they should have done from a sense of right, and of sound statesmanship. It is the same old posture of affairs, wherein our rulers do wrong from choice and right from necessity.

— Speech, Washington, 1885

If [federal officials] can protect the rights of European American men, they can protect the rights of African American men; if they can defend the rights of American citizens abroad, they can defend them at home; if they can use the army to protect the rights of Chinamen, they can use the army to protect the rights of African American men. The only trouble is the will! the will! the will! Here, as elsewhere, "Where there is a will there is a way."

—Speech, Washington, 1886

We warn the American people, and the American government to be wise in their day and generation. The time may come that these whom they now despise and hate, may be needed. These compelled foes may, by and by, be wanted as friends. America cannot always sit, as a queen, in peace and repose. Prouder and stronger governments than hers have been shattered by the bolts of the wrath of a just God. We beseech her to have a care how she goads the sable oppressed in the land. We warn her in the name of retribution, to look to her ways. . . .

— The North Star, 1849

The presence of [deprived citizens] in any section of this country, constituting an aggrieved class, smarting under terrible wrongs, denied the exercise of the commonest rights of humanity, and regarded by the ruling class of that section as outside of the government, outside of the law, outside of society, having nothing in common with the people with whom they live, the sport of mob violence and murder, is not only a disgrace and scandal to that particular section, but a menace to the peace and security of the whole country.

— Pamphlet,

Fellow-citizens! We want no aggrieved class in America. Strong as we are without the African American, we are stronger with him than without him. The power and friendship of seven millions of people scattered all over the country, however humble, are not lo be despised —— Our legislators, our Presidents, and our judges should have a care, lest, by forcing these people outside of law, they destroy that love of country which is needful to the Nation's defense in the day of trouble.

— Speech, Washington, 1883

. . .let us have peace, but let us have liberty, law and justice first. Let us have the Constitution, with its Thirteenth, Fourteenth, and Fifteenth amendments, fairly interpreted, faithfully executed and cheerfully obeyed in the fullness of their spirit and the completeness of their letter. . .When the supreme law of the land is practically set at naught, when humanity is insulted and the rights of the weak are trampled in the dust by a lawless power;

when society is divided into two classes, as oppressed and oppressor, there is no power and there can be no power, while the instincts of humanity remain as they are, which can provide solid peace.

— Speech, New York City, 1878

What Abraham Lincoln said in respect of the United States is as true of the African American people as of the relations of these States. They cannot remain half slave and half free. You must give them all or take from them all. Until this half-and-half condition is ended, there will be just ground of complaint. You will have an aggrieved class, and this discussion will go on.

Until the public schools shall cease to be caste schools in every part of our country, this discussion will go on. Until the African American man's pathway to the American ballot box, North and South, shall be as smooth and as safe as the same is for the European American citizen, this discussion will go on. Until the African American man's right to practice at the bar of our courts, and sit on juries, shall be the universal law and practice of the land, this discussion will go on. Until the courts of the country shall grant the African American man a fair trial and a just verdict, this discussion will go on. Until color shall cease to be a bar to equal participation in the offices and honors of the country, this discussion will go on.

Until the (cades-unions and the workshops of the country shall cease to proscribe the African American man and prevent his children from learning useful trades, this discussion will go on. Until the American people shall make character, and nor color, the criterion of respectability, this discussion will go on— In a word, until truth and humanity shall cease to be living ideas, and mankind shall sink back into moral darkness, and the world shall put evil for good, Inner for sweet, and darkness for light, this discussion will go on. Until all humane ideas and civilization shall be banished from the world, this discussion will go on.

— Speech, Washington, 1883

In this period, Douglass—despite his denunciation—became an elder statesman. He was named Marshal of the District of Columbia and Minister to Haiti. He moved to a mansion in Anacostia, Washington, D. C. After the death of his first wife, he married a European American woman who was a clerk in his office in the District of Columbia. But he continued to press the claims of African American people. He had one foot in the grave on the day a young African American student came to him and asked: "Mr. Douglass, what shall I do with my life?" The Old Warrior pulled himself up to his full height and his eyes blazed with the fury of his youth as he said,

"Agitate!"
"Agitate!"
"Agitate!"

On a cold gray day, February 20, 1895, the Great Agitator slumped to the floor in his mansion at Anacostia Heights, Washington, D. C. By nightfall he was dead. The legislatures of several Northern states passed resolutions of regret. The legislature of North Carolina adjourned for the day to mark the death of one of the greatest African American men produced in this country. At his funeral in Washington, John Hutchinson sang the abolitionist song his brother Jesse had dedicated to Douglass:

I'll be free, I'll be free, and none shall confine
With fetters and chains this spirit of mine;
From my youth I have vowed in God to rely,
And, despite the oppressor, gain freedom or die.

A few days later, the African American people of Americus, Georgia, held a meeting and voted to contribute to a national fund to erect a monument in Douglass' honor. "No people," these maids and laborers and cotton pickers said, "no people who can produce a Douglass need despair."

Some fifty-eight years later, Mary Church Terrell, the great woman leader, echoed this sentiment in an Ebony magazine article in which she called Frederick Douglass the greatest of all Americans.

Since that time Frederick Douglass has become a central figure of the African American liberation struggle, a fact noted by poet Robert E. Hayden, who wrote:

> When it is finally ours, this freedom, this liberty, this beautiful
> and terrible thing, needful to man as air,
> usable as earth; when it belongs at last to our children,
> when it is truly instinct, brain matter, diastole, systole,
> reflex action; when it is finally won; when it is more
> than the gaudy mumbo jumbo of politicians:
> this man, this Douglass, this former slave, this African American
> beaten to his knees, exiled, visioning a world
> where none is lonely, none hunted, alien,
> this man, superb in love and logic, this man
> shall be remembered. Oh, not with statues' rhetoric,
> not with legends and poems and wreaths of bronze alone,
> but with the lives grown out of his life, the lives
> fleshing his dream of the beautiful, needful thing.

Part Five

African American Women Writers Eighteenth and Early Nineteenth Century

Brenda Wilkerson

Chapter Twenty-Six
Phillis Wheatley

(1753 ? - 1784)

In the summer of 1761, a ship named the *Phillis* arrived in Boston. A small and fragile girl, no more than eight years old, stood shivering at the dock. Sickness and fear consumed her trembling body, which she attempted to cover with an old piece of carpet.

Kidnapped from Africa and sold into slavery, Phillis was named for the slave ship on which she was brought to America. Her birthplace is unknown, but research has placed the point of her capture on the west coast of Africa, the present-day nations of Senegal and Gambia. How frightening it must have been for Phillis—first, to be torn away from her family and village, and then to endure the cruel voyage.

This young girl was destined to become one of America's brightest stars. A future poet and author of the first collection of poetry by an African American, she was at that moment a piece of property awaiting the highest bidder. Along with approximately seventy-five other Africans, she was part of the human cargo of Captain Peter Gwinn, who worked for Timothy Fitch, slave merchant and owner of the *Phillis*.

Along with the small number of survivors, young Phillis had been splashed with a bucket of water and was presented for sale at the Boston docks. Among the speculators at the Boston slave auction was Susannah Wheatley, wife of John Wheatley, a wealthy Boston tailor. The mother of eighteen-year-old twins, Mary and Nathaniel Wheatley, Susannah was in search of a young servant of "healthy" appearance.

Something about the trembling and half-naked girl captured her attention. Perhaps it was Susannah's own poor health, or that of her fragile daughter, Mary, that evoked such pity and made her choose the sickly girl.

Phillis Wheatley's tribal and religious African roots are not known. But based on Phillis' point of capture and on her own early recollections, some historians believe that she was a member of the Fulani, a Muslim tribe of western Africa. As a girl, she shared a story of a faint memory of her mother kneeling before the sunrise, a Muslim ritual.

Whatever religious grounding young Phillis may have had, it was displaced by the influence of Christianity, the religion of her owners, whose customs she accepted as her own.

Phillis quickly adjusted to life in the Wheatley household, where she would remain for seventeen years. The Wheatleys recognized the young slave girl's hunger for knowledge and encouraged her. Eighteen-year-old Mary Wheatley, who was sickly like Phillis, became a constant companion. The two spent extended periods of time reading the Bible and studying poetry. Phillis Wheatley soon learned to read English, and by age nine was studying Latin and the Bible.

When Phillis arrived in America, 230,000 Africans and future African Americans lived in the colonies.

Some 16,000, like Phillis, were enslaved in New England, where they worked primarily as servants and were allowed to learn to read and write. But most were enslaved in the South, where they labored on rice, cotton, and tobacco plantations. Southern "slave codes" denied

African Americans many privileges: learning to read or write, defending themselves against abuse by European Americans, testifying against them in court, and owning property.

At age twelve, she began to write poetry. The Wheatleys provided paper, pen, and ink and allowed her to burn a candle until late into the night. because of her poor health, Phillis was virtually cut off from other African Americans, so she found companionship in words.

The Wheatleys treated Phillis differently from their other slaves. They assigned her light household duties, such as the dusting and polishing of furniture or the arranging of tables for dinner parties. They even scolded Prince, their driver, for keeping Phillis up front beside him in the cold, damp weather, instead of letting her sit inside their carriage.

The other close relationship that Phillis was able to develop with another slave was with Obour Tanner. They met in Rhode Island, where their owners spent their vacation. Like Phillis, Tanner was educated by her owners and was a devout Christian. The two young women established a long friendship through their letters.

Phillis Wheatley started to gain recognition in 1770 with the publication of a verse she wrote in 1767 in memory of Reverend George Whitefield, a famed Methodist evangelist. In 1768, she wrote a patriotic verse, "On the Arrival of the Ships of War, and Landing of the Troops," in response to the arrival in Boston of British troops sent to quell colonial unrest.

Phillis became a source of great pride to the Wheatley family, and they began to invite prominent Bostonians to meet and hear her. Among those invited was Eunice Fitch, wife of the merchant upon whose slave ship Phillis had arrived in America. Governor Thomas Hutchins and legislator John Hancock gave the aspiring young artist books to encourage her.

In 1773, Nathaniel Wheatley had cause to travel to England on business. The family decided that Phillis Wheatley would accompany him on the trip. They had a special reason. American printers had refused to publish the writings of a slave girl, so Nathaniel Wheatley took Phillis to London to publish her book. She gave it the title *Poems on Various Subjects, Religious and Moral, by Phillis Wheatley, Negro Servant to Mrs. Wheatley of Boston.*

Her visit to London was glorious. To Phillis's surprise, word of her accomplishment as a poet had reached England before her arrival. London society embraced her. She became a protégée of both Lady Huntingdon and Lord Dartmouth, who was then mayor of London. Other dignitaries who welcomed and encouraged her included Benjamin Franklin, who later became a prominent political figure in America, and Brooke Watson, who would become the mayor of London.

Unfortunately, Susannah Wheatley became severely ill, and Phillis's stay in London came to an end. She left London a few weeks short of the publication of her book. She was approximately twenty years old when she returned to Boston in September 1773. It would prove an eventful month for Phillis Wheatley. She was emancipated by John Wheatley and her book was released.

Some individuals who believed that people of African heritage were incapable of "thinking," let along "writing," questioned that Phillis was the genuine author of the book. So her mistress, Susannah Wheatley, needed to prove that Phillis was indeed the true author. Thus, a certificate signed by prominent European American men of New England was printed in the book. It read in part: "We whose names are under-written, do assure the world that the poems specified in the following pages were (as verily we believe) written by Phillis, a young African American girl." Susannah Wheatley died shortly afterward.

Phillis Wheatley continued to write poetry right up to the beginning of the American Revolution.

She wrote to and was acknowledged by General George Washington in 1775. The general invited her to visit his headquarters, which she did the following year. Altogether, Phillis would publish five books of poetry and letters.

Following the death of John Wheatley in 1778, Phillis, who had remained part of the Wheatley household, was now on her own. That same year she married John Peters.

Stories about her husband vary. Some say that John Peters held a variety of jobs—lawyer, grocer, banker, and doctor —but that he was unsuccessful in all of these occupations. Others labeled him a ne'er-do-well who shunned hard labor. It is difficult, however, to determine Peter's true character given the prejudice of the day. Whatever the true story, serious financial problems landed him in debtor's jail in 1784.

Phillis gave birth to three children, two of whom died as infants. Her third child died in 1784.

Destitute and living in a boardinghouse in Boston, Phillis died.

Announcement of her funeral was placed in two local papers: "Last Lord's Day, died Mrs. Phillis Peters (formerly Phillis Wheatley) aged 31, known to the world by her celebrated miscellaneous poems. Her funeral is to be this afternoon at four o'clock....Her friends and acquaintances are desired to attend." Sadly, no one came.

Although Phillis Wheatley's five books were ignored for years after her death, and often dismissed as being too sentimental and patriotic; today her work is given the special honor it deserves. Indeed, a debt of gratitude is owed this early American poet for her discipline and determination. With the site of her grave unknown, the city of Boston honored her some two hundred years after her death by erecting a monument in her name.

A POET SHARES HER FEELINGS

"In every human breast, God has implanted a principle,
which we call love of freedom;
it is impatient of oppression and pants for deliverance. I
will assert that same principle
lives in us."

—Phillis Wheatley

Chapter Twenty-Seven
Sojourner Truth

(1797 - 1883)

Unlike Phillis Wheatley, most slaves faced endless days of labor and harsh treatment. Slaves who dared show defiance were subjected to severe beatings and other savage acts of punishment. Many African Americans risked all by running away. Among those who ran was the bold and brave woman who came to be known as Sojourner Truth.

Sojourner Truth was born in Ulster County, New York, in 1797. Her name was Isabella, and she was owned by a Dutchman named Ardinburgh. During her youth, she was separated from her parents and passed through a succession of cruel masters, two of whom were named Baumfree and Hurley. Tall of stature and large of frame, she was exploited for her size and made to work excessively hard.

She watched her mother's grief as her siblings were sold away to other masters. Sojourner grew up to experience the same horror of giving birth to children, only to have them torn from her arms. It is not known how many children she had, but when she escaped in 1826, she took only an infant son with her.

Fleeing with her child in the middle of night, Sojourner crept through dangerous forests and swamps, terrified of being tracked by bloodhounds and bounty hunters. She knew what could happen if she were caught alive. Punishments for escapees ranged from beatings after which a solution of salt and vinegar was poured on open wounds, to the cutting off of body parts, such as toes and finger.

As Sojourner and other slaves stole their way through the nights, sympathizers—both African American and European American—risked their own safety, giving shelter, food, and water along the way. As a fugitive slave, she made her way safely to New York and was emancipated the following year, 1827.

In 1843, while working as a maid in New York City, Sojourner became convinced that she had been called to go out into the world and "travel about the land spreading truth to the people." Changing her name to Sojourner Truth, she became a preacher. Sojourner testified. Describing the suffering she had lived through, she soon became a major spokesperson for the abolitionist movement. Along with Frederick Douglass and William Lloyd Garrison, she became a significant leader in the struggle for emancipation.

Some people mocked her and spread rumors that she was a man disguised in women's garments. To dispel these rumors, she once publicly revealed her breast, then told the stunned audience, "It is not my shame, but yours that I should do this."

Nothing could stop Sojourner Truth. One day as she attended a women's right meeting in Akron, Ohio, clergymen argued that women should not have the right to vote. One dared to say that the fact that Christ was a man proved God considered women inferior to men. Sojourner rose to speak. Some of the suffragettes worried that a former slave was not a proper spokesperson for them and would only bring ridicule to their cause. They gestured for her to return to her seat. But the president of the group, Frances Dana Gage, ignored them and welcomed Sojourner to the podium.

"Ain't I a Woman?," the courageous speech Sojourner gave that day, June 21, 1851, became etched in American history:

> The acclaimed European American author of the era, Harriet Beecher Stowe, wrote a special tribute to Sojourner in the *Atlantic Monthly*. In the 1863 article, Stowe said, "I do not recollect ever to have been conversant with anyone who had more of that silent and subtle power which we call person presence than this woman."

During the Civil War, Sojourner Truth helped recruit soldiers and aided in relief efforts for freed men and women escaping from the South. As an adviser to President Abraham Lincoln, she used her influence to bring about the desegregation of streetcars in Washington, D.C.

Sojourner Truth never learned to read or write, but she often said, "I cannot read a book, but I read the people." In 1850, with the help of friends and family, she worked with Olive Gilbert to write and publish *Narrative of Sojourner Truth;* and she updated it with the assistance of Frances Titus.

The expanded version, *Book of Life,* includes personal letters, newspaper stories of events in which she participated, and expressions of appreciation for her work sent to her from around the world. The narrative was reprinted in 1878, 1881, and 1884 with the title *Narrative of Sojourner Truth; A Bondswoman of Olden Time, With a History of Her Labors and Correspondence Drawn from Her "Book of Life."*

"AIN'T I A WOMAN?"

> "That man over there says that women need to be helped into carriages and lifted over ditches, and to have the best help everywhere, Nobody ever helps me into carriages, or over mud-puddles, or gives me any best place.
>
> Well, I'm a woman, ain't I?

Look at my arms. I have ploughed , and planted, and gathered into barns, and no man could head me!

And ain't I a woman?

I could work as much and eat as much as a man, when I could get it—and bear the lash as well.

And ain't I a woman?

I have borne…children, and seen most sold off to slavery, and when I cried out with a mother's grief, none but Jesus heard me!

And ain't I a woman?"

—Sojourner Truth

Sojourner Truth, one of America's greatest reformers, died at home in Battle Creek, Michigan, in 1883.

Chapter Twenty-Eight

Harriet Jacobs

(1813 - 1897)

Born in Edenton, North Carolina, Harriet Jacobs was orphaned at an early age, a common situation for enslaved children. Eventually, she would also be separated from her brother, John. Harriet was never left totally alone, though. When her parents died, she was raised by her freed grandmother and a sympathetic mistress who taught her to read.

Harriet was barely eleven years old when her mistress died, and she was then turned over to an evil new master, Dr. James Norcom. She became the victim of his horrendous sexual abuse. She accepted the affection of another European American man who helped protect her.

With him, she gave birth to a son and a daughter. Still fearful, however, she fled alone, finding refuge in hiding at her grandmother's home. In a stroke of luck, the apparently abandoned children were given to Harriet's grandmother.

Harriet remained in her grandmother's home for seven years, hiding in a tiny attic. She passed the years reading the Bible, sewing, and sneaking moments with her children. Through the help of friends, letters from her were directed to her owner from distant places; it did not occur to anyone to look for her at her grandmother's house.

Harriet Jacobs finally escaped and worked her way north. Reunited with her daughter, she found employment as a nursemaid to the infant child of editor, poet, and magazine writer Nathaniel Parker Willis.

Jacobs wisely sought out anti-slavery activists in Rochester, New York, one of whom was her brother, John. Jacobs went to live with him, and together they operated an anti-slavery reading room and bookstore. It was located above the office where abolitionist and former slave Frederick Douglass published his newspaper, the *North Star.*

Through Jacob's association with Douglass, she met Amy Post, an abolitionist and early feminist. It was Amy Post who, upon hearing Jacobs's story, urged her to consider sharing it with others. Because of the widespread response to the publication of *Uncle Tom's Cabin,* the anti-slavery novel by Harriet Beecher Stowe, Jacobs solicited the support of the author, hoping that she would be interested in her story.

No such support or interest, however, was forthcoming, Jacobs's story received little public attention except for that of abolitionist sympathizers.

Harriet Jacobs began writing her autobiography in the form of a novel, *Incidents in the Life of a Slave Girl* (1861). She published *Incidents* under the pseudonym of Linda Brent.

She explained that there was no motive for secrecy on her own account—but that she felt the need to disguise important people and places because of the sensational nature of the story she wished to tell. She had no way to predict what the response to her book would be from either African Americans or European Americans.

Incidents describes the painful sexual exploitation of African American girls and women under slavery. It took tremendous courage to tell such a sad and personal story—for although experienced by many, few could or would tell it Some were too afraid, and some were too embarrassed. Most suffered in silence.

From 1862 to 1866, Harriet Jacobs worked in Washington D.C., with black Civil War refugees. After the war ended, she went to Savannah, Georgia, and continued to work in war relief efforts among African Americans. Upon returning to Washington, she became one of the founding organizers of the National Association of Colored Women. Harriet Jacobs remained in Washington until her death on March 7, 1897.

INCIDENTS IN THE LIFE OF A SLAVE GIRL

"I have not written my experiences in order to attract attention to myself; on the contrary, it would have been more pleasant to me to have been silent about my own history. Neither do I care to excite sympathy for my own sufferings. But I do earnestly desire to arouse the women of the North to a realizing sense of the condition of two millions of women at the South, still in bondage, suffering what I suffered, and most of them far worse. I want to add my testimony to that of abler pens to convince the people of the Free States what Slavery really is. Only by experience can anyone realize how deep, and dark, and foul is that pit of abominations."

—Harriet Jacobs

Chapter Twenty-Nine
Frances E. W. Harper

(1825 - 1911)

Frances Ellen Watkins Harper's novel *Iola Leroy (1892)* was the best selling novel by an African American in the nineteenth century. It is the saga of education, light-skinned, free blacks who are sold into slavery. Iola and her brother join the Union army as a nurse and a soldier, respectively, and then reunite, older and much wiser, after the long Civil War.

Born on September 24, 1825, in Baltimore, Maryland, Frances Ellen Watkins was the spirited only child of free parents. Orphaned by age three, she was raised by an aunt and uncle. Frances uncle was a minister, writer, and educator who made sure that his niece read the Bible and practiced writing every day. At age thirteen, Frances was hired out to do domestic work, but she continued to study during her leisure time.

Frances loved words and in 1845 published a book of poetry titled *Forest Leaves.* Unfortunately, no copy of the book remains today. She continued to write and eventually produced four novels and numerous volumes of poetry, short stories, and essays during her long, rewarding life.

France's first career was as a teacher. Hired as the first female teacher at Union Seminary, a school organized by the African Methodist Episcopal Church, she later taught in Little York, Pennsylvania.

Because of the Fugitive Slave Laws, Frances Watkins and all free African Americans traveling around the country risked being seized in any slaveholding state and declared a slave. Living with such restrictions frustrated her. And more than this, it troubled her to read news stories of those who suffered daily with slave codes and worse. Frances decided to resign from her teaching position in the 1850s and dedicate all her time to fighting slavery.

Writing became Frances's weapon. "Eliza Harris," written in response to Harriet Beecher Stowe's 1853 publication of *Uncle Tom's Cabin,* brought praise from abolitionists Frederick Douglass and William Lloyd Garrison. Both men began reserving space for her protests in their publications. They also wrote complimentary introductions to some of her writings. Frances was hired as a speaker by the Maine Anti-Slavery Society, which led to other speaking invitations from other abolitionist groups.

The author's publication of *Poems on Miscellaneous Subjects* in 1854 (which featured an introduction by William Lloyd Garrison) sold more than 10,000 copies in its first printing. Reprinted more than twenty times during her lifetime, it also became a favorite among young militant poets of the 1960s because of its fiery tone. Many young blacks were inspired to write protest poetry against segregation after discovering Frances Watkin's protest poems and essays.

As emancipation seemed further out of reach than ever, Frances Watkins grew more militant. When abolitionist John Brown failed in his attempt to start a slave rebellion at Harpers Ferry, Virginia (now West Virginia), in 1859, Frances led a campaign of support for him. There was no chance of securing the freedom of John Brown, his sons, or the black men who took part in the failed raid. But Frances felt she could at least write to the families of the men who awaited the gallows. She also helped raise financial support for the families. As Watkins wrote in a newspaper editorial, "It is not enough to express our sympathy by words. We should be ready to crystallize it into action."

In 1860, the author married Fenton Harper, a widower with three children. They lived on his farm in Columbus, Ohio, where Frances gave birth to a daughter. Fenton Harper died four years after their marriage. With debts absorbing most of her husband's assets, Frances Harper returned to the lecture circuit. She also became one of the many teachers who traveled south after the Civil War to teach newly freed slaves.

In her collection *Sketches of Southern Life (1872)*, Harper creates a sixty-year-old ex-slave, Aunt Chloe, a witty character who tells the story of slavery and Reconstruction—and how she triumphs in the end. The conversational style that Harper used to tell these stories would be used by future writers such as the famous poet Langston Hughes. In her Philadelphia newspaper column, Harper used the same technique, imaginary conversations, this time between a female college graduate and her aunt, to comment on the ideas of the day. Above all, Harper wanted "to awaken the hearts" of Americans to injustice, religion, and morality.

Frances Harper was co-founder and officer of the National Association of Colored Women and she also served with the National Council of Women, the Universal Peace Union, the Women's Christian Temperance Union, and other clubs and organizations.

The author died of heart disease on February 20, 1911, and was eulogized at the Unitarian Church in Eden Cemetery, Philadelphia.

A PROTEST POEM
The Slave Auction

The sale began—young girls were there,
Defenseless in their wretchedness,
Whose stifled sobs of deep despair
Revealed their anguish and distress

And mothers stood with streaming eyes,
And saw their dearest children sold;
Unheeded rose their bitter cries,
While tyrants bartered them for gold.

—Frances E.W. Harper

Chapter Thirty
Ida B. Wells-Barnett

(1862 - 1931)

The Civil War in no way ended injustice toward African Americans. They needed people to speak out and speak up for their new rights. One of the most courageous voices was that of Ida B. Wells-Barnett, a crusading journalist and early feminist.

Ida, the eldest of Lizzie Bell and James Wells' eight children, was born in Holly Springs, Mississippi, just six months before President Lincoln issued the Emancipation Proclamation freeing all slaves in the Confederacy.

Her parents rejoiced in her freedom. James Wells became a leader in the Freedmen's Bureau, an organization established by the government in 1865 to help former slaves rebuild their lives. He and Lizzie Bell also helped set up a school for black children.

Northern church missionaries, many of whom made great sacrifices entering the hostile atmosphere of the South, came to help. Ida was one of their first students.

All these positive experiences made Ida feel strong and confident. So she was prepared when tragedy struck. At age sixteen, Ida's childhood ended abruptly. Both her parents and her youngest brother died of a yellow fever epidemic in 1878. Ida became responsible for her siblings.

After graduating from Rust, a high school and industrial school in Holly springs Mississippi, and passing the teacher's exam, she began a career as a teacher, earning $25 per month. She later moved to Memphis for a higher-paid position.

Wells somehow found time to attend classes at Fisk, a historically black college, which led to another big change in her life. She discovered journalism. She wrote for the student newspaper. She also became editor of the *Evening Star* and the *Living Way,* two African American church publications. The more jobs she had, the more money she could send home to her family.

Using the pen name Iola (from her friend Frances Harper's novel), Wells often wrote about race. She frequently got her subject matter from her own personal experiences. For example, she refused to sit in the Jim Crow car on a train in the South. She sued the railroad company and won, but her case was later overturned by a Tennessee state court. She wrote about the railroad lawsuit in the church publications. She also wrote about the inequality between the public education of African American children and that of European American children in the South.

By 1891, local European American politicians learned that Wells was the writer behind these politically charged articles, and she was fired from her teaching position. Not to be silenced, Wells purchased part interest in a newspaper the *Memphis Free Speech.* She became editor and eventually sole owner.

Ida B. Wells' writing was very plain and direct. On her decision to write this way, she said, "I had an instinctive feeling that the people who had little or no school training should have something coming into their homes weekly which dealt with their problems in a simple, helpful way. So in weekly letters to the *Living Way,* I wrote in a plain, common-sense way on the things which concern our people."

As African Americans struggled to establish their rightful place in America at the turn of the century, European Americans grew increasingly resentful. Mob violence became commonplace.

Envy over African Americans who attempted to build decent housing for themselves and anger over African Americans competing for jobs and establishing businesses were only some of the resentments that exploded into senseless assaults on African American lives.

In March 1892, three African American businessmen were lynched in Tennessee for attempting to establish a grocery store that competed with one owned by a European American merchant. Local papers asserted that the cause of the lynching was an assault by African American men on European American women.

The outraged and brave Ida B. Wells dared to write in response: "Nobody in this African American section believes that old threadbare lie."

Wells asserted instead that the lynchings were to discourage financial independence of African Americans and the idea that European American women could be interested in African American men. These statements brought out a mob. Fortunately, she was away visiting Frances Harper at the time. Not only was the office of *Free Speech* destroyed, but Wells' partner, J. C. Fleming, was run out of town and Wells was warned not to return.

Establishing herself in New York, she continued her crusade against racial injustices in a newspaper, the *New York Age,* of which she later became editor and part owner. Publication of "A Red Record" (1895), one of many pamphlets she wrote, helped raise public awareness and action. The tone and writing style of "A Red Record" would be repeated years later in the speeches of civil rights advocates such as Dr. Martin Luther King, Jr.

When African Americans were bared from participation in the Chicago World's Fair, Wells joined Frederick Douglass and others in leading a protest campaign. She also began a campaign to have the word *Negro* capitalized in the press, pointing out that French, German, Dutch, and Japanese were always capitalized.

In 1895, she married Ferdinan Barnett, a Chicago lawyer and editor of the *Chicago Conservator.* The couple became partners in social action.

Ida B. Wells-Barnett is reported to have crusaded with all four of her children when they were infants, nursing them along the way. A founding member of the National Association for the Advancement of Colored People, in 1898 she presented to President William McKinley resolutions drafted against lynching.

She organized one of the first African American suffrage groups, and in 1930, co-founded the National Association of Colored Women and the National Afro-American Council. She also ran as an independent candidate for Illinois state senator.

By the time of her death in Chicago on March 25, 1931, she was known nationally and internationally. Her autobiography, *Crusade for Justice,* edited by her daughter Alfreda M. Duster, was published in 1970.

Part Six

African American Inventors

Otha Richard Sullivan

Introduction

In every century, African American discoverers and inventors have made their marks on history. Each of these African American inventers left a special legacy. Yet their inventiveness and ingenuity are known to only a few.

Some have helped save the lives of countless individuals. You've probably heard of Dr. Charles Drew, who invented the apparatus for preserving blood helping millions of people, saving lives during war and peacetime. Dr. Daniel Hale Williams, the first physician to perform open-heart surgery, was also an African American. Dr. Earl Shaw, a physicist, was the co-inventor of a laser device that has helped hospitals throughout the world provide radiation therapy for cancer patients.

African American inventors have also helped improve every mode of transportation from the bicycle to the space shuttle. Otis Boykin, for instance, contributed to the development of the guided missile William Harwell invented the space shuttle retrieval arm. Adolph Shamms invented a multistage rocket.

Other African American inventors have made immeasurable contributions to the industrial growth of America. Dr. George Washington Carver's discoveries of hundreds of new ways to use peanuts and sweet potatoes saved southern farmers from poverty. Jan Matzeliger's invention of the shoe lasting machine helped build a multi-billion-dollar industry.

Lewis Latimer pioneered in the field of electric lights, helping to bring in a new era in American life.

In every era, Americans could thank African American inventors for making their lives safer. Early in the twentieth century, for example, Garrett A. Morgan invented the gas mask as well as the first traffic signal, for which he sold the rights to the General Electric Corporation.

African Americans contributions have been diverse: fountain pen, dust pan, clothes dryer, cellular phone, lawn sprinkler, elevator, pencil sharpener, galvanic battery, home security machine, player piano, toilet, postal letter box, golf tee, guitar, gas burner, eggbeater, air conditioner, train alarm, typewrite, horseshoe, and thousands of other practical inventions.

Sarah Goode, the first recorded African American woman inventor, received a patent for a folding cabinet bed. Sarah Boone invented an ironing board. Henrietta Bradberry invented a method of discharging torpedoes in wartime.

The ingenuity is not new. The history of African American inventors goes back to the first stone tools invented in Africa millions of years ago!

In the early days of the United States, prior to the Emancipation Proclamation, few African Americans could get patents to prove that they owned their inventions. Only free people could receive patents. One of the first patents granted to an African American went to Henry Blair, a free man of Maryland, for a corn planter and cotton planter in 1834 and 1836. Enslaved African Americans used their ingenuity to make inventions for which their masters claimed the credit.

In modern times, African Americans have patented thousands of inventions that range from the lawn mower of J.A. Burr to a floppy disk for computers by John P. Moon and a computerized blood pressure devise by Dr. Michael Croslin.

Chapter Thirty-One
Norbert Rillieux

(1806- 1894)

Like Benjamin Banneker, Norbert Rillieux lived in the shadow of slavery. He was born on March 17, 1806, on a large planta-tion in New Orleans, six years before Louisiana became a state. His father, an affluent French immigrant, was the master of the plan-tation. Norbert's mother, Constance Vivant, was a free mulatto there.

As a child, Norbert was curious and asked lots of questions. He espe-cially wondered how machines around the plantation worked. Norbert's father, who had developed a steam-operated cotton-baling press, was quite proud of him and wanted him to receive the best education possible.

The best schools in the city of New Orleans refused to admit African Americans, so he sent Norbert to Paris to study at L'Ecole Centrale, where there were no racial restrictions.

In France, Norbert confirmed his father's hopes. He was an excep-tionally bright student who, on graduation, taught mechanical engineering at his school, making him the youngest teacher there. He set about studying sugar refining, a thriving industry back home in New Orleans.

In 1830, at age twenty-four, Rillieux published research on the new steam engines that were causing a revolution around the world.

After spending a few years in Paris, Rillieux returned to the United States. Louisiana's rich soil, sun, and rain produced abundant crops of sugarcane. But the sugar-refining process was slow, dangerous, and primitive. Known as the "Jamaica Train," the process produced a dark, crude form of sugar that resembled molasses. Slaves were forced to pour the hot sugarcane juice back and forth from one large kettle into another in order to increase evaporation of the liquid.

Rillieux knew that a steam engine could be designed to produce the same amount of evaporation as the Africans' dangerous labor and perhaps to even get better quality sugar in the end by controlling the temperature. In Rillieux's patent dated August 26, 1843, he described his idea this way:

> "The first improvement is…connecting a steam engine with the evaporating pan or pans in such manner that the engine will be operated by the steam in its passage to the evaporating pan or pans, and the flow of steam be so regulated by a weighted or other valve as to reach the said pan or pans at the temperature required for the process."

The big break that Rillieux needed to test his design idea finally arrived with the chance to upgrade the sugar refinery at a large plantation called Myrtle Grove. His evaporator was a huge success.

Built by the firm of Merrick and Towne of Philadelphia, it required only one workman to manage the valves that processed the sugarcane juice through the equipment.

When Norbert Rillieux arrived in Paris, the Industrial Revolution was in full force. This was a revolution in manufacturing. Before the revolution, people made products slowly, using small machines or tools. To operate the machines, manufactures depended on workers (including slaves) or animals, and the energy of the wind or running water.

Then inventors figured out how to make bigger machines using the energy of steam. The new steam engine, invented in 1765, provided the means with which people could produce more things at a lower cost than ever before. Rillieux's studies prepared him to play a big role in this revolution.

Norbert Rillieux's invention took the sugar industry by storm. It reduced the price of sugar for consumers nearly everywhere. Sugar refineries throughout Louisiana, Cuba, and Mexico began installing the new device. Eventually, manufacturers of soap, gelatin, glue, condensed milk, and paper also found ways to use Rillieux's evaporator in their factories.

Now forty years old, the inventor was firmly on his way. Rillieux secured a second patent on December 10, 1846, to protect his "new and useful improvements in the method of heating, evaporating, and cooling liquids."

As time passed, however, Rillieux was confronted with more and more restrictions. Freemen were not permitted to send their children to New Orleans public schools. Laws prohibited freemen from attending meetings of slaves for fear that they might help a slave escape or revolt.

Free African Americans had to get permission to walk in the streets of New Orleans. The state of Louisiana required both free and enslaved African Americans to carry passes.

Norbert Rillieux went back to Paris in 1854, as the conflict in the United States over slavery intensified. In 1857, when a former slave named Dred Scott sued for his freedom, the Supreme Court decided that African Americans were not citizens at all. According to then-Chief Justice Roger B. Taney, African Americans were no more than property, and had no rights that European American people had to respect.

When Rillieux developed a way to help New Orleans deal with its yellow fever epidemic by draining the swamps and depriving the disease-breeding mosquitoes of their breeding grounds, he was turned away by the New Orleans Sewage Department. They would not accept the word of an African American. Ironically, the city put Rillieux's plan to use some years later, but by then he had become disgusted with his treatment and had returned to Paris.

In 1881, still living in exile from his home in Louisiana, Rillieux again turned to inventing and patented yet another improved process of heating liquids with their own vapors in several stages to produce refined sugar. He even went to Egypt to supervise the installation of his latest devices for using steam more efficiently.

Rillieux never returned to the United States to live. When he died on October 8, 1894, he was buried in a vault in the Pere Lachaise Cemetery in Paris.

Chapter Thirty-Two
Benjamin Montgomery

(1819 - 1877)

Hitched like a horse to a wagon, eighteen-year-old Benjamin T. Montgomery walked nearly a thousand miles from Virginia to Mississippi while his master rode along in comfort. The brutal trip took several weeks.

Montgomery had been born a slave in Loudon County, Virginia. His new master, Joseph Davis, was the brother of Jefferson Davis, who was destined to become president of the Confederate States of America.

Arriving at Hurricane Plantation at Davis Bend in Warren County, Mississippi, Joseph Davis put Montgomery to work. Intelligent and dependable, Montgomery had been a mechanic in Virginia. Davis soon made him a general manager and mechanic and encouraged him to learn new skills.

Davis let Montgomery spend time in the plantation library so that he could learn how to read, survey land, and draw architectural plans. Montgomery used his knowledge to construct several large buildings and improve the machinery on Davis's plantation.

Like many other grand plantations, Hurricane was built near a river. In the late 1850s, Montgomery invented a better propeller for the river steamboats that navigated the shallow waters around the plantation.

Unlike other propellers that gave the boats their thrust and forced them along in the water, Montgomery's was constructed on the "canoe paddling principle." The blades could cut through water at any angle and with much less resistance than other propellers. Montgomery dreamed of eventually powering his new propeller with a steam engine to really test its advantages.

Joseph Davis and his brother, Jefferson, seeing the possibilities, attempted to have Montgomery's propeller patented. But since the Dred Scott decision in the Supreme Court , slaves could not apply for or receive a patent—and a master could claim a slave's creation. By law, a slave was no longer considered to be a person. Slaves were just personal property without any rights at all.

The Davis brothers were not pleased that they could not patent Benjamin Montgomery's work for themselves. They tried again in the early 1860s, when eleven southern states pulled out of the Union to form the Confederate States of America, commonly known as the Confederacy. Jefferson Davis, now president of the Confederacy, recommended this law to the Confederate Congress:

> "In the case the original inventor or discoverer of the art, machine or improvement for which a patent is solicited, is a slave, the master of such a slave may take oath that the said slave was the original inventor; and shall receive a patent for said discovery or invention, and have all the rights to which a patentee is entitled by law."

Montgomery was prohibited from receiving patents, but he continued inventing things. He improved the cotton bale presses on the Davis plantation and encouraged other people to create practical inventions, too. One of those people was Peter R. Campbell, born a slave in 1841 on Hurricane Plantation. After his emancipation, Campbell invented a special steam-powered press. He applied for a patent on April 1, 1879.

In 1884, nearly twenty years after the Civil War, Montgomery finally exhibited his propeller at the Cotton Centennial in New Orleans, Louisiana. He also showed it at the Chicago World's Fair in 1893, and at the Southern Exposition in Atlanta in 1895.

African Americans had to exhibit their inventions separately from European American exhibitors. Even so, Montgomery's propeller was well received.

An inventive spirit seemed to run through the Montgomery family. Benjamin's brother, Peter T. Montgomery, also an inventor, secured a patent for a device for holding books or documents to be read or copied.

Isaiah Montgomery, son of Benjamin Montgomery, founded the all-African American town of Mound Bayou, Mississippi.

Chapter Thirty-Three
Elijah McCoy

(1843 - 1929)

During the Civil War years (1861-1865), long before, and long after, few businesses could even imagine hiring African Americans, particularly as engineers or in other skilled trades. Even the railroad industry, which hired more African Americans than any other industry did, expected them to lay tracks and work in the train yards.

Elijah McCoy, trained as a mechanical engineer, had bigger plans, but he took a job as a fireman on the Michigan Central Railroad. Still, it proved a stepping-stone toward his dream.

McCoy was born free in Colchester, Ontario, Canada, on May 2, 1843. His parents, George and Mildred McCoy, had been slaves in Kentucky and had escaped to Canada on the Underground Railroad, the famous network of individuals, homes, and farms that sheltered fugitive slaves on their way to freedom.

After a few years, McCoy's family returned to the United States, to Ypsilanti, Michigan. There, Elijah went to grammar school and worked in a machine shop.

Even as a young child growing up with eleven brothers and sisters, McCoy was fascinated with machinery. His parents sacrificed to send him to Edinburgh, Scotland, so that he would have a chance to learn mechanical engineering. After learning everything he could as an apprentice, McCoy returned to Michigan and headed to the city of Detroit, ready and eager to find engineering work on his own.

He took the best job he could find, on the railroad. His duties included oiling the engines of the locomotives. In those days, engines had to be periodically turned off and lubricated, or oiled, by hand. Otherwise, they would break down or catch fire. Oiling helped because it reduced the friction that made the screws, gears, levers, and other moving parts wear down.

Children, some of whom were orphans, were also hired to oil the locomotive engines by hand. Called "grease monkeys," they did dangerous work that could injure or kill them, and it often did. They were paid just pennies a day and had to sleep on the dirty, oily floors where they worked.

McCoy quickly grasped the need for a safer and more efficient method for oiling machinery. And he worked daily in his crude machinery shop to develop a device that would lubricate seam engines without stopping their operation and without endangering anyone.

Finally, he figured out the answer. It turned out to be amazingly simple—a drip cup filled with oil attached to an engine or machine. He patented his device on July 2, 1872. Within a year, McCoy had improved the device further and had received a second patent. He assigned all or part of these patents to other people in exchange for money to pay for his workshop, and he continued to assign patents to others from then on.

Around 1920, Elijah McCoy agreed to let some businessmen form the Elijah McCoy Manufacturing Company in Detroit, Michigan, make and sell his inventions.

McCoy himself worked as a patent consultant to the railroad and other industries and businesses. Other companies tried to copy McCoy products, but none met the McCoy standard for excellence. If people wanted the best quality, they learned to ask for the "real McCoy" by name.

At first, locomotive engineers were reluctant to use the drip cup because it was developed by an African American. But the device was so effective that they changed their minds. Within a short time, railroads shipping lines, and factories throughout the world bought the McCoy lubricating cup. McCoy used the money he earned to develop more devices for locomotives.

Eventually, Elijah McCoy's inventions were recognized throughout the world. He held patents in numerous foreign countries, including Russia, France, Germany, Austria, and Great Britain. Altogether, by 1926 McCoy had received more than forty patents for his lubricating devices and other inventions, which ranged from special tires to lawn sprinklers.

McCoy lived to be quite old. Businessmen made millions from his inventions, far more than he ever made for himself. In his later years, with fairly little money and perhaps a few regrets, he spent a lot of time working with young people, counseling and encouraging them to pursue careers in science and technology. He died in Detroit, Michigan, at age eighty five.

Chapter Thirty-Four
Lewis Howard Latimer

(1848 - 1928)

By the end of the nineteenth century, the gaslight was becoming obsolete because of the increased use of electricity. Lewis Latimer, born free in Chelsea, Massachusetts, a town near Boston, on September 4, 1848, played a vital part in that transformation.

It is hard to imagine that the parents of a pioneer in the use of electricity had to escape from slavery. Making a bold dash to freedom, Virginia slaves George and Rebecca Latimer sneaked onto a steamer in Norfolk, Virginia, that was headed for Baltimore.

They hid in the ship's hold. Landing safely in Baltimore, they took a train to New York. The light-skinned George Latimer posed as a Virginia planter, and Rebecca posed as his servant. They were heading for Boston, far from the slave South.

Shortly after Latimer arrived in Boston, a man who knew his former owner, James B. Gray, spotted him and alerted Gray of his whereabouts. Gray then traveled to Boston to take Latimer back. George Latimer was arrested on October 18, 1842, as a fugitive slave.

News of his arrest spread and came to the attention of abolitionists Frederick Douglass, William Lloyd Garrison, and the Reverend Samuel Caldwell, who were famous leaders of the movement. With the help of abolitionist citizens of Boston, Garrison and Douglass were able to raise $650 to purchase Latimer's freedom. After a month in jail, George Latimer was released.

Even with their hard-earned freedom, life remained difficult for George and Rebecca Latimer. They had four children, George Junior, Margaret, William, and young Lewis, who tried to do his part to help the family by selling copies of the *Liberator,* William Lloyd Garrison's abolitionist newspaper.

When Lewis was ten years old, George Latimer deserted the family. Some historians believe that he felt vulnerable, a risk to his family because of his notoriety. George had never gotten over his fear of being captured by slave-catchers.

Lewis Latimer's boyhood was filled with all the uneasiness and strife of the times. His mother sent him and his brother William to a rural school, but Lewis ran away at age fifteen and enlisted in the Union Navy, to join the fight to abolish slavery. He lied about his age to qualify. On September 16, 1864, Latimer was made a "landsman" (seaman) on the USS *Massasoit* and fought at sea. His brothers fought with the Union's land forces.

Honorably discharged on July 3, 1865, Latimer returned to Boston and went to work for Crosby and Gould, patent lawyers, where he eventually became a top draftsman.

When Alexander Graham Bell, inventor of the telephone, needed drawings for his patent application, it was Latimer who made them.

At the age of twenty-six, Latimer began to create inventions of his own and got his first patent: "Water Closets For Railroad Cars," U.S. Patent Number 147,363.

But it was the 1879 invention of the electric lamp by Thomas Edison that captured Latimer's imagination.

Experimenting along with Joseph V. Nichols on ways to improve Edison's lamp, Latimer developed superior filaments of carbon.

Ever since he was a boy, Lewis Latimer had loved drawing. When he saw that his new employers Crosby and Gould needed drawings to accompany the inventors' patent applications, he had an idea. As soon as he had saved enough money, he bought a secondhand set of drafting tools and set about teaching himself to use them. He quickly became extremely proficient.

His employers admired his work. They also liked his personality. Latimer was polite and resourceful and had a positive attitude. Other people liked working with him, too. This combination of qualities won him a promotion to chief draftsman.

On September 13, 1881, Latimer and Nichols received a patent for their own electric lamp. It was definitely time for a move. After eleven years of working as a draftsman for Crosby and Gould, Latimer took a job as a draftsman with Hiram Maxim, chief engineer for the United States Electric Lighting Company, located in Bridgeport, Connecticut. Latimer saw the future in the exciting new science of electricity, and he wanted to be part of the action.

Within a year, Latimer had invented the "Globe Supporter for Electric Lamps," patented on March 21, 1882. His invention was in great demand. He was asked to install incandescent electric plants in New York City and Canada. He was the only person at the U.S. Electric Lighting Company who knew every aspect of producing the light bulbs. In 1881, Latimer went to London to set up an incandescent lamp department for the Maxim-Weston Electric Company.

While discrimination against African Americans permeated society and European Americans were unwilling to accept that an African American man could create, much less surpass, the efforts of European

Americans, Latimer quietly made one pioneering advance after another behind the scenes.

Latimer wrote a famous book called *Incandescent Electric Lighting*. In it, he carefully explained electric lighting:

> "If the electric current can be forced through a substance that is a poor conductor, it will create a degree of heat in that substance which will be greater or less, according to the quantity of electricity passing through it."

> "Upon this principle of the heating effect of the electric current is based the operation of the incandescent lamp... While the copper and platinum wires readily conduct the current, the carbon filament offers a great deal of resistance to its passage and for this reason becomes very hot, in fact it is raised to white heat or incandescence, which gives its name to the lamp."

In 1884, Thomas Edison, the most famous scientist of the era, invited Latimer to become a member of the Engineering Department of the Edison Electric Light Company in New York City.

Edison had previously attempted to interest Granville T. Woods, another African American inventor, in joining the Edison Company. Woods preferred to be his own boss. But Latimer wanted to work in a team again, as he had for most of his career. He joined Edison and served as the chief draftsman. His work helped to protect Edison's patents against infringements such as copying by other companies.

Latimer achieved many dreams. In 1873 he had married Mary Wilson. He delighted in their two daughters Louise Rebecca and Emma Janette. He was asked to join the original Edison Pioneers, the group of twenty-eight men who helped build the electric light industry.

When he died on December 11, 1928, after a long illness, the Edison Pioneers aptly described Latimer's contributions as a scientist: "a great work for all people under a great man."

Chapter Thirty-Five
Andrew Jackson Beard

(1849 - 1941)

"I never went to any school in my life," declared Andrew J. Beard, another self-taught African American inventor. In his day, a formal education was not necessary for a person with a talent for invention. "All the education that I have is gotten by contact with people in the world."

Like Elijah McCoy, Beard worked for a railroad company at a time when the railroad industry was growing rapidly. People were his best inspiration. Watching them gave him the idea for the "Jenny-Coupler," a device that probably saved thousands of train workers' lives and limbs.

Beard was born in slavery in Jefferson County, Alabama, in the tiny town of Eastlake, a short distance from Birmingham. When he gained his freedom with emancipation in 1865, he set out on his own, trying out one enterprise after another and building on each success.

"I farmed five years," he said. "I visited Montgomery in 1872 with a load of apples drawn by oxen. I had fifty bushels, which I sold at an average of four dollars per bushel. It took me three weeks to make the trip. After this venture I quit farming and…built my first flour mill…I watched how people worked, and that was the way I succeeded in building flour mills.

"During my work there," he continued, "I began turning in my mind to the making of plows, and in 1881 I patented one of my own." He sold his plow patent in 1884 for $4,000, invented another plow, and on December 15, 1887, sold its patent for $5,200. He then went into the real estate business, buying land and houses. Over time, he accumulated the sum of $30,000.

Eventually, Beard, like many African American men, got a job in the railroad industry. In an Alabama rail yard, he witnessed many accidents, especially ones that happened while men were "coupling" railroad cars. Coupling was a dangerous operation: workmen had to run along the top of a freight train, quickly climb down between two cars, and try to insert a pin to join the cars as they came together.

As the men worked, the cars would crash together and become firmly coupled. If a workman's hands or arms got in the way, they would be smashed beyond recognition, ending a career and creating desperate living conditions for the man and his family. Workers were not protected by insurance.

Though Beard had no formal training in either metalworking or engineering except what he had gotten by watching others over the years, he tried to develop an automatic system that would not require a person to be involved in bringing the railroad cars together.

Working on this problem at home day after day, often barely eating and sleeping, Beard found an answer in 1897. He got a patent and sold the rights for more than $50,000 to a New York manufacturing firm. He went on to get four other patents for inventions that benefited the railroad industry, and he left some money in his will to a school for African American children in Montgomery.

Thousands of inventors might be working on the same problem at the same time. That was certainly true for Andrew Beard, who was one of thousands of people who received patents for train coupling devices.

His was one of the best, and a manufacturer paid him for the rights to produce it.

Some of the other African Americans who invented important devices for the railroad industry had to go to court to protect their claims to their discoveries. For example, on April 3, 1883, H.H Reynolds had patented a ventilator for passenger cars that kept out the dust and soot that surrounded the moving car. The *Baltimore Afro-American* newspaper reported the following story:

> "Reynolds was a porter on one of the Pullman cars. Opening and shutting the windows as he did so often for his passengers, he devised a screen to keep the cinders out.
>
> Pullman (whose company manufactured these special sleeping cars) heard of it and Reynolds was sent for. He explained his invention to the car magnate, and the interview resulted shortly afterward in the adoption of this ventilator on all the Pullman cars. Reynolds claimed the invention, but Pullman did not recognize the claim. Reynolds sued, and got a verdict for ten thousand dollars."

Chapter Thirty-Six

Jan Earnst Matzeliger

(1852 - 1889)

A life-size portrait of Jan Earnst Matzeliger, a major inventor during the Industrial Revolution in the United States, looks down on gatherings at the North Congregational Church in Lynn, Massachusetts, where he was once a member.

Matzeliger was born on September 15, 1852, in Paramaribo, Surinam, a country on the northern coast of South America. His mother, a native of Surinam, was enslaved, and his father was a Dutch engineer in charge of the government machine shops. Matzeliger began working as an apprentice in these shops when he was just ten years old. Young Jan showed outstanding mechanical ability that predicted his later gift for invention.

Matzeliger grew increasingly restless with his life in Surinam, and by the time he was nineteen, he was ready to leave. He became a sailor on an East Indian merchant ship. During his two years at sea, he had visited many ports, but he left the ship for good in Philadelphia. For the next couple of years he took odd jobs, one of which was as an apprentice shoemaker.

In 1876, Jan Matzeliger left Philadelphia and went to Boston, where he stayed for about a year. He then moved to Lynn, Massachusetts, a town that was known for its shoe industry, and he began working for Harney Brothers, a shoe manufacturer. His job was to operate a shoe-sole sewing machine and to clean the factory floors. This was not the exciting life he had imagined that he would live, but it was a beginning.

Matzeliger had little formal education and was not fluent in English, but he wanted to make a good life for himself. At night, he went to an adult education class in order to learn English. He became an avid reader, spending hours studying physics and other subjects. He also painted pictures and tried to join a church in Lynn. The Episcopal, Unitarian, and Catholic churches turned him away. They did not admit African Americans. Only the members of North Congregational Church would accept him. Matzeliger never forgot this.

Work filled Matzeliger's days and occupied his lively mind. He noticed that *lasting*, the job of connecting the shoe upper to the sole, had to be done by hand and it seriously limited the number of shoes produced in a day. At best, a worker could last no more than fifty pairs a day. Matzeliger was optimistic that he could invent a machine that could do the job faster. "The object is to perform by machinery and in a more expeditious manner, the operations which have been heretofore performed by hand," he wrote later.

Without any encouragement, Matzeliger watched the lasters at work, and at night, using their scraps, he tried to duplicate their motions. Maybe, he thought, he could find a better way of doing their job. Surely a machine would be more efficient.

Matzeliger must have seemed like a dreamer to anyone who knew about his project. He probably knew that other inventors were trying to devise a shoe-lasting machine, too. A pessimist would have quit. Matzeliger had the opposite reaction. He began to work every night on his invention, making drawings and experimenting with scraps of wood, string, and cigar boxes.

Six months of persistent work paid off in a crude model of a lasting machine. Matzeliger showed it to his employer, who offered $50 for the model. He refused the money. There would be a much bigger reward ahead if his invention worked.

Through several more years of sleepless nights and rising expenses, Matzeliger kept experimenting. To save money for the project he sometimes spent only five or six cents a day on food. Finally, he accepted an offer from two businessmen, Melville S. Nichols and Charles H. Delnow: in exchange for a two-thirds interest in the invention, they gave him the money he needed to finish the project.

On March 20, 1883, Jan Matzeliger claimed the reward for his determination and ingenuity: U.S. Patent Number 274,207 for the first perfected shoe-lasting machine.

A major invention makes a big difference. Jan Matzeliger's machine was awesome. This one machine cut the cost of producing shoes in half. By 1890, American shoe manufacturers increased their earnings from $220 million to more than $442 million.

This was a towering tribute to Matzeliger's genius. What others saw as an impossible dream, Matzeliger had achieved. By 1889, the machine was in great demand worldwide. It increased by ten times the daily output of one worker.

A school was established in Lynn to train boys to operate the machine. More than two hundred youths were graduated each year and sent throughout the country and the world to teach others how to use the machine.

The machine was so efficient that it made the craft of shoe lasters obsolete. It could turn out 150 to 700 pairs of shoes in one day.

Matzeliger's invention was one of the most important inventions during the Industrial Revolution in America.

In 1886, Matzeliger became seriously ill. What at first appeared to be a cold turned out to be tuberculosis. It was a dreadful price to pay for the years of hard work and poverty.

Bedridden for three years, he continued to paint and experiment. He died on August 24, 1889, at age thirty-seven and was buried in the Pine Grove Cemetery at Lynn, Massachusetts. He had never married, but he had one foster son.

Always generous and friendly, Matzeliger bequeathed the North Congregational Church much of his stock in the companies that held the rights to his machine—provided that the money never be shared with the Roman Catholic, Unitarian, and Episcopal churchgoers who had turned their backs on him.

As the patent historian Henry Baker recalled "…Years afterward North Church became heavily involved in debt, and remembering the stock that had been left to it by this African American member, found, upon inquiry, that it had become very valuable through the importance of the patent under the management of the large company then controlling."

"The church sold the stock and realized from the sale more than enough to pay off the entire debt."

Chapter Thirty-Seven
Daniel Hale Williams, M.D.

(1856 - 1931)

On July 9, 1893, at Providence Hospital on the south side of Chicago, doctors and nurses thought that they had witnessed a miracle. Dr. Daniel Hale Williams had successfully operated on a man who had been stabbed in the heart. Until that moment everyone thought that open-heart surgery was impossible. But Dr. Williams took the risk and, in doing so, took medical science to a higher level.

Dr. Williams was born in the small community of Hollidaysburg, Pennsylvania, on January 18, 1856, the fifth of seven children. His father, a barber, was active in the abolitionist movement. But Daniel's father died early, and his mother could not take care of all the children by herself. So when most youth would be entering fourth grade, Daniel was sent to Baltimore, Maryland, to become an apprentice to a shoemaker.

He was unhappy in Baltimore and ran away to rejoin his family. They had moved to Rockford, Illinois, to be close to his mother's family. They struggled to stay together, but they could not. For the next seven years, Daniel was on his own, apprenticed as a barber.

The family stayed in touch, encouraging one another whenever they could. Daniel moved to Edgerton, Wisconsin, and opened his own barbershop at the age of seventeen, with the help of his eldest sister, Sally. Four years later, he graduated from high school. He had struggled to go to school and to support himself at the same time. He never gave up.

Inspired by his older brother who had become a prominent lawyer, Williams took a job as a clerk in a law office, but he was bored. Then one day he read about Dr. Henry Palmer, a local surgeon.

Dr. Palmer had been the director of a large military hospital during the Civil War and was the former surgeon general of Wisconsin. Palmer's work sounded so interesting that in 1878 at age twenty-two, Williams quit his job and became an apprentice to Dr. Palmer, so that he could become a doctor himself. At the time, a person could open a medical practice after only a two-year apprenticeship under a licensed physician.

At first, Daniel simply cleaned Dr. Palmer's office and did menial tasks. After a few months, however, Dr. Palmer recognized Daniel's intellect and discipline and gave him a chance to read medical books and journals. With Dr. Palmer as his guide, Daniel learned to practice medicine.

Before 1890, few doctors in America were trained at a medical college. But young Dr. Williams had heard of the prestigious Chicago Medical College, now known as Northwestern University Medical School. He applied, was accepted, borrowed $100 from a bank, and headed for Chicago.

In 1883, Williams graduated at the top of his class. His training equipped him with knowledge of the latest techniques in surgery and in the prevention and care of common diseases.

Dr. Williams was unable to gain an internship in area hospitals after graduation, because he was an African American. When he performed surgery, he was required to do so in the homes of his patients.

Dr. Williams opened a small medical office at the corner of Thirty-First Street and Michigan Avenue in an African American neighborhood in Chicago. He did not yet have a lot of experience as a doctor, but he knew all about two of the newest advances in medicine.

In France, Dr. Louis Pasteur had recently discovered that germs, micro-organisms too tiny to see with the naked eye, caused certain infections and diseases. And in England, Dr. Joseph Lister had introduced the practice of antiseptic surgery to fight germs.

These were such new ideas that some doctors didn't believe in them. But young Dr. Williams saw their value, and he practiced antiseptic surgery from the start.

Their kitchens or dining rooms became his operating rooms. At the time, it was common for patients to die of infections following surgery. But using the recent discoveries of Pasteur and Lister, Dr. Williams kept his patients infection-free. They affectionately began to call him "Dr. Dan."

At the time, African Americans had few options available for medical care. In general, they were admitted to the charity wards of city hospitals where they were segregated, neglected, and even used for experimentation. Some lost their lives because hospitals refused to provide treatment.

Dr. Williams was fascinated by the idea of opening his own hospital. In May 1891, after months of organizing and fund-raising among African American and European American supporters, Dr. Williams opened Provident Hospital and Training School for Nurses to patients of all races/cultures. His days of performing operations in kitchens and dining rooms were over.

Provident Hospital was a success until it was hit financially by the depression of 1893. Frederick Douglass, the great abolitionist, came to the rescue. At the Chicago World's Fair, Douglass asked all African Americans to dig deep into their wallets and purses to save Provident

Hospital. Contributions flowed in to the hospital from all over the world.

On July 9, 1893, Dr. Williams faced the greatest challenge of his medical career. James Cornish, a local stockyard worker, had been stabbed in the chest in a barroom brawl. He was rushed to Provident Hospital with a one-inch knife wound in the chest.

When Dr. Williams was summoned to the hospital, he had a tough choice to make. He could use traditional treatments—cleaning the wound and letting the patient rest—even though they did not usually save victims of stab wounds. Or he could use his skill as an experienced surgeon.

The patient was near death. Dr. Williams opened the chest and cut through the tissue, muscle, and cartilage around the heart. He found that the knife had penetrated the heart. His staff, four European American and two African American physicians, were sure that simply opening the chest would cause sudden death. No other physician had dared to enter the chest cavity of a living patient. But using a salt solution, the substance commonly used to guard against infection, Dr. Williams repaired the damage.

Mr. Cornish remained in Provident Hospital for fifty-one days. Even though the first few days for Cornish were quite rocky, he recovered and was released. After a period of recuperation, he returned to his job.

Dr. Williams's medical first was not known for three and a half years. He did not see a need to make an official report of the lifesaving surgery. When the word spread, newspapers everywhere hailed him as a genius.

In 1894, Howard University's Freedmen's Hospital in Washington, D.C., offered Williams the position of chief surgeon at the two-hundred-bed hospital. There, he trained African American doctors and nurses for four years.

In 1898, Dr. Williams resigned from Freedmen's Hospital. He and his wife, Alice, returned to Chicago where he continued his work as chief surgeon of Provident Hospital, which had grown from twelve beds to sixty beds. Finally, in 1912, Dr. Williams became the first African American to be appointed associate attending surgeon at St. Luke's Hospital, the wealthiest and largest hospital in Chicago.

Dr. Williams received many honors. The American College of Surgeons selected him as a charter member in 1913, its first African American. Hoard University and Wilberforce University, two historically African American colleges, awarded him honorary degrees.

Dr. Williams and his wife retired in 1920 to Idlewild, Michigan, a resort community for African Americans. Alice died a year later of Parkinson's disease. Dr. Williams suffered a stroke five years later and was partially paralyzed. He died at the age of seventy-five.

Chapter Thirty-Eight
Granville T. Woods

(1856 - 1910)

"The greatest African American inventor, equal, if not superior, to any inventor in the country," declared the *Catholic Tribune* in 1886. The newspaper was referring to Granville T. Woods.

Inspired by the way electricity was transforming the world, Woods had unraveled the mysteries of electric currents and begun to change the world himself.

The son of Tailor and Martha Woods, Granville was born free in Columbus, Ohio, on April 23, 1856. When he was only ten, he quit school to help his family and went to work in a machine shop. Out of his hands-on education grew an enthusiasm for inventing.

At age sixteen, Woods moved to Missouri and took a job as a fireman and engineer on the railroad. An avid reader during his leisure time, he borrowed books on electricity from the local library. Friends and co-workers recognized his hunger for scientific knowledge and gave him all the books they could find on the subject. Woods practiced at work what he had learned from books.

Moving to Springfield, Illinois, and then to New York City, Woods found work wherever he could, first in a steel mill and then in another machine shop. But his heart was set on going to an electrical and mechanical engineering school where he could take real courses, and eventually he did.

With his new knowledge, he secured a job as an engineer on *Ironsides*, a British steamship. He worked on this ship for two years, until a job as an engineer on the Danville and Southern Railroad took him away.

By 1881, Woods was ready for a new challenge and opened an electrical equipment factory in Cincinnati, Ohio. After years of working in positions that were beneath his abilities, he believed that he could fare better as his own boss. He worked diligently for two years.

On June 3, 1884, at the age of twenty-eight, Woods received his first patent. It was for an improved steam-boiler furnace for steam-driven engines. On December 2, 1884, he received another patent, this time for a stronger, clearer telephone transmitter. It set a new direction for his imagination.

In 1885, Woods patented a device that combined the telegraph with the telephone. Woods called it a "telegraphony." Instead of reading or writing the Morse code signals, an operator could speak near the telegraph key. This device made it possible to receive both oral and signal messages clearly over the same line without making changes in the instrument and without understanding Morse code.

Woods' telegraphony was purchased by the American Bell Telephone Company of Boston, Massachusetts, for a large sum of money.

Woods continued to explore the power of telegraphy. His next invention, patented on November 15, 1887, allowed conductors and engineers on moving trains to send and receive messages for the first time.

With this success, the inventor formed the Woods Electric Company. Orders for his devices came in from around the world. In 1890, Woods moved to New York City and joined his brother, Lyates Woods, also an inventor. They made a brilliant team. By 1907, Granville Woods would have some sixty patents to his credit.

New Yorkers, including the Woods brothers, loved to go to shows. But theaters had become fire hazards. Why? The electrical system that slowly dimmed the lights and controlled the other electrical equipment could easily become overheated.

Woods decided to focus on the problem. Through careful study and experimentation, he discovered a way to dim the lights using a separate generator. By controlling the strength of the electrical current, this system eliminated the overheating problem. Woods patented his theater lighting system on October 13, 1896.

A few of Woods' inventions stood out from the rest. Some people considered the "third rail" to be his greatest invention. Used in subway systems throughout the world, the third rail put electrical conductors along the path of the train so that the cars would receive the current directly without needing an electric engine. On January 29, 1901, Woods received a patent for the "third rail," and he sold this invention to the General Electric Company of New York shortly after.

Other people believed that Woods' air brake technology was just as important as the third rail. Starting in 1902, he had developed several devices that led to the automatic air brake. Woods eventually sold this system to the Westinghouse Air Brake Company of Pennsylvania.

Called the "African American Edison," Woods faced as many difficulties as victories and never rested on his laurels. Once, in 1892, he was arrested and kept in jail in connection with charges he himself had brought against the American Engineering Company for stealing one of his patents. Legal fees he could barely afford and powerful enemies in business and politics made his life a struggle right to the end.

He died of a stroke in 1910 and was buried in New York City.

Woods had to defend his patents from other inventors' claims. Once he sued the Thomas Edison company and won. A newspaper reporter wrote the following article explaining the patent in question:

> "Mr. Woods...still continues to add to his long list of electrical inventions. The latest device he invented is the synchronous multiplex railway telegraph. By means of this system, the railway dispatcher can note the position of any train on the route at a glance. The system also provides for telegraphing to and from the train while in motion. The same lines may also be used for local messages without interference with the regular train signals."

> "The system may also be used for other purposes. In fact, 200 operators may use a single wire the he same time. Although the messages may be passing in opposite directions, they will not conflict with each other. In using the device there is no possibility of collisions between trains as each train can always be informed of the position of the other while in motion."

> "Mr. Woods has all the patent office drawings for these devices as your correspondent witnessed. The patent office has twice declared Mr. Woods the prior inventor."

Part Seven

African American Entrepreneurs

Jim Haskins

Introduction

The more than thirty people profiled in the next pages are just a sample of the many clever and skilled African Americans who have beaten the odds and succeeded in business. They are men and women who represent three centuries of success. The actual number of successful African American entrepreneurs, particularly in modern times, could fill many more such collections.

Africans arrived in North America with many strong traditions, including clever business practices. As far back as 3000 B.C., Nubian traders had prospered selling ebony, gold, cattle, and ivory to Egyptians. In the fifth century A.D. the African kingdom of Ghana was known far and wide for its iron industry and was trading more gold than any other civilization of the time. But in North America, slavery and European American prejudices against free African Americans prevented most African Americans from continuing their business traditions.

In 1788, J.P. Brissot de Warville, a Frenchman traveling in America, wrote that "if…African Americans here are limited to the small retail trade, let us not attribute it to their lack of ability, but rather to the prejudices of the European Americans who put obstacles in their way."

Chief among those obstacles in 1788, and for nearly another century, was slavery. Even those African Americans who were free faced nearly insurmountable barriers. They were denied an education and barred by law or custom from equal jobs, credit at banks, and other means for success in business. Forced to devote all their energies to sheer survival, most had few chances to use their intelligence or skills for anything else. Those who did could enrich themselves, buy freedom for themselves and their families, or help fight slavery.

After the Civil War and the Emancipation Proclamation, African Americans had greater opportunities to become entrepreneurs. What does an entrepreneur do? With boldness, initiative, skill, and luck, entrepreneurs see people's needs and start businesses to fill them.

By 1900, scores of African Americans owned small businesses. In that same year, the renowned educator Booker T. Washington formed the National Black Business League at a convention attended by some 400 African Americans from thirty states.

Between 1900 and World War I, the number of African American businesses more than doubled, from 10,000 to 25,000. In the same period of time, African American banks increased in number from four to fifty-one. By 1929, the League estimated that 65,000 African Americans owned businesses in the United States.

For a while, that number continued to grow, despite the obstacles that discrimination and segregation represented. In fact, in some cases segregation by law or custom aided African American

businesspeople, for African American consumers were denied service at European American business establishments. Ironically, the civil rights movement and federal laws outlawing segregation meant the death of some African American businesses, as formerly segregated businesses opened their doors to African American consumers.

Beginning in the 1960s, the government helped many African Americans to start new businesses or improve enterprises they had already begun. In the 1980s, government support waned. But today there are few areas of enterprise in which African Americans are not represented.

Even though age-old prejudices and lack of equal opportunity continue to place obstacles in the way, there are now over 1,000,000 African American-owned businesses in the United States.

Today, as in the past, it takes a determined individual to be a successful entrepreneur. As the biographical sketches in the following pages show, there have been many such individuals in African American history.

Chapter Thirty-Nine
Marie-Therese Metoyer

(1742 - 1816)

African Americans were entrepreneurs in America from very early times. Years before the Declaration of Independence, one of the most successful of all was born. Marie-Therese Metoyer took her first breath in Nachitoches, Louisiana, when Louisiana was still a French colony. Known as Coincoin, a name given to second-born daughters by the Ewe people of western Africa, she probably had at least one parent who was an Ewe. Her parents, Francois and Francoise, were slaves and had been married in Natchitoches. In the French colonies, slave marriages were legal.

Coincoin's family was owned by Louis Juchereau de Saint-Denis, a commandant in the French army and founder of the army post where they lived. When he died, his ownership of Coincoin passed on to his widow and then to his son, who gave her to his daughter, Marie. During those years, Coincoin gave birth to five children, each one baptized in the Catholic Church. All were sold away from her, but she never forgot them.

Marie de Saint-Denis rented Coincoin to Claude-Thomas-Pierre Metoyer, a French merchant on Isle Breelle in the Red River Valley of

Louisiana. Watching Coincoin toil as a servant in his household, Metoyer fell in love with her, and together they had four children. Eventually Metoyer purchased and freed her, along with their new-born child. She remained with him another eight years, bearing three more children—all legally free because she was now free, too.

In 1786, Claude-Thomas-Pierre Metoyer married someone else. But first he arranged for Coincoin to receive a small plot of land and an annual sum to support herself and her children who were free. At the age of forty-four, Coincoin began a new life. One of the first things she did was to purchase her eldest daughter, Marie-Louise. She had been crippled in a shooting accident and cost only $300. Coincoin's plan was to buy back all of her other enslaved children, but first she had to make more money.

Coincoin planted tobacco and indigo and raised cattle and turkeys, all of which she sold. She also trapped bears and sold their hides and grease.

In 1762, France ceded a large part of Louisiana Province to Spain, including all territory west of the Mississippi River. By 1794, Coincoin had established herself financially and secured land from the Spanish government. Coincoin obtained a grant of 64 acres of piney woods on Isle Brevelle.

There she herded cattle and raised crops, profiting handsomely from her hard work and smart business practices. While building her ranch, Coincoin became a slave owner herself. Freed African Americans were often permitted to purchase African American slaves who were not family members, but they were not always allowed to set them free. Coincoin probably provided better food, clothes, and protection for her slaves than other owners might have. Still, it seems strange that someone who loved freedom so much had slaves of her own.

It is impossible to know what was in Coincoin's mind, but it is likely that she had several reasons for owning slaves. Most practically, she needed help. There may not have been enough freed

African Americans in the area to hire, and she certainly could not have hired European American help.

She may also have concluded that owning slaves would make European Americans believe that she supported slavery. European Americans, sometimes with good reason, suspected free African Americans of aiding slave insurrections. They would have no suspicions against someone who also owned slaves.

Now she could purchase more of her children. They were scattered throughout western Louisiana and eastern Texas. She would have to travel to find them and negotiate their sale. Nearly all their owners were willing to sell them, for cash or on credit Sadly, one daughter, Francoise, was not obtainable, but Coincoin and her heirs managed to purchase Francoise's children.

In 1802, at the age of sixty, Coincoin offered to forfeit the annual payment Metoyer gave her in exchange for the freedom of their first three children. Metoyer agreed, and Coincoin at last realized her dream of freedom for her entire family.

By the time of Coincoin's death in 1816 at the age of seventy-four, she owned sixteen slaves. Coincoin descendants inherited her energy, spirit, and talent for business. Before the Civil War, they built an agricultural empire on Isle Brevelle that included nearly 20,000 acres of land, a dozen homes, and ironically, 500 slaves.

Coincoin's home on Isle Brevelle, Melrose Plantation, still stands. It has been designated a National Historic Landmark.

Chapter Forty

Paul Cuffe

(1759 - 1817)

Unlike Marie-Therese Metoyer, Paul Cuffe was born free. In 1795, he sailed his 69-ton schooner *Ranger* into Norfolk, Virginia, to purchase a cargo of corn. He later wrote in his auto-biography of the day the ship dropped anchor and he and his crew of African Americans went ashore:

> "The people were filled with astonishment and alarm. A vessel owned and commanded by an African American man, and manned with a crew of the same complexion, was unprecedented and surprising. The European American inhabitants were struck with apprehensions of the injurious effects on the minds of their slaves suspecting that he [Cuffe] wished secretly to kindle the spirit of rebellion, and excite a destructive revolt among them."

Cuffe was angered by this kind of reaction. He was one of the few African American men of his time to own a ship. But he did not let the concerns of European Americans—in Norfolk or elsewhere—interfere with his plans. He went about his business, purchased his cargo, and set sail for Connecticut, his home.

Paul Cuffe was born on the island of Cuttyhunk, off the coast of New Bedford, Massachusetts. He was the seventh of ten children of Cuffe Slocum and his wife, Ruth Moses, a Wampanoag Indian. Cuffe Slocum had been born in Africa and brought to the North American colonies as a slave. But he had managed to purchase his freedom from his master in Dartmouth, Massachusetts, and his children were born free.

Cuffe Slocum died when Paul was only thirteen. Although still a boy, Paul knew he would have to provide for himself. First, he found a tutor and learned to read and write. Then he studied navigation. At the age of sixteen, he went to sea, shipping out on a whaler bound for the Gulf of Mexico.

During Cuffe's third voyage, in 1776, the Revolutionary War broke out. His ship was captured by the British, and he spent three months in a New York prison. Cuffe settled in Westport, Connecticut, after his release from prison. Because going to sea during the war was hazardous, he worked as a hired hand on a farm. Meanwhile, he continued to study navigation and to look for ways to make a better living.

He and his brother, John, built an open boat with which they could trade with towns on the Connecticut shore, but rough seas could trade with towns on the Connecticut shore, but rough seas and pirates loyal to England made that entrepreneurial venture too dangerous. The brothers returned to laboring on a farm as the war continued.

Paul Cuffe was still determined to make a living as a merchant mariner. Twice, he built small boats and attempted to trade. His first boat was seized by American pirates who supported the British. During his second attempt, he failed to sell his cargo of goods. Finally, on his third attempt, he managed to make such a good profit that he was able to buy an 18-ton craft and hire help.

A few years after the Revolutionary War, Cuffe married Alice Pequit, who, like his mother, was a Wampanoag Indian. He rented a small house in Westport and used his new boat to sail to Ontario, Canada, where he bought a cargo of dried codfish. Back home, he sold his cargo quickly.

The Cuffes were keenly aware that one reason behind the revolt of the colonies against England was the charge of "no taxation without representation." If the colonists refused to pay taxes to England because they had no say in how the English government was conducted, why should the Cuffes pay taxes to the state of Connecticut? As African American men, they could not legally vote or own a business, so they refused to pay taxes.

When state authorities arrived to seize the Cuffes' property, they found none to seize. In December 1780, Paul and John Cuffe were jailed for nonpayment of taxes. Released from prison the following spring, the Cuffes pursued their cause, putting the issue before a town meeting in Taunton, Connecticut, where they had been jailed.

The Cuffes, along with five other African Americans, demanded that free African Americans have the same rights as European Americans to own businesses and vote or else be relieved of taxation. The Cuffes finally had to pay the taxes they owned, but they had put up a courageous fight for the same rights for which the European American colonists had gone to war.

Over the next ten years, often in partnership with one of his brothers-in-law, Michael Wainer, also a seaman, Cuffe made even greater profits and built even larger vessels.

He then entered the expanding whaling business, sailing on the 42-ton schooner *Mary* in 1793. He then traveled to Philadelphia to exchange whale oil and bone for hardware to outfit the *Ranger,* the 69-ton schooner that he piloted to Norfolk, Virginia, on what was probably his first trip south.

Cuffe took the corn he bought in Virginia and sold it in Westport. When the market for corn was not good, he dealt in gypsum, a mineral used in the making of plaster. He traded in whatever commodity would bring him profits.

Cuffe's longest voyage of trade was on the 268-ton *Alpha*. With its African American crew of seven, he sailed south to Wilmington and Savannah, then across the ocean to Helsingor, Denmark, and Goteborg, Sweden, and returned to Philadelphia with passengers and freight.

By the time Captain Paul Cuffe was fifty years old, he owned a small fleet of ships. He built a schoolhouse for Westport with his own money on his own land and then donated both land and building "freely...to the use of the public."

Every year, however, he became more and more outraged over slavery, which he described as the "evil of one brother making merchandise of and holding his brother in bondage." He eventually decided that the best course for freed slaves was to return to their native Africa.

One day in the fall of 1810, he and a crew of nine African American seamen set said for Sierra Leone in western Africa. He stayed there three months, taking notes on the country's possibilities as a home for African Americans from North America. He made one more visit to Sierra Leone before returning there in 1815 on the *Traveller* with thirty-eight African American emigrants and a cargo of supplies to get them started in their new home.

Cuffe's health soon failed, and he died in October 1817. His dreams of an African nation of African American emigrants from America would be carried forth by others and bear fruit in the settling of Liberia by African American freedmen in 1821. But there would never be a large exodus of free African Americans from the United States.

The Cuffe Farm at 1504 Drift Road in Westport, Connecticut, is now a National Historic Landmark.

Chapter Forty-One
James Forten

(1766 - 1842)

James Forten knew Paul Cuffe as an adult, and like Cuffe, Forten was filled with the revolutionary spirit of his times.

Forten was born free in Philadelphia. His father, Thomas Forten, had also been freeborn and had purchased his wife's freedom with his wages as a sail maker in the employ of Robert Bridges.

James Forten was only seven when his father fell to his death while working on the tall sails of a ship. His family survived the sudden tragedy, and life went on.

James Forten attended a Quaker school as a boy. The colony of Pennsylvania had been established by the Quakers, a religious sect formally known as the Society of Friends. The Quakers believed in the equality of all people and had early on allowed African Americans to attend their schools.

After the Revolutionary War, Forten became an apprentice to Robert Bridges, the Philadelphia sail maker who had employed his father. Forten was such a skilled and responsible worker that by 1786 he had been named foreman of the sail making loft. Twelve years later, in

1798, he became its owner. More than forty workers, both African American and European American, were employed in his factory.

At the age of fourteen, Forten enlisted in the navy, where he served as a powderboy, loading cannons aboard the *Royal Lewis,* a privateer, or private ship commissioned by the American navy. The *Royal Lewis* was captured by the British navy, and its crew, which included some twenty African Americans, was taken as prisoners. Forten became friends with the British captain's son. The boy asked Forten to go back to England with him to live a life of wealth and aristocratic privilege.

Forten paused and answered, "I am a prisoner here for the liberties of my country. I never shall prove a traitor to her interests. " He was transferred to the British prison ship *Jersey* and later released in a general prisoner exchange.

Sometime after 1800, Forten invented a device that helped control the sails on ships and that opened the door to the modern sailing industry. The exact date is not known because Forten never patented his invention. He secured contracts from the United States Navy to outfit its vessels, and he quietly made a fortune.

Forten could have made even more money had he been willing to work with the slave traders.

But he refused to outfit slave vessels with sail rigging or with his sail-handling device. Instead, he used much of his wealth in good causes. For instance, he joined other African American Philadelphia businessmen in various endeavors to help the poor.

He gave a lot of money to support the *Liberator,* an anti-slavery newspaper founded by William Lloyd Garrison, and he helped to build its subscription list. A strong supporter of the United States government, his largest customer, he helped to recruit African American soldiers to serve in the War of 1812.

Forten's friends asked him to be chairman of the African American People's Convention, which met at Bethel Church in Philadelphia on August 10, 1817. Forten, along with 3,000 others, adopted this basic resolution: "We will never separate ourselves voluntarily from the African American slave population of this country; they are our brethren by ties of shared blood, suffering and wronged; we feel there is more virtue in suffering privation with them, than fancied advantage for a reason."

Forten was not in favor of colonization in Africa. "We are contented in the land that gave us birth and for which many of our fathers fought and died," he said. He had more faith in offering money to master mechanics to take African American children as apprentices than in settling another country

At Forten's death in 1842, his sail loft enterprise was estimated to be worth $100,000, a vast sum for any American at that time.

Chapter Forty-Two
Pierre Toussaint

(1766 - 1853)

As successful in his time and place as James Forten was, Pierre Toussaint, like Forten, began his entrepreneurial life as an apprentice.

Toussaint was born a slave on a plantation in Haiti when that island was a French possession prized for its sugarcane crop. A house servant, Toussaint was encouraged to read and write and was treated well by his owners, the wealthy and aristocratic Jean and Marie Berard. But the cruelty of other slave owners led to unrest in Haiti.

The Berards, accompanied by Toussaint, fled to New York. Fully expecting the slave revolt in Haiti to be put down by French troops, Jean Berard had brought only enough money to maintain his family comfortably in New York for one year.

Soon after settling in a rented house on Reade Street, Jean Berard apprenticed twenty-one-year-old Toussaint to a Mr. Merchant, one of the city's leading hairdressers. Toussaint quickly mastered the art of making the elaborate hairstyles that were in vogue for wealthy women, but he had to walk to their homes to do his work, because African Americans were not allowed to ride the city's public horsecars.

The situation in Haiti grew worse. Frightened by the rumors of impending disaster, Jean Berard sailed to Haiti to save his property. Berard never returned to New York; he died of pleurisy, a disease of the lungs, on his plantation. Not long after his death, his plantation was destroyed. Although French troops eventually put down the rebellion, the French hold on the island had been broken. In 1803, Haiti became an independent African Frenchman republic.

Having barely adjusted to the news of Jean's death and the conditions in Haiti, Marie Berard learned that her husband's investments in a New York City business were wiped out when the firm collapsed. Penniless, she asked Toussaint to sell some of her jewelry. He refused, offering instead to provide for the household's weekly expenses. He sometimes earned $1,000 per year per client at a time when a man was considered wealthy if he made $10,000 a year.

Although he had every right to be free, Toussaint was sensitive to Madame Berard's feelings and to appearances, and he always acted the dutiful slave. Marie Berard remarried, but her new husband, Gabriel Nicolas, also a refugee French planter from Haiti suffered financial reverses.

Pierre Toussaint continued to support the household. In fact, he put off his own plans to marry a young Haitian girl, Juliette Noel, because he felt that he could not marry her while he was responsible for the Nicolas household.

Marie Nicolas died when Toussaint was forty-five years old. On her deathbed, she informed him that she had provided for his freedom in a legal document dated July 2, 1807.

Pierre Toussaint wasted no time in marrying Juliette, but otherwise, he continued to live much as he always had, attending early mass each morning before he went to work. He used his money to help the poor. He provided much of the support for the Prince Street Orphanage, New York's first Catholic institution for homeless children, and he helped raise funds to build St. Patrick's Cathedral and St. Vincent de Paul Church.

Pierre and Juliette took orphans into their home. Toussaint also put his life on the line to nurse victims of cholera and yellow fever, crossing quarantine barriers to reach sufferers in the city's early ghettoes.

He continued to work well into his later years. One of his customers said, "Toussaint, you are the richest man I know. Why not stop working?" Toussaint replied, "Then, Madame, I should not have enough for others." He continued to work until Juliette died in 1851. Not long afterward, Toussaint himself became ill. He died on June 30, 1853, at the age of eighty-seven.

Pierre Toussaint was first buried in the cemetery of Old St. Patrick's Church on Mott Street. His remains now lie in a crypt beneath the floor of St. Patrick's Cathedral on Fifth Avenue in New York City. Catholic church officials had come to believe that the good man they reburied there was very likely a saint.

Chapter Forty-Three

"Free Frank" McWorter

(1777 - 1854)

Frank McWorter built an entire town in the pursuit of complete freedom for his family. He was born a slave in Union County, South Carolina, a frontier outpost. His mother, Juda, had been born in western Africa. Evidence indicates that Juda's owner, George McWhorter, was Frank's father.

Around 1795, George McWhorter purchased land in Pulaski county, Kentucky, some two hundred miles northwest of Union County, South Carolina. Kentucky law stated that in order to own the land, the buyer must live on it, fence two acres, and cultivate a crop of corn. So George McWhorter sent eighteen-year-old Frank and three other McWhorter slaves to Kentucky to establish his claim to the land.

During that year in Kentucky, Frank met Lucy, who belonged to William Denham, a relative of the McWhorters. Four years later Frank and Lucy chose to be man and wife, although slaves in Kentucky were not allowed to marry. Because their respective masters lived some distance away from each other, Frank and Lucy were able to live together under a single roof. Over the course of the next eighteen years, however, they had thirteen children, all of them the legal property of Lucy's owner.

The years passed. They were hard but never boring. Frank got George McWhorter's permission to hire out his own time as a jack-of-all-trades, agreeing to pay an annual fee for the privilege. After George moved his family south to Wayne County and left Frank in charge of the Pulaski County farm, Frank had even more time to work for himself. But it was the War of 1812 that led him to establish his own business.

In its fight against Great Britain, the United States needed huge quantities of saltpeter, the principal ingredient in gunpowder. Kentucky was the nation's leading producer of saltpeter, and the Rockcastle caves, rich in potassium nitrate, or niter, saltpeter's basic ingredient, were only a short distance away from the McWhorter farm in Pulaski County.

Frank worked the farm by day and devoted his nights to mining and producing saltpeter. After the War of 1812, as the demand for saltpeter declined, Frank also went into the business of making salt. In those days, salt-making even on a small scale could be profitable.

George McWhorter died in 1815. Before his death he had promised to free Frank, but he had made no provision in his will for Frank's emancipation. McWhorter's heirs agreed to free Frank, on payment of $500, more money than Frank had yet saved.

That year, Lucy gave birth to their thirteenth child, Solomon. By 1817, she was pregnant again. Frank did not want his fourteenth child born in slavery, and by then he had earned enough to buy Lucy's freedom. He purchased her for $800. As a consequence, their child, Squire, born the following September, was the first member of their family to be born free.

In 1819, Frank purchased himself, paying $800. His owners had decided to raise his price! No matter. Rather than choose a surname, he proudly had his name listed as Free Frank in the 1820 census. From then on, Frank paid whatever price freedom demanded.

Ten years later, in 1829, Free Frank purchased freedom for his twenty-five-year-old son, Frank Junior, by trading his saltpeter works to the Denham family. Three years earlier, young Frank had escaped and made it safely to Canada. But Free Frank wanted his son with him, and so he bought his freedom.

Now that Free Frank had traded away his main source of income, he had little reason to stay in Kentucky. It was no longer a frontier. In 1830, he sold the land he had acquired and moved the free members of his family—Frank Junior and Squire, Commodore, and Lucy Ann, three children who had been born free after 1817—to Illinois, a free state. They traveled by ox-drawn wagon, crossed the Ohio River on a flatboat, and settled in Hadley Township in Pike County on the Illinois frontier.

By the time they reached Illinois, Free Frank and his family had dropped the "h" in their last name and were known as the McWorters. The family, who at the time were the only African Americans in Pike County, bought land and began to raise hogs and horses for cash money to buy Frank and Lucy's children who remained in slavery.

Four years later, in 1835, Frank purchased his son Solomon for $550. Two daughters and their children remained in slavery. (Frank and Lucy's other slave children had died by this time.) Money was scarce, and time seemed to be running out.

Then Free Frank had his best moneymaking idea yet. He decided to establish a town, primarily because selling lots was the best way to obtain cash money. he bought land and had it surveyed, or plotted. He named the town New Philadelphia. Free Frank was a deeply religious man, and it is possible that he took the name from a passage in Revelation, in which God says: "To the angel of the church in Philadelphia. I know your deeds; that is why I have left before you an open door which no once can close."

New Philadelphia was one of six towns founded by single proprietors in Pike County at that time. Free Frank quickly opened a store and worked with county officials to build cross-county roads nearby. He had sold eight town lots by 1841; the purchasers included European Americans.

With the increased prosperity of the county in the middle 1840s, New Philadelphia grew. Soon it had a stagecoach stop and a post office.

The Underground Railroad, an informal network of African Americans and European Americans who helped escaped slaves from the South reach freedom in Canada, was active by the 1840s. In New Philadelphia, the McWorters aided many fugitives. They built a secret room in the basement of their home as a hiding place, and McWorter's sons often helped lead the fugitives to Canada.

By 1850, Free Frank and his family owned over 600 acres of land valued at more than $7,000. Only 3,000 of the nation's nearly 440,000 free African Americans owned land.

In that year, Free Frank purchased two of his grandchildren and the wife of his son Squire. By 1854, he had purchased four more family members.

Free Frank McWorter died on September 7, 1854, at the age of seventy-seven. He had not lived to accomplish his dream of freeing his entire family, but his will provided for his work to go on.

His sons carried out his wishes, and within three years they purchased a total of seven more grandchildren and great-grandchildren. Altogether, fifteen members of the Frank McWorter family were freed from bondage, at a cost of more than $14,000.

Chapter Forty-Four

Thomas L. Jennings

(1791 - 1859)

W hile slaves and freemen such as Free Frank McWorter were taking advantage of the few opportunities available to them in the South and Midwest, enterprising African Americans in the cities of the Northeast were also finding ways to prosper. They, too, faced extraordinary obstacles.

As Edgar J. McManus wrote in *A History of Negro Slavery in New York,* African Americans were "in a very real sense a population in quarantine, trapped in a system of racial bondage in many ways as cruel and intolerable as slavery." But many within the city's small, cultured African American middle class managed to thrive.

Thomas L. Jennings of New York City was one of them. He operated a boarding house, but his tailoring and dry cleaning business brought him more success. In 1821, at the age of thirty, he patented a dry cleaning process known as "dry scouring." Jennings is believed to be the first African American to have received a patent for an invention.

The first U.S. Patent Act had been enacted in 1790, one year before Jennings was born. It was meant to encourage innovation by making detailed information about inventions known to the public. It also protected the inventor from unauthorized use of his or her invention. The patent office did not keep records of an inventor's race/culture. There may have been earlier inventions patented by African American people, but Jennings's is the first to be verified. He received his patent on March 3, 1821.

Jennings used the profits from his successful businesses to support many causes. Abolitionism, or the movement to abolish slavery, was one of the most important to him.

The first abolition society was formed in Philadelphia in 1775. The Declaration of Independence and the creation of the new nation based on the idea that all men were created equal brought the issue of slavery to the forefront.

Those who were against slavery demanded its end. Inspired by the great religious revival that swept the country in the early part of the nineteenth century, with its moral urgency to end sinful practices and its vision of human perfection, abolitionists declared that slavery was a moral evil that had to be wiped out.

Jennings was a leading member of the National Colored Convention Movement, whose first Annual Convention of the People of Color was held at Wesleyan Church in Philadelphia on September 15, 1831. Its purpose was to "devise ways and means for the bettering of our condition." He was also a founder of the first African American organization, the New York African Society for Mutual Relief, chartered on March 23, 1810, whose purpose was to raise funds to aid the widows and orphans of its deceased members.

He attended Abyssinian Baptist Church, which in the next century would have the largest African American congregation in New York City and be the political power base of its pastor the Reverend Adam Clayton Powell Jr., who served in Congress from 1945 to 1970.

Jennings was proud of his culture and thought he was as much an American as any other citizen of the still-new United States. Like

James Forten in Philadelphia, he was against the idea of African American emigration to Africa. At a meeting of the New York African Society for Mutual Relief in 1828, Jennings said:

> "Our claims are on America; it is the land that gave us birth. We know no other country. It is a land in which our fathers have suffered and toiled. They have watered it with their tears and fanned it with their sighs."

> "Our relation with Africa is the same as the European American man's is with Europe. We have passed through several generations in this country and consequently have become naturalized."

> Our habits, our manners, our passions, our dispositions have become the same. The same mother's milk has nourished us both in infancy, the European American child and the African American have both hung on the same breast. I might as well tell the white man about England, France or Spain, the country from whence his forefathers emigrated, and call him a European, as for him to call us Africans. Africa is as foreign to us as Europe is to them."

Jennings and his wife lived at 167 Church Street, and they had several children. Thomas L.. Jennings Jr., studied dentistry in Boston and established a practice in New Orleans. Matilda Jennings, a dressmaker, married and lived in San Francisco.

In 1854, Jennings's sister, Elizabeth, brought suit against the Third Avenue Railway Company for discrimination after a conductor put her off a train reserved for "whites".

Her lawyer was young Chester A. Arthur, fresh out of law school. His law firm, Culver, Parker, and Arthur, had established a reputation for handling abolitionist causes and believed Elizabeth had a strong case.

Thomas L. Jennings spearheaded the fundraising drive to pay Elizabeth's legal costs. One of his appeals, addressed "To the Citizens of

Color, Male and Female, of the City and State of New York," pointed out that no actual law forced persons of African descent to ride in segregated trolley cars marked COLORED and that it was really a matter of custom, tradition, and transit company rules. The case, the appeal went on, "will bring up the whole question of our right…in the public conveyances."

In winning her suit, Elizabeth effectively ended discrimination in transportation in New York City. Chester A. Arthur went on to become president of the United States.

Thomas L. Jennings died in 1859, four years after his sister won her case

Chapter Forty-Five
William A. Leidesdorff

(1810 - 1848)

The only individual in this collection to inherit wealth, William Alexander Leidesdorff, was born in Concordia on the island of St. Croix in the Danish West Indies (now the U.S. Virgin Islands). He had a Danish father and an African mother named Anna Marie Sparks. He had a privileged childhood on his wealthy father's plantation, and although no record of his education exists, he became fluent in several languages, including French and German.

As a young man, Leidesdorff worked in his father's cotton business, sailing ships to such ports as New York City and New Orleans. Reportedly, a failed love affair spurred Leidesdorff to set out for California. His ship, the *Julia Ann*, arrived in Yerba Buena (later renamed San Francisco), via New Orleans in 1841.

h Hawaii, and purchased two 300-foot lots on the corner of Clay and Kearney Streets. He later built Yerba Buena's first hotel on that property.He soon made Yerba Buena his home, established himself in trade wit

With the aim of obtaining additional large land grants from Mexico, Leidesdorff became a naturalized Mexican citizen in 1844 and acquired

313

from the Mexican government a 35,000-acre estate, which he named Rio Del Rancho Americano. There, he raised cattle and horses, and by 1846, he had 4,500 head of cattle and 250 horses.

Also in 1846, he obtained a grant for a lot at the foot of California Street in Yerba Buena, renamed San Francisco that same year. Here, he built a warehouse for the export of tallow, which was used in the making of candles, and of hides, which were used to make clothing and shoes. The following year, he acquired property on Montgomery Street, near California Street, and built a home.

His entrepreneurial ventures became legendary. He purchased a 37-foot steam boat, *Sitka,* to operate for commercial purposes on San Francisco Bay.

It was the first steamboat ever seen in that bay, and Leidesdorff became known as the "Robert Fulton of the West." He hosted the first recorded public horse race in California—in a meadow near Mission Dolores.

In 1845, even though Leidesdorff was a Mexican citizen, the U.S. consul to Mexico, Colonel Thomas David Larkin, appointed him vice-consul, making Leidesdorff probably the first African American diplomat in the history of the United States.

Leidesdorff held that position in 1846 when the American explorer John C. Fremont led American settlers to set up a republic at Sonoma. Leidesdorff supported Fremont.

Meanwhile, Mexico and the United States had gone to war, although the news had not yet reached California. The *Californios* in the north supported the United States' effort and worked with the U.S. troops who arrived to occupy the main population centers. Leidesdorff arranged a fancy dress ball at his home to entertain the American leaders.

Inhabitants of southern California were not as cooperative as those in the north. In fact, they resisted U.S. forces until 1847, when they were defeated.

314

Mexico formally ceded California to the United States the following year; and in 1850, it was admitted to the Union as the thirty-first state.

Originally part of New Spain, as the Spanish empire in the Americas was called, California had been colonized by Spain. The settlers were known as the *Californios.* The *Californios* built mansions supposedly for the purpose of bringing Christianity to the native Indians, whom they forced to work as manual laborers.

Mexico won its independence from Spain in 1821 and later took control of California. Under Mexican rule, the native Indians were released from their servitude. Many mission lands were subsequently given to *Californios,* who built vast estates called *ranchos* and raised cattle. Colonization of California was still largely Mexican when William A. Leidesdorff arrived in 1841.

Yerba Buena was a small, sparsely populated port in 1841, but that was soon to change. Founded as a military outpost by Juan Bautista in 1776, it was quickly becoming a popular stopping place for ships on their way to the Far East. Also, the first American immigrants began to arrive in California by overland routes in 1841, and Leidesdorff must have sensed the business opportunities they represented.

In 1848, the same year that Mexico ceded California to the United States, gold was discovered in California not far from Leidesdorff's ranch. But Leidesdorff did not live to take advantage of the new business opportunities it presented. An epidemic of typhus hit the San Francisco area that year, and on May 18 Leidesdorff became one of its victims.

When Leidesdorff died, his estate was deeply in debt. But the later discovery of gold on his ranch made the property very valuable. Leidesdorff's estate was eventually awarded to a European American army captain, Joseph Folsom, who became wealthy as a result.

The high regard in which his fellow San Franciscans held this first African American resident of their town is evidenced by the fact that by 1856, a street had been named after him. Three blocks long today, it is, quite fittingly, located in San Francisco's Financial District.

Chapter Forty-Six
David Ruggles

(1810 - 1849)

Nineteenth-century New York City was America's greatest city. It was also strongly segregated. Out of a population of some 515,000, about 14,000 were of African descent. African Americans were restricted in voting, denied jobs, refused service in restaurants, forbidden to serve as jurors, and excluded from membership in professional organizations. Slavery was abolished in New York State in 1827, but African American New Yorkers remained a few steps above slavery.

David Ruggles, the first publisher of an African American magazine, arrived in New York in 1827. Born of free parents in Norwich, Connecticut, on March 15, 1810, he left home at the age of seventeen and moved to New York, where he started a grocery business.

Almost immediately, the abolitionists' campaign against the moral evil of slavery captured the young man's imagination, and he became involved as a traveling agent for the *Emancipator,* their weekly newspaper.

In 1834, Ruggles opened a bookshop and circulating library at 67 Lispenard Street in New York City, thereby becoming the first

African American bookseller. He soon began to publish pamphlets condemning African American oppression.

He thrived on fighting for justice. When the New York Committee of Vigilance was founded by leading European American and African American citizens, Ruggles became its director. The committee helped runaway slaves get settled in New York or travel farther north, to Boston or Providence or Canada. It also watched out for slave hunters and kidnappers, and it gave legal aid to people tried in court as runaways.

The most famous person Ruggles' committee helped was Frederick Douglass, one of the most powerful orators in the cause and a newspaper publisher himself.

Ruggles' anti-slavery activities were apparently too much for some of New York's pro-slavery European Americans. In the fall of 1835, Ruggles' bookshop was destroyed by fire. It was suspected that pro-slavery European Americans were responsible. But Ruggles would not be intimidated. The November 24, 1835, issue of the *Emancipator* contained the following advertisement:

> Agency Office, 67 Lispenard Street, New York—The friends of Human rights are respectfully informed that in consequence of the destruction of my books, pamphlets, and stationery by fire, I am compelled for the present to discontinue the sale of books and the circulating library, but will abide in the same place, and continue my agency for all Anti-Slavery Publications.

Less than two months later, an attempt was made to kidnap Ruggles and sell him into slavery. Early one morning, he was awakened by a knock on the door. From the other side a man who identified himself as "Mr. Nash" claimed he had urgent business with Ruggles. But a suspicious Ruggles refused to open the door. Foiled, the man returned with reinforcements, who battered down the door of the house. By that time, however, Ruggles had escaped.

Ruggles continued to create businesses to help African American people. In 1837, he established a newspaper called the *Mirror of Liberty*. the following year, he opened a reading room for African Americans at 36 Lispenard Street "because African Americans were not given free privileges in the libraries of New York."

Ruggles edited yet another newspaper, the *Genius of Freedom*, in New York between 1845 and 1847. He died two years later at the age of thirty-nine, nearly fifteen years before slavery was ended in the United States.

Chapter Forty-Seven
Elizabeth Keckley

(1818 - 1907)

Elizabeth Keckley was born Elizabeth Hobbs to a slave family in Dinwiddie Courthouse, Virginia. She was only in her mid-teens when she was sold to a slave owner in North Carolina and forced to leave her family.

In her new place of enslavement in North Carolina, Elizabeth was raped, probably by her owner, and later gave birth to a son. Then, when Elizabeth was eighteen, she and her son were repurchased by the daughter of her original owner, who took them to St. Louis, Missouri, to live.

In all probability, Elizabeth was sought out by a member of her original owner's family because of her exceptional skills as a seamstress. She started a dressmaking business in St. Louis that eventually became so prosperous that it supported her owners and their five children, as well as herself and her own son.

Elizabeth wanted to be free, and one reason why she married James Keckley was because he claimed to be free. She later learned that he had lied to her about his status. The couple separated, but Elizabeth kept his name for the rest of her life.

Elizabeth Keckley worked for the abolitionist cause, helping other African American women form an organization to aid former slaves seeking refuge in the capital. She secured donations from Mrs. Lincoln as well as from such prominent African American abolitionists as Frederick Douglass and Wendell Phillips. The Contraband Relief Association, as her organization was known, changed its name to the Freedmen and Soldiers' Relief Association of Washington when African Americans were allowed to join the army.

Nearly 180,000 African Americans fought in the war between the North and the South. Sadly, Keckley's son, who was light-complected enough to serve in a European American regiment in the Union Army, was killed in action.

In 1855, when Elizabeth was thirty-seven years old, she secured loans from her dressmaking clients to purchase her freedom for $1200. She continued in her dressmaking business in St. Louis for another five years, until she had earned enough money to pay back the loans.

In 1860, Keckley moved first to Baltimore, Maryland, and then to Washington, D.C. She employed twenty girls in her business in the nation's capital, and her clients included Mrs. Jefferson Davis, whose husband was at that time a senator from Mississippi.

Introduced to Mary Todd Lincoln on the day after President Lincoln's inauguration, Keckley soon became the First Lady's dressmaker. Within months, seven southern states had seceded from the Union, and Keckley's former client, Mrs. Davis, became the First Lady of the Confederate States of America.

Elizabeth Keckley moved into the White House, serving as Mary Todd Lincoln's dressmaker, personal maid, and confidante. Keckley told an interviewer, "I dressed Mrs. Lincoln for every levee. I made every stitch of clothing that she wore. I dressed her hair. I put on her skirts and dresses."

"I fixed her bouquets, saw that her gloves were all right, and remained with her each evening until Mr. Lincoln came for her. My hands were the last to touch her before she took the arm of Mr. Lincoln and went forth to meet the ladies and gentlemen on those great occasions."

After President Lincoln was assassinated in 1865, Mary Todd Lincoln and her children moved out of the White House. Keckley moved, too, but continued to make dresses for and remained a close personal friend of Mary Todd Lincoln until 1868.

Mrs. Lincoln was shocked when Keckley's memoir, *Behind the Scenes; or, Thirty Years a Slave, and Four Years in the White House,* was published that year. Written in collaboration with James Redpath Whoran, a lecture agency, the book described Keckley's life as a slave and the brutality she'd been forced to endure in North Carolina as well as life at the White House, including the personalities of the Lincoln's and their family dynamics. Mary Todd Lincoln considered the book a betrayal of her friendship.

Keckley spent her last years supported by a pension paid to her because her son had died fighting for the Union cause. The rest home in which she died on May 26, 1907, was one she had helped found for others.

In spite of the controversy that raged around it, Keckley's book proved to be a valuable resource for Lincoln scholars. Its accuracy has rarely been questioned.

Chapter Forty-Eight
Richard Henry Boyd

(1843 - 1922)

Like Elizabeth Keckley, Richard Boyd was born a slave but rose on the winds of freedom and personal initiative. At his birth on March 15, 1843, in Nexubee County, Mississippi, he was given the name Dick Gray. During the Civil War, he accompanied members of his owner's family into battle. But after emancipation, in 1867, he changed his name to Richard Henry Boyd and set out on his own.

At first, the future entrepreneur became a minister in the predominantly European American Texas Baptist Convention of churches. To Boyd, the times probably seemed hopeful, because new laws were passed to give African Americans the right to vote as equals. But events proved otherwise.

In 1870, Boyd organized, largely with his own funds, the first association of African American Baptists in the state of Texas. He started with six churches but steadily built the association until it represented most African American Baptist congregations in the state.

By 1896, Boyd had become a real power in both state and national Baptist circles. When the United States and other nations began building a canal across the Isthmus of Panama to facilitate shipping between the eastern and western United States and between the United States and Latin America, for instance, Boyd oversaw the building of four churches and one school in Panama.

During the post-Civil War period called Reconstruction (1865-1877), African Americans briefly enjoyed the right to vote and hold office. Like most European Americans, however, members of the Texas Baptist Convention were officially against Reconstruction reforms But Richard Henry Boyd did not falter in his faith or lose hope. He resisted the racism by forming a separate group for African American churches.

Also in 1896, Boyd established and became secretary of the National Baptist Publishing Board in Nashville, Tennessee. Four years later, he moved his family to Nashville and oversaw the publication of the first Baptist literature for mass consumption. At Boyd's urging, the board also published literature for African American Baptist Sunday schools.

In large part because of Boyd's domination of the church's successful publishing firm, some leaders of the national church wanted to incorporate the National Baptist Convention and make it more of a business. Boyd led the fight against incorporation, and when the dust settled, he found himself the sole owner of the publishing company. Boyd's own books, a total of fourteen about the Baptist denomination, were published by his company.

Although Boyd did not want his church to become a business, he liked starting businesses. He even started businesses outside the church. He was the founder in 1904 and first president of the One Cent Savings Bank and Trust Company (later renamed the Citizen's Savings Bank and Trust Company of Nashville).

The following year, he and his son, Henry Allen Boyd, established the Nashville Globe Printing Company and the weekly African American newspaper, *Nashville Globe and Independent*.

Boyd also originated the idea of making African American dolls for African American children. His National Negro Doll Company was the first in the nation to make ethnic dolls.

Boyd died of a cerebral hemorrhage and stroke on August 19, 1922, at the age of seventy-nine.

His son, Henry Allen Boyd, succeeded him as Publisher and President of the *Globe and Independent* and took control of the publishing firm. He also ran his father's bank, which, unlike many other African American-owned banks, managed to weather the Great Depression a decade later.

Part Eight

African American Healers

Clinton Cox

Introduction

The story of African American healers in the United States is a story as fascinating as that of any group in this country's history. These doctors, nurses, and researchers were and are determined to help relieve the suffering of others. This is their story.

Their story is a journey: a journey from Colonial America to the present, from slave ships and fields to the most modern laboratories and operating rooms in the world. There were African American healers throughout American history.

In the early years, for example, an African American man named James Durham, though born into slavery in 1762, managed to study medicine. He discovered an effective method for treating diphtheria, one of the most widespread diseases of his time.

In the 1800s, African American doctors ministered to escaping slaves, served in the Union army in the Civil War, and founded medical schools. One of the healers was an African American teenager, Susie King Taylor. She helped nurse African American Union army soldiers in the Civil War.

Entering the twentieth century, the number of African American medical students grew slowly but steadily. Dr. Charles Richard Drew became a pioneer in the development of blood plasma during World War II. By the 1980s, there were African American specialists and health administrators in fields ranging from heart surgery and oncology (the study and treatment of cancers) to ophthalmology (eye-related disorders) and psychiatry.

In modern times, neurosurgeon Dr. Benjamin Carson, a young man who came out of a Detroit ghetto, has become "one of the acknowledged miracle workers of modern medicine".

All of these healers possessed a courage, talent, and compassion that has rarely been surpassed. "He never turned a deaf ear to a cry for help," a friend once said of the great African American surgeon, Dr. Daniel Hale Williams. Those words could easily apply to the healers we are about to meet: men and women whose dreams of helping others could not be denied.

Chapter Forty-Nine
Dr. James Durham

(1762 - ?)

James Durham of New Orleans, Louisiana, the first African American doctor in the United States, hurried through the streets of Philadelphia, eager to meet Dr. Benjamin Rush. Rush, a signer of the Declaration of Independence and the foremost medical man of his day, was just as eager to meet the twenty-six-year-old African American.

Although Dr. Durham had only been fourteen years old when Dr. Rush had signed the Declaration of Independence, the younger man's reputation for healing was now well known. And Dr. Rush had an urgent problem. How could he keep more people from dying in the terrible diphtheria epidemic that was sweeping the city of Philadelphia?

The epidemic of diphtheria had killed 119 people in Philadelphia in a single day. Physicians looked on helplessly as patients died from the dreaded disease. Rush had already lost his sister and three pupils. Doctor Durham, however, had developed a successful treatment for diphtheria.

Benjamin Rush wanted to learn how Durham had saved so many people. Perhaps Dr. Durham's knowledge could help him stop the diphtheria epidemic.

Like other members of the African American population, Durham was struggling to make a place for himself in the new nation. He had been born in Philadelphia, but the place Durham (sometimes spelled Derham) was trying to make was unusual for anyone in those times, and especially for a African American man: He was struggling for acceptance as a doctor.

Durham had been born into slavery, but he had learned to read and write. Like most doctors in this country, he had learned his profession by studying under other doctors.

While still a small child, he was put to work mixing medicines by a physician who bought him and by yet another doctor, who taught him to perform "some of the more humble acts of attention to his patients."

Finally, when he was twenty-one, the determined Durham managed to buy his freedom and begin his own medical practice in New Orleans. His fluency in French, Spanish, and English made him one of that city's most popular doctors, and he soon became one of its most distinguished ones as well.

Durham finally met Rush on that day in 1788, and gave him such good information that Rush ended up reading the young man's paper on diphtheria before the College of Physicians of Philadelphia. "I have conversed with him upon most of the acute and epidemic diseases of the country where he lives," Rush said later, "and was pleased to find him perfectly acquainted with the modern simple mode of practice in those diseases. I expected to have suggested some new medicines to him, but he suggested many more to me."

Durham returned to New Orleans in 1789. There, he managed to save the lives of more yellow fever victims than most doctors of his time, losing only eleven of sixty-four patients during an epidemic that raged through New Orleans.

Only three years later, however, the city of New Orleans limited his work because he did not have a formal medical degree. He continued to write to Dr. Rush, but today no one knows what happened to Dr. Durham after 1802. Despite his achievements, the idea that African American people were incapable of understanding medicine remained widespread in the decades to come.

In the face of often incredible odds, however, many African American men and women wrote their names into history as outstanding doctors, nurses, and researchers.

Several decades before Rush and Durham met, the most important medical discovery in Colonial America was contributed by an African American man. The man's name was Onesimus, a young African held as a slave by the Puritan clergyman Cotton Mather.

During one of the periodic smallpox epidemics that swept the colonies, Onesimus told Mather "…Cut the Skin, and put in a drop… nobody have Small Pox any more." He then showed Mather the scar he had received.

Traditional healers in Africa had apparently used smallpox inoculations for centuries, injecting a mild case of the disease as a protection against a fatal attack.

Mather published the information he had received from Onesimus in *Some Account of What Is Said of Inoculating or Transplanting the Small Pox*, in 1721. This was almost thirty years before Edward Jenner, the Englishman who is credited with developing the smallpox vaccine, was born. Mather was greeted with ridicule by most of the leading physicians of his time when he urged them to trust the method described by Onesimus.

But a doctor named Zabdiel Boylston tried it on his son and two of his slaves during an epidemic that swept Boston that same year. When it worked on them, Boylston inoculated another 241 people. Only 6 later caught smallpox. (Thomas Jefferson tested a smallpox vaccine many years later by injecting it into 200 slaves, including 80 of his own. When none of them died, European Americans allowed themselves to be injected.)

The method Onesimus passed on to Boylston was also used to inoculate American soldiers during the Revolutionary War, saving many of them from the ravages of smallpox

Chapter Fifty

James McCune Smith, M.D.

(1813 - 1865)

James McCune Smith was born free in New York City to a successful merchant and a mother who had managed to buy her freedom. Knowing that their son would need to be well educated in order to succeed, his parents sent him to the city's African Free School. This school had been established for African American children in 1786 by the New York Manumission Society.

James was so bright that when the Marquis de Lafayette visited the United States in 1824, the youth was called on to welcome the Revolutionary War hero to the school. Still, it was difficult for James to succeed. In spite of his intelligence, he was refused admittance to any American college because of the color of his skin. He finally enrolled in the University of Glasgow in Scotland, as several other aspiring African American doctors would do in the coming years, and received his M.D. degree in 1837. That made him the first African American to earn a medical degree.

For the next twenty-eight years, Smith waged war on sickness. He became the first African American man to own a pharmacy in the United States. He build up a prosperous medical practice in New

York City. He served on the medical staff of the city's Free Negro Orphan Asylum.

At the same time, he found time to fight for "the elevation and enfranchisement of the free African American people on this, the soil which gave them birth, and through their enfranchisement, the emancipation of the African American slaves of the South."

Called the most scholarly African American writer of his time, Smith wrote eloquent denunciations of slavery. He published his writing in the *Colored American,* a newspaper that he edited and in the *North Star,* the crusading newspaper owned by his friend the abolitionist Frederick Douglass.

As civil war between the North and the South grew ever closer, Smith and several other African American doctors intensified their struggle against slavery. Several years after Smith's death, Frederick Douglass paid tribute to these healers.

"On all occasions, in season and out of season, there were brave and intelligent men of color all over the United States who gave me their cordial sympathy and support," Douglass wrote.

"Among these, and foremost, I place the name of Doctor James McCune Smith…He was never among the timid who thought me too aggressive and wished me to tone down my testimony to suit the times. A brave man himself, he knew how to esteem courage in others."

Smith fearlessly challenged the theories that powerful people used to defend slavery and racism. When Senator John C. Calhoun of South Carolina, the country's foremost pro-slavery spokesman, argued that African Americans should be kept in slavery for their own good, Dr. Smith demolished Calhoun's argument.

Calhoun argued that the recent census listed certain towns as having several mentally ill African American residents. Dr. Smith calmly compared the census findings with actual population statistics and discovered that there were no African American people at all in some of the towns. Dr. Smith proved that the director of the census, who was a friend of Calhoun's, had simply made up the census figures to support pro-slavery arguments.

One observer noted several months later that as a result of Smith's replies to the senator, "we have heard nothing [more] about Calhoun's learned argument."

The Civil War that Smith and the others prepared themselves for began in 1861 and ended in 1865, the year Smith died. He had lived long enough to see the end of slavery.

Chapter Fifty-One
Major Martin Robinson Delaney

(1812 - 1885)

Martin Robison Delany was born free in Charlestown, Virginia (now West Virginia). His father, Samuel Delany, was an African American slave. His mother, Pali Peace Delany, was a free African American woman.

They taught him to be proud of his grandfathers: an African chieftain on his father's side and an African prince on his mother's side. Both had been captured, sold to slavers, and brought to America.

Young Martin was eager to go to school. It was against the law for any African American person to learn to read or write, because slave owners feared that educated African American people would find a way to gain their freedom.

Pali Delany, however, was determined that their children would be educated. She arranged for a northern peddler to teach Martin and his four siblings. When her European American neighbors discovered that her children could read, she was threatened with imprisonment.

Mrs. Delany hurriedly moved the family to Pennsylvania. Samuel Delany eventually bought his freedom and joined his family. When Martin was nineteen, he hiked across the Allegheny Mountains to live in Pittsburgh so he could attend night school in the basement of the African Methodist Episcopal Church.

Martin made Pittsburgh his home. In 1843, Delany married Catherine Richards, and the couple had seven children: six sons and a daughter. True to his pride in his heritage, Delany named each of the children after an African American person in history.

The sons were named after Toussaint L'Ouverture, Charles Lenox Remond, Alexandre Dumas, Saint Cyprian, Faustin Soulouque, and Rameses Placido, while the daughter was named Ethiopia Haile Delany.

At first, Martin worked as a journalist. He founded *The Mystery,* a weekly newspaper that fought for equal rights for African American people and women. It was the first African American newspaper west of the Allegheny Mountains. After *The Mystery* folded in 1847, Delaney joined the abolitionist newspaper *North Star,* as co-editor with Frederick Douglass.

Delany toured Ohio, Michigan, and several eastern states to gather news and subscribers for the paper. He sent back letters every week, which Douglass published, describing the lives of the free African American people he met. Once, in a village in Ohio, Delany was almost lynched by a pro-slavery mob.

During those years, Delany joined the Pittsburgh Anti-Slavery Society and the Underground Railroad, where he risked his life to help fugitive slaves escape.

The *North Star* could not support two editors, however, so Delany left. Finding himself unemployed, the journalist decided to study medicine. His applications to New York and Pennsylvania medical schools were rejected, but in 1850 he was admitted to the medical school of Harvard College.

Delany studied medicine for one term, but was not allowed to continue after pro-slavery students passed a resolution condemning his presence. He nevertheless managed to become a physician later by apprenticing under sympathetic European American doctors in Pittsburgh.

In 1854, just three years after being banned from Harvard, Dr. Delany was praised for his service during a cholera epidemic in Pittsburgh, and was also asked to advise European American authorities about the medical needs of poor African Americans and European Americans.

He would go on to practice medicine for the next thirty-five years, combining the healing of sick bodies with an equal determination to cure the ills of slavery and injustice.

Meanwhile, the seemingly timeless Delany had organized resistance to the Fugitive Slave Act of 1850, moved briefly to Canada where he helped abolitionist John Brown contact possible recruits for an anti-slavery guerrilla army, and traveled back and forth across the country speaking against slavery.

Delany believed fervently in the achievements and hopes of African Americans. But he was becoming increasingly pessimistic about the future. He was disappointed by the failure of European American abolitionists to protest his expulsion from Harvard. He also felt that the security of every African American man, woman, and child in the United States was threatened by the Fugitive Slave Act, which made it illegal for anyone to refuse to help return a fugitive slave to captivity.

Delany decided it was probably not possible that African American people would ever be accepted as equals in American society. He began to believe they would be better off in another land and should consider emigrating. With typical energy, he set out to find a way to make a new life in Africa for African Americans.

In April of 1861, the Civil War exploded between the North and the South. Dr. Delany suddenly had reason to hope for a better future for African Americans. He joined Frederick Douglass in trying to persuade President Abraham Lincoln to enlist African American men as soldiers, but Lincoln refused. Finally, in 1863, Lincoln changed his mind and gave permission for Massachusetts to raise the all-African American Fifty-fourth Massachusetts Volunteer Regiment.

Dr. Delany was one of the recruits for the regiment, along with Douglass and several other African American abolitionists.

Delany's son Toussaint L'Ouverture joined the regiment, as did Douglass's sons, Lewis and Charles. Delany himself was commissioned a major in the 104th U.S. Colored Troops in 1865, making him the first African American staff officer in the United States Army.

He spent most of his military career recruiting for the 104th and 105th regiments in South Carolina.

Delany pursued several careers that earned him a reputation as a great crusader against slavery. In 1854, Dr. Delany organized the National Emigration Convention in Cleveland, Ohio, consisting of more than one hundred African American men and women.

In 1858, the convention chose Delany as chief commissioner of an expedition to Africa's Niger River Valley. His mission was to find land for a settlement for African Americans. In Ahbeokuta, a city-state in present-day Nigeria, the *alake* (king) signed a treaty with Delany giving members of "the African race in America" the right to start a self-governing colony.

Delany returned to the United States in 1861 and wrote the *Official Report of the Niger Valley Exploring Party*. The convention failed to sign up settlers for the colony in Ahbeokuta after all.

Dr. Delany, however, would become famous as the Father of Black Nationalism.

After the war, Delany remained in South Carolina where he became an assistant commissioner in the Freedmen's Bureau, which was established to help ex-slaves.

He had moved his family to the campus of Wilberforce University in Xenia, Ohio, during the war. They continued to live there while he worked in South Carolina for the Freedmen's Bureau. Delany later became active in politics, running unsuccessfully in 1874 for lieutenant governor in South Carolina.

Major Delany turned his restless, inquiring mind to other pursuits. In 1879, he published *Principia of Ethnology: The Origin of Races and Color.* The book was a blend of archaeology, anthropology, and biblical history. He also wrote a novel called *Blake.*

Delany left the South in 1880, still dreaming of returning to Africa as soon as his children were self-supporting. But that dream would never become a reality. He tried unsuccessfully to obtain a government appointment in Washington, then finally rejoined his family at Wilberforce, where he died on January 24, 1885. He was seventy-three years old.

Dr. Martin Robison Delany could boast of many accomplishment in a lifetime of striving, but perhaps his most lasting legacy to African Americans was the one he felt most strongly: unflagging pride of race and self in a land where both were under constant attack.

Douglass once said of the grandson of an African chieftain and an African prince, "I thank God for making me a man, but Delany thanks him for making him an 'African American' man."

Chapter Fifty-Two

John S. Rock, M.D.

(1825 - 1866)

D r. John S. Rock was typical of African American doctors such as Martin Delany who combined their practice of medicine with the struggle against slavery and discrimination.

Rock was born to free parents in Salem, New Jersey, and they were able to send him to the Salem public schools. After graduating, he taught in a one-room schoolhouse and gave private lessons. But he had a bigger dream for himself.

During this same period, 1844 to 1848, the young teacher was studying medicine with two European American doctors. At last he was ready to enter medical school. To his disappointment, he was turned down because of his race.

He then studied dentistry under a European American dentist. Finally, in 1852, Rock succeeded in getting an M.D. degree. It is not certain what school he attended, but it was probably the American Medical College in Philadelphia, which was only a few years old at the time.

Dr. Rock then moved to Massachusetts, where he was admitted to the state's medical society. He gained prominence in his new home in the 1850s, as an abolitionist who helped fugitive slaves. Working with a vigilance committee that met in the home of African American abolitionist Lewis Hayden, Dr. Rock gave his medical services to sick fugitives.

He was also active in a campaign that resulted in the desegregation of Boston's public schools in 1855.

Difficulty in speaking led him to undergo an operation of his throat. The operation helped some, but Rock decided to seek further relief in France. When Secretary of State Lewis Cass ruled that African American people could not receive passports because they were not considered citizens, Massachusetts granted Rock a passport and he spent eight months in France, studying the language and literature, and undergoing another throat operation.

Upon his return to the United States, he again launched into the struggle against slavery and the concept of African American inferiority. Far from being inferior, Rock declared in one of his many speeches denouncing the treatment of African Americans, "Black is Beautiful."

In an 1858 speech given to commemorate Crispus Attucks Day, celebrating the African American Revolutionary War hero, Rock predicted the Civil War. He declared that "sooner or later the lashing of arms will be heard in this country and the African American man's services will be needed."

By the end of 1863, there were more than sixty all-African American regiments in the Union army. Before the war was over, almost 190,000 men would serve in more than 140 African American regiments, officially labeled United States Colored Troops (U.S.C.T.). Approximately 38,000 of them died.

African American soldiers suffered a casualty rate 35 percent greater than that of European American soldiers, due in large part to a lack of medical care for the sick and wounded. European American doctors usually refused to serve in African American units, and African American doctors were turned down when they tried to volunteer.

The clashing of arms came in 1861, and Dr. John Rock joined other African American leaders in trying to persuade officials to accept African American men in the military. Lincoln's initial refusal to allow them to enlist led Rock to declare: "I confess I do not understand how it is, that when the national life has been assailed, he had not availed himself of all the powers given him…"

When Lincoln finally gave permission for Massachusetts to form the all African American Fifty-fourth Volunteer Regiment, an eager Rock became one of its principal recruiters.

He also helped recruit the all-African American Fifty-fifth Infantry Regiment, and spoke out against the practice of paying African American soldiers less than European American soldiers. His voice, along with those of other African American abolitionists and a few European American ones, helped reverse the policy of unequal pay.

As the Civil War dragged on, Rock's struggles against legal racial discrimination finally convinced him that he needed to become a lawyer as well as a doctor. This decision resulted in his making history in 1865, when he became the first African American admitted to practice law before the U.S. Supreme Court.

Following that triumph, Rock was given a welcome on the floor of the House of Representatives. The welcome was probably the first time an African American lawyer was accorded that honor. Preparing to return to Boston, however, Rock was arrested at the Washington train station for not having the pass that all African American people were required to carry. But this incident was turned into a victory when Rep. James A. Garfield of Ohio (later to become the nation's twentieth president) introduced a bill that ended the pass system.

Rock's health had bothered him since his throat trouble years before, and now it deteriorated rapidly, finally ending in tuberculosis. He died in his mother's home in Boston on December 3, 1866.

Dr. John S. Rock was only forty-one years old when he died. He had worn himself out in the struggle for racial equality. "I believe in the equality of my people," he once said. And his short but fervent life was proof of that belief.

Chapter Fifty-Three
Dr. Alexander T. Augusta

(1825 - 1890)

Alexander Augusta was a native of Norfolk, Virginia. Though born free, he had to struggle for an education . For example, he learned to read in secret because Virginia law forbade teaching any African American person to read. His teacher was Daniel Payne, who later became a bishop of the African Methodist Episcopal Church.

As a young man, Augusta moved to Baltimore where he earned his living as a barber. He used his earnings to pay for tutoring in medicine. Hoping to become a doctor, Augusta moved to Philadelphia to enroll in the University of Pennsylvania's medical school. To his surprise, he was rejected. Yet all was not lost. Professor William Gibson of the medical school allowed Augusta to study medicine in his office.

Still determined to earn a medical degree, Augusta moved to California where he earned more money for his education, but again was unable to gain acceptance to a school. Like Dr. James McCune Smith and many other African American doctors in the nineteenth century, he finally traveled to a foreign school: The University of Toronto's Trinity Medical College in Canada.

Enrolling in 1850, Augusta graduated in 1856 with a Bachelor of Medicine degree. He stayed in Toronto for approximately six years, conducting a private practice and heading the Toronto City Hospital. After a while, he quit the hospital in order to direct an industrial school. He continued his private practice in Canada, while gaining skills as an administrator.

A few months after the Civil War broke out, Augusta tried to join the Union army's volunteer medical service. Like other African American doctors, he was turned down, but he refused to be discouraged. Finally, he appealed directly to President Lincoln, after Lincoln gave permission for African American men to serve.

"I was compelled to leave my native country,…on account of prejudice against colour, for the purpose of obtaining a knowledge of my profession," he wrote the president on January 7, 1863, "and having accomplished that object…I would like to be in a position where I can be of use to my race."

A month after finally being commissioned, Augusta boarded a train in his native land dressed in his uniform with the oak-leaf straps of a major. He was immediately attacked by several men enraged at the sight of an African American officer. They punched him and tore off one of the straps.

Augusta got off the train and went to the nearest provost guard. He was escorted back to the station by soldiers and a squad of detectives. Even with such protection, however, Augusta was attacked again. He was finally seated on the train only when his escorts drew their revolvers.

When the Army Medical Board turned down Dr. Augusta's request to serve in the Union army, he journeyed from Toronto to Washington, D.C., to plead his case.

"I have come near a thousand miles at a great expense and sacrifice," he wrote to President Lincoln and the medical board, "hoping to be of some use to the country and my race/culture at this eventful period."

Finally, on April 14, 1863, the board found Augusta "qualified for the position of Surgeon" with a rank equivalent to that of a Major. August would later be promoted to Lieutenant Colonel, making him the highest ranking African American officer in the Civil War.

Augusta was assigned to the Seventh U.S.C.T. The Seventh would go on to fight in ten major battles, including Deep Bottom, James Island, Bermuda Hundreds, Chapin's Farm, Petersburg, and Richmond.

But Doctor Augusta spent only a few months with the regiment. He was transferred after six European American surgeons and assistant surgeons, who were all commissioned after Augusta, wrote President Lincoln: "Judge our Surprise and disappointment, when upon joining our respective regiments [the letter writers were assigned to the Seventh, Ninth, and Nineteenth U.S.C.T.] we found that the *Senior Surgeon* of the command was an African American.

"....Such degradation, we believe to be involved, in our voluntarily continuing in the Service, as Subordinates to an African American officer. We therefore most respectfully yet earnestly, request, that this *unexpected, unusual,* and most unpleasant relationship in which we have been placed, may in *some way* be terminated. "

Lincoln did not respond to the letter, but Augusta was transferred to Baltimore to examine African American recruits. He retained his rank as surgeon in the Seventh, however, leading to more protests from European American officers who were blocked from advancement because he outranked them.

Augusta's transfer from the regiment helped him make medical history. He was appointed to run Camp Barker, the forerunner of Freedmen's Hospital in Washington, D.C., thereby becoming the first African American person in the United States to direct a hospital.

The hospital was necessary because thousands of escaped slaves sought refuge in the nation's capital, where they lived in overcrowded shelters rampant with disease. Out of an estimated 31,500 African Americans in Washington and its environs, almost 23,000 needed medical treatment.

Camp Barker was opened on a temporary basis to help these "freedmen" and, in 1868, Freedmen's Hospital was established to permanently "care for the national needs of African Americans who because of the lack of facilities, were inadequately cared for in their respective states."

At least 1 million African American patients were treated by both African American and European American doctors in the more than one hundred hospitals and dispensaries set up by the Freedmen's Bureau during the Civil War, including Camp Barker. When the war ended, African American doctors and nurses were more desperately needed than ever—a need the hospitals and dispensaries of the Freedmen's Bureau had partially filled during the war.

Augusta spent several months after the war in charge of a hospital in Savannah, Georgia, where "medical gentlemen of the first eminence in that city…often came to the hospital to observe cases interesting to the profession, and to join with him in uncommon surgical operations."

In 1868, Augusta was elected to the faculty of the newly organized medical department of Howard University to teach anatomy, becoming the first African American faculty member in an American medical school. Augusta also served on the staff of Freedmen's hospital until 1877.

Despite Augusta's qualifications and accomplishments, he and other African American physicians were refused admission to the Medical Society of the District of Columbia. The refusal was especially painful for him because he knew that such racial obstacles would become widespread and hinder young African American doctors in the future.

Augusta left Freedmen's in 1877 to set up a private practice in Washington. He maintained the practice until his death on December 21, 1890.

Dr. Alexander T. Augusta was buried in Arlington National Cemetery, the final resting place of so many of the nation's heroes. It was a fitting honor for the man who had been so determined to serve his country and his people.

Chapter Fifty-Four
Susie King Taylor

(1848 - 1912)

During the Civil War, countless African American women served as nurses to soldiers. The nurses were paid only what they could earn by doing odd jobs around the camps. Susie King (later to become Susie King Taylor) is one of those rare African American Civil War nurses whose name has come down to us.

Born into slavery in Georgia in 1848, to Hagar Ann Reed and Raymond Baker, Susie spent the first years of her life on the Isle of Wight, just off the coast of Georgia. When she was seven, she was given permission by her owners to move to Savannah, where she lived with her grandmother.

There Susie learned to read and write, in spite of the fact that such learning was illegal and carried the threat of whipping for any African American child who was caught. Harsh penalties were also imposed on any adult who taught African Americans to read.

But just as Dr. Martin Delany's mother had found a northern peddler to educate him, Susie King Taylor's grandmother found a neighbor who was willing to educate Susie; a free African American woman who ran a secret school for African American children.

"We went every day about nine o'clock, with our books wrapped in paper to prevent the police or European American persons from seeing them," Susie said of her trips to the secret school with her brother. "We went in, one at a time, through the gate…After school we left the same way we entered, one by one…"

Susie also studied with an African American nun named Mary Beasley and with two European American youngsters who were willing to teach her. She often used her newfound knowledge to write passes in the name of her grandmother's employer, helping her grandmother to evade the curfew that applied to African American people. According to Susie, "all African American persons, free or slaves, were compelled to have a pass…for at nine o'clock each night a bell was rung, and any African American persons found on the street after this hour were arrested by the watchman, and put in the guard-house until next morning.."

Shortly after the Civil War began, Susie joined her uncle's family in escaping to St. Catherine's Island, which was under Union control. She then moved to St. Simons Island and established a school for African American children and adults. Many of the men on St. Simons were recruited to serve in the all-African American First South Carolina Volunteers (later renamed the Thirty-third U.S. Colored Troops). The regiment was composed almost entirely of escaped slaves. It is recognized as the first African American regiment officially mustered into the Union army. (The Fifty-fourth "Glory" Regiment, officially called the Fifty-fourth Massachusetts Volunteer Regiment, was the first all-African American regiment mustered in the North.)

In 1862, fourteen-year-old Susie married Sergeant Edward King, one of the new recruits from St. Simons, and journeyed with him to camp. The new Mrs. King spent most of her time teaching the soldiers in her husband's Company E to read and write "when they were off duty. Nearly all were anxious to learn…" She also washed their clothes, ran a school for children, and even learned how to fire a musket. But her biggest desire was "to care for the sick and afflicted comrades."

She soon received an opportunity to care for many wounded soldiers. In January 1863, almost 500 members of the regiment sailed on a raid up the St. Mary's River, which divides Georgia and Florida. "Braver men never lived," the regimental surgeon declared after seeing them rout a Confederate cavalry unit. "One man with two bullet-holes through the large muscles of the shoulders and neck brought off from the scene of action, two miles distant, two muskets; and not a murmur escaped his lips."

Whenever the wounded men returned to camp, Susie King would hurry to the regimental hospital. There she met Clara Barton, future founder of the American Red Cross. "Miss Barton was always very cordial toward me, and I honored her for her devotion and care for those men,"

Mrs. King said years later. The two women often made the rounds of the hospital together nursing the men and doing whatever they could to make the soldiers comfortable.

In February 1865, the First South Carolina was ordered into Charleston as Confederate soldiers set fire to the city and fled.

In 1863, after the famous attack of the Fifty-fourth Massachusetts on Fort Wagner, South Carolina, with its terrible loss of life, Clara Barton said she watched "the wounded, slowly crawling to me down the tide-washed beach...I can see again the scarlet flow of blood as it rolled over the black limbs beneath my hands, and the great heave of the human heart before it grew still."

"It seems strange how our aversion to seeing suffering is overcome in war, "Susie King said of her experiences treating these and other African American soldiers. "How we are able to see the sickening sights... and instead of turning away, how we hurry to assist in allevi-ating their pain, bind up their wounds, and press the cool water to their parched lips, with feelings only of sympathy and pity."

The African American soldiers extinguished the fires while European American residents jeered them and African American residents cheered them. When Major Martin Delany spoke at Zion Church, the city's largest African American congregation, thousands of people packed the pews, aisles, and doorways to hear him. Men, women, and children even came to his room at night to see an African American man wearing the uniform of a United States Army officer. Sick and wounded soldiers were moved into a mansion in the city, and Susie continued to nurse them until the regiment was mustered out on February 9, 1866.

The young woman who was only thirteen years old when the war began spent four years and three months nursing the men she always remembered fondly as her "comrades." She never received a penny for her work, but took joy in being able to help the suffering.

Susie and her husband moved to Savannah in early 1866, where she "opened a school at my home on South Broad Street…as there was not any public school for African American children."

"I had twenty children at my school, and received one dollar a month for each pupil." She was forced to lose the school after about a year when a free school took most of her students.

Sergeant King, who was an excellent carpenter, could not get much work because of racial prejudice. He died in September 1866, leaving the pregnant Susie "to welcome a little stranger alone."

In the years to come, Mrs. King supported herself and her child by doing laundry and cooking. In 1879, she married Russell L. Taylor, but almost nothing is known about her second husband. She made her home in Boston, where she received letters from some of "the comrades" and was pleased to learn that "all are doing well."

In February 1898, she traveled to Shreveport, Louisiana, where her son lay seriously ill. The "little stranger" Sergeant King never saw was now an actor, in town to appear in a play called *The Lion's Bride*. Susie wanted to take him back to Boston, but he was too weak to sit up all the way, and the European American railroad employees refused to sell her a sleeper ticket.

"It seemed very hard," Susie said, "when his father fought to protect the Union and our flag, and yet this boy was denied, under this same flag, a berth to carry him home to die, because he was a Negro." Her son died a few weeks after her arrival, and she returned to Boston alone.

In 1902, Susie King Taylor published her autobiography, *Reminiscences of My Life in Camp: A Black Woman's Civil War Memoirs*. "I sometimes ask, 'Was the war in vain?'" she wrote, referring to the treatment of her son and of African Americans in general. "Has it brought freedom, in the full sense of the word, or has it not made our condition more hopeless?"

Susie King Taylor died in 1912, just ten years after her book came out. But despite all she had been through and the pain she had experienced, she still expressed hope for a better tomorrow.

"Justice we ask," she declared, "to be citizens of the United States, where so many of our people have shed their blood with their European American comrades, that the stars and stripes should never be polluted."

Chapter Fifty-Five

Rebecca Lee (Crumpler), M.D.

(1833 - ?)

In 1849, Elizabeth Blackwell became the first woman to graduate from an American medical school. The daughter of English immigrants who held strong abolitionist views, Blackwell was an outspoken advocate of racial equality and tried to open up the medical profession to African American women.

It was another fifteen years, however, before the first African American woman graduated from a medical school in the United States: thirty-year-old Rebecca Lee (Crumpler).

Lee had dreamed of becoming a doctor since childhood. The aunt who raised her was a healer in their Pennsylvania community. Though Rebecca's aunt was not formally trained, the relief she was able to bring the sick made a powerful and permanent impression on her young niece.

"I early conceived a liking for and sought every opportunity to be in a position to relieve the suffering of others," Dr. Lee remembered toward the end of her life.

From 1852 to 1860, she worked as a nurse in Massachusetts. The people she nursed were so impressed by her ability that they recommended her to the Female Medical College. She was awarded the Doctoress of Medicine degree from Boston's New England Female Medical College in 1864.

The Civil War ended soon after she graduated from college, and the eager young doctor moved to Richmond, Virginia, to help treat thousands of the newly freed African Americans. There she encountered obstacles based on both race and sex, but was determined to succeed.

In 1867, Rebecca Cole (1846-1922) became the second African American woman to graduate from an American medical school, receiving her degree from the Female Medical College of Pennsylvania (now known as the Medical College of Pennsylvania).

After graduation, Cole went to work as resident physician at the New York Infirmary for Indigent Women and Children. Founded in 1854 by Elizabeth Blackwell, her sister Emily, and Dr. Marie Zakrzewska, the infirmary was established because female doctors in the United States were routinely barred from practicing in hospitals, which were all controlled by males.

In 1867, Elizabeth Blackwell hired Rebecca Cole as resident physician. Cole quickly recognized the close connection between poverty and illness. Whereas many doctors believed that high mortality rates among the poor were due to ignorance, Cole blamed slumlords for creating the crowded conditions that led to sickness and death.

The twenty-one-year-old doctor was soon assigned by Blackwell to visit families in the slums, in what was the first medical social service program in the country. This position of "sanitary visitor" perfectly suited Cole who loved teaching poor mothers how to take better care of their families despite the conditions they were forced to live in.

Cole worked in the infirmary for several years, then became superintendent of the Home for Destitute Colored Women and Children in

Washington, D.C. She eventually moved to Philadelphia (her birthplace), where she opened an office, directed a residence for the homeless, and joined with fellow physician Charlotte Abby to establish a center that provided both medical and legal services to poor women and children.

Dr. Rebecca Cole died in Philadelphia on August 14, 1922, after a career of helping the poor than spanned more than fifty years.

Druggists refused to fill her prescriptions, male doctors snubbed her, and jokes were made that the M.D. stood for "Mule Driver." Dr. Lee persevered, and, in the years to come, became widely respected for her devotion to the study of diseases afflicting women and children.

After several years in Richmond, Dr. Lee moved back to Boston. She had kept personal journals throughout her career and, in 1883, published a book based on the journals: *A book of Medical Discourses in Two Parts.* The book offered medical advice to women on how best to care for themselves and their children.

It is not known when or where this African American pioneer died, but countless people were helped because of her desire to relieve the suffering of others.

Chapter Fifty-Six
Charles Burleigh Purvis, M.D.

(1842 - 1929)

In the 1870s and 1880s, something had to be done if the masses of African American people were to have any hope of receiving adequate medical treatment.

Death rates of African American adults in the South were routinely twice as high as those of European American adults, while the mortality rate of African American children under the age of five was often three times as high as that of European American children. In many southern communities, one-quarter to one-third of the former slaves had died by the mid-1870s.

Determined to do all they could to provide better treatment for their underserved people, African American doctors began to found their own hospitals, professional societies, and medical schools. From 1882 to 1900, they opened six medical schools in the South and trained approximately 1,000 doctors. Although many of these doors to education would close in the twentieth century, this was a brave beginning of a new era.

One of the men who would train African American doctors, as well as one of the most remarkable physicians in the United States in the last half of the nineteenth century, was Dr. Charles Burleigh Purvis. Purvis was one of eight children born to Harriet Forten, daughter of abolitionist, inventor, and businessman James Forten Sr., and Robert Purvis Sr., wealthy abolitionist and civil rights leader.

Charles's father was a founder of the American Anti-Slavery Society, while his mother was a founder of the Female Anti-Slavery Society. The determination of his parents to end racial injustice as passed on to Charles, who would spend his adult life as a doctor, medical educator, and hospital administrator proving that "brain development knows no race, or complexion."

Charles attended Quaker schools in Bayberry, Pennsylvania, for his early education. He also learned much from the prominent anti-slavery leaders who were frequent guests in his parents' home.

When Charles was eighteen, his parents sent him to Oberlin College in Ohio, where he studied from 1860 to 1863. He then enrolled in Wooster Medical College (later renamed Western Reserve Medical School) in Cleveland. During the summer of 1864, he worked as a military nurse at Camp Barker, which Dr. Augusta had directed a few months earlier, and saw firsthand how desperately the ex-slaves needed medical care.

Purvis graduated from Wooster Medical College in 1865. His experiences at Camp Barker may have led to his next step: enlisting in the Union army as an acting assistant surgeon. Purvis served in the Union army from 1865 to 1869, spending most of his time treating sick freedmen in Washington, D.C. He was one of only six African American physicians in the city.

After serving in the Union army for four years, he was appointed to the medical faculty of Howard University, joining Dr. Augusta. That made them the only African American teachers of medicine in the United States. Dr. Purvis's reputation grew quickly. He was a major influence at the school for the next fifty-seven years.

Medical schools need a great deal of money to keep their doors open. During the national financial crisis of 1873, the Howard University board of trustees announced that the university medical school might have to close its doors. It could no longer pay its professors.

"While I regret the University will not be able to pay me for my services," Dr. Charles Purvis wrote Howard president Oliver O. Howard, "I feel the importance of every effort being made to carry forward the Institution and to make it a success.

Charles Purvis, Alexander Augusta, and one other faculty member stayed on as volunteers. These courageous doctors went on to train more than half the African American doctors of their era. For thirty-three years, Dr. Purvis taught at Howard while receiving virtually no salary. His generous personal sacrifice saved the medical school.

Purvis was known as a harsh taskmaster. He demanded that his students and colleagues keep abreast of the latest medical developments, and was impatient with anyone who did not meet his exacting standards. As a result Purvis was greatly respected but also feared as "a very ferocious man who barked rather than spoke."

On July 2, 1881, when President James A. Garfield was shot by an assassin at the Washington train station, Purvis was the first physician to treat the mortally wounded man. That action helped lead to Purvis's appointment a few months later as surgeon in chief of Freedmen's Hospital, making him the first African American to head a civilian hospital. (Dr. Augusta had been in charge of a military hospital).

Purvis served at Freedmen's for almost twelve years, overseeing its growth in both size and importance. Under his leadership, the hospital became the teaching hospital for Howard University. It served thousands of patients a year, including a growing number from southern states who were denied admission to local hospitals because of their race.

360

Always the warrior for racial equality Purvis joined with Dr. Alexander Augusta in 1869 to fight the American Medical Association's European Americans-only membership policy. It was a fight that African American doctors would not win until decades after Purvis had died. "We are all Americans, European Americans and African Americans…," Purvis declared. "As African Americans nothing is demanded, as American citizens every enjoyment and opportunity is demanded."

Purvis moved to Boston in 1905 and was admitted to the Massachusetts Medical Society. He resigned from the faculty of the Howard Medical School in 1907, but remained on its board of trustees until 1926.

Dr. Charles Burleigh Purvis died on January 30, 1929, in Los Angeles, California. He had spent sixty-five of his eighty-seven years training doctors and fighting for better medical care for African Americans.

Part Nine

African American Musicians

Eleanora E. Tate

Introduction

America's major musical gifts to the world were created in African American neighborhoods. These gifts include spirituals, gospels, ragtime, blues, jazz, rhythm and blues, rock and roll, even hip-hop. All found their beginnings in the homes and communities in the United States where the sons and daughters of Africa lived:

In Georgia's slave quarters. In Tennessee's sharecropper shanties. On Harlem's 125 Street, and in New Orleans's Storyville red-light district. On Kansas City's Eighteenth and Vine and Memphis's Beale Street. In Alabama's cotton and tobacco fields, the Mississippi Delta, and Florida and Texas juke joints.

In New York brownstones, Philadelphia and Harlem churches, and Baltimore row houses. On St. Louis Mississippi River levees, in Chicago's South Side public housing projects, and in proper middle-class parlors east, west, north, and south. Wonderful music emerged from the artists living in or escaping from these environments.

Wherever African American musicians went, their music retained their unique flavorings of home, love, God, and hope and carried their messages to the world. Their musical expressions give us a unique perspective on American history from its beginnings to the present day.

African American music began with African people's unconquerable spirit and will to survive in a new land despite enslavement. Slave traders who ripped the sons and daughters of Africa from their beds and villages also separated them from most of their physical belongings. Most had to leave without even a comb.

But the African's drum was allowed to come; the slave traders thought music and dancing would keep their stolen cargo happy and docile. When they discovered that the drum was the major means of communication among the Africans, whose many languages kept them apart, the drum, too, was banned.

But even without a physical drum, these heroic peoples kept the memories of their families and their music with them. Their bodies and their voices became their musical instruments until they could build their own again. They also found spiritual sustenance in memories of their traditional Gods, and in the promise of freedom through the God they were taught to worship in America.

Strengthened spiritually and mentally by their memories and new beliefs, they were able to endure and survive their troubles by praising their God through song, with rhythm supplied by clapping their hands and moving their feet. Those songs became "plantation songs," "slave songs," "jubilee songs," work songs and spirituals, created by many unknown individuals inspired by God and biblical stories.

Slave holders who allowed their slaves to worship as Christians tried to control how they did it. But determined to sing and "hold praise in their own way," slaves would "huddle behind soaking wet quilts and rags that had been hung to form a sort of tabernacle" to muffle the sound. Other times, they would "take an iron pot or kettle, turn it upside down, place it in the middle of the cabin floor or at the door step, then prop it up slightly to hold the sound .

The oldest African American music is the most enduring. It contains the most compelling messages for freedom. Spirituals such as "Go Down, Moses"; "Didn't My Lord Deliver Daniel?"; "Swing Low,

Sweet Chariot", "Steal Away"'; and "This Little Light of Mine" were "seeking-emancipation songs" from slavery. African Americans developed this music during colonial times and during the Civil War years.

But even after emancipation, they were not really free. So the spirituals remained as meaningful as they were beautiful. African American musicians like the Fisk Jubilee Singers and concert singers like Matilda Joyner (also know as Sissieretta Jones) made these songs popular with a wide audience outside the South following the Civil War.

Deep into the twentieth century, great African American singers such as Roland Hayes, Paul Robeson, Marian Anderson, and Jessye Norman kept the old songs alive in concerts and churches. Some of the spirituals became the "freedom songs" of the civil rights movements of the 1950s and 1960s.

Along the way, African Americans invented new musical forms. When slave songs, spirituals, work songs, and chants came together at the turn of the century, the new sounds of gospel, ragtime, and blues were born. African Americans continued to improvise and create new ways of expressing themselves through their music, and in modern times have given us the unforgettable sounds of jazz, rock and roll, soul, and rap.

Throughout history, African American musicians contributed to many of the musical traditions of the world. Some of the earliest African American musicians performed European classical music. You will find African American musicians bringing their unique talents to classical music today as well as to Latin-flavored music and all types of American popular music.

Chapter Fifty-Seven
Elizabeth Taylor Greenfield

(1809 - 1876)

Among the earliest African Americans to make a splash in American music was Elizabeth Taylor Greenfield. Despite the absence of an African American role model in concert music, this dedicated star became known around the world as an "African nightingale" for her remarkable singing voice.

Elizabeth Greenfield was born in Natchez, Mississippi, in 1809 to an enslaved couple named Taylor. Elizabeth's father was a native African. He and Elizabeth's mother lived on the homestead of Mrs. Holliday Greenfield, a wealthy woman from Philadelphia, Pennsylvania.

Although Mrs. Greenfield was a Quaker, she owned slaves. When she decided to move back to Pennsylvania, she freed Elizabeth's parents and sent them to Liberia, but she kept baby Elizabeth. The child lived with Mrs. Greenfield for several years, then moved in with one of her own relatives, Mary Parker.

At a young age Elizabeth showed "a propensity for singing and probably did so at her local church." By the time Elizabeth was in her late teens, she had a basic understanding of music and was probably amazing her friends with her songs. In the meantime, Mrs. Greenfield had grown old. At Mrs. Greenfield's request, Elizabeth became her companion and live-in housekeeper, but she never stopped singing.

One of Mrs. Greenfield's neighbors, Miss Price, heard Elizabeth singing and was so impressed that she gave Elizabeth music lessons. Miss Price's interest in Elizabeth was valuable because it introduced Elizabeth to other European Americans who encouraged her with her music.

With Mrs. Greenfield's support, Elizabeth began singing at private parties in the Philadelphia area. Mrs. Greenfield died in the mid-1840s. Her will stated that $1,500 was to be set aside for the return of Elizabeth's mother from Liberia, and that $100 was to be given annually to Elizabeth throughout her lifetime. Mrs. Greenfield's relatives and attorneys, however, contested the will so vigorously that Elizabeth never received any money.

But the young songstress persevered. In 1849, Elizabeth received her first "break." A prominent Philadelphia musician and bandmaster hired her to sing in Baltimore. While in Baltimore, she also looked for jobs as a music teacher. When she heard that the "Swedish nightingale" Jenny Lind was scheduled to sing in Buffalo, New York, in 1851, Greenfield began saving her money to pay for her travel there. While on a boat en route to Buffalo, she met and sang for Buffalo resident Mrs. H. B. Potter, who invited her to sing for her friends at her Buffalo mansion.

A group of Buffalo residents sponsored Elizabeth in a series of concerts for the Buffalo Music Association. The first concert was held October 22, 1851. The concerts were so successful that Elizabeth was nicknamed the "Black Swan" after Jenny Lind. Greenfield went on to sing in non-slaveholding states and in Canada. She was a soprano whose range was over three and one-fourth octaves. She often amazed her audiences by singing the song "Old Folks at Home" first as a soprano, and then as a baritone.

Despite her popularity, Greenfield suffered many instances of racism in the North. On March 31, 1853, for example, she was scheduled to sing at the Metropolitan Hall in New York before 4,000 people. No other African American people were allowed.

Someone threatened to "burn the house" if a "African American woman sang" there. Police had to be brought in to protect the building. Greenfield sang, even though she was frightened.

Mindful of the exclusion of her own people, she gave a follow-up concert to help the Home of Aged Colored Persons and the Colored Orphan Asylum.

That same year, she went to London, England, to sing, but had problems with the promoter over money. Author Harriet Beecher Stowe, who was in town at the same time to publicize her book *Uncle Tom's Cabin,* went to hear her sing. Stowe helped introduce Greenfield to the Duchess of Sutherland and to Sir George Smart, the Queen of England's musician.

This led to more concerts, and Greenfield also received musical training from Sir George. On May 10, 1854, she gave a command performance at Buckingham Palace for England's Queen Victoria.

Queen Victoria said that Greenfield had "a most wonderful compass of voice, ranging over fully three octaves with fine, clear high notes..."

Upon Greenfield's return to the United States, she continued touring, sang again in Canada, and completed another tour of the northern United States in 1856. Between tours, she taught music to other rising stars in Philadelphia. She stopped touring when anti-African American sentiment rose over the Dred Scott decision and the Civil War began. Her last extended tour was in 1863.

When Elizabeth Taylor Greenfield was not on the road, she was involved in social and religious activities in support of other African

Americans, the homeless, the Freedman's Society, African American churches, and orphans. She died in Philadelphia on March 31, 1876.

Elizabeth Taylor Greenfield not only organized a Black Swan Opera Troupe, but also wrote her autobiography. *The Black Swan at Home and Abroad,* or *A Biographical Sketch of Miss Elizabeth Taylor Greenfield, the American Vocalist.* It was privately printed in 1855.

Chapter Fifty-Eight
Edmund Dede

(1827 - 1903)

Edmund Dede was born in New Orleans on November 20, 1827. His parents were free Creoles of color who had moved to New Orleans from the French West Indies around 1809. New Orleans, an aristocratic city since its earliest days, was an international seaport. Its population was primarily made up of French, English, Spanish, and Italian people, free African American people, and enslaved African Americans.

This variety of ethnic groups made for a rich mix. People of mixed heritage sometimes called themselves Creoles. Even among the Creoles, however, distinctions were made between white Creoles, Creoles of color, and light-skinned and dark-skinned Creoles. Some of the earliest composers of American music had this mixture of New Orleans roots.

Young Edmund, who was a dark-skinned Creole, first took music lessons from his father, a bandmaster for a local military group, and learned how to play the clarinet. He studied violin under Ludovico Gabici, a European American teacher, and Christian Debergue, a free Creole of color. Charles Richard Lambert also instructed young

Edmund. Lambert was a New York-born free African American musician, music teacher, and conductor of the New Orleans Free Creoles of Color Philharmonic Society.

From around 1848 to 1851, Edmund Dede lived in Mexico where he continued his musical education. Because of an illness, Dede returned to his hometown in 1851, where he created and probably published the piece "Mon Pauvre Coeur" (My Poor Heart), known to be the "oldest piece of sheet music by a New Orleans Creole of color."

In 1857, with money saved from his job as a cigar-maker, Dede traveled to England and then to Paris, France, where he entered the Paris Conservatory for advanced musical study. From there, he worked as an orchestra conductor of the 'Alcazar in Bordeaux.

Being in France was much like being back home for Dede because of New Orleans's French roots. Like many other free Louisiana Creoles of color who had moved to France, Dede also experienced less racial prejudice in France than he had in the United States. In 1864, he married a French woman named Sylvie Leflat.

Dede was a popular, prolific musician. While living in Bordeaux, for example, he wrote over 250 dances and songs, as well as numerous comic operas. He was also known for his ballet music, "Ables," "Les Faux Mandarins," and "La Sensitive." His overture "Le Palmier" was performed in New Orleans on August 22, 1865.

He returned to the United States in 1893 to visit relatives. The boat he was on wrecked in rough weather, and he lost his prized Cremona violin. He was rescued with the other passengers and taken to Galveston, Texas, where he was "acclaimed by the best musicians of that section, both European American and African American."

Dede traveled to several American cities, including Chicago, giving violin concerts, before returning to France in 1894. Edmund Dede died in 1903.

Chapter Fifty-Nine
Thomas "Blind Tom" Greene Bethune

(1849 - 1908)

Today, musicians with physical disabilities are acknowledged and respected. In past years, however, a talented musician with a disability was looked upon as an oddity. If the musician was also African American and a slave, he or she was often exploited or, in extreme cases, treated cruelly. But the blind pianist and composer Thomas Green Bethune rose above his limitations.

Bethune was known to millions of Americans and Europeans as "Blind Tom," the "human mockingbird." Tom had no formal schooling on the piano or in music. He would listen to the sounds in the countryside around him, memorize them, and play them back on the piano perfectly. Tom flabbergasted audiences with his talent for over thirty years.

Thomas was born sightless and into slavery to Charity Wiggins on May 25, 1849, on the Wiley Edward Jones plantation near Columbus, Georgia. Thomas, his mother, and his siblings were soon sold to a Columbus plantation owner names James N. Bethune.

As a child, Thomas did not play much with other children. His play-mate was the piano. When he was only four years old, he was discovered at the Bethune family piano, perfectly playing back songs he had heard. The technical term for his ability is "absolute pitch." Tom had a phenomenal musical memory. He would memorize and then re-create notes and songs of all the sounds he had heard from the trees, the wind, and the birds. Some said he could even reproduce the sound of thunder.

His talents shocked everyone, and James Bethune, being a capitalist, declared himself the manager of this "unusual" slave child. By age eight, young Tom was already performing at concerts that his master organized in the Columbus area. Bethune's wife was a music teacher, and she and her daughters would play piano selections by Bach, Bee-thoven, Chopin, Mendelssohn, and others for Thomas to play back. And he did, steadily increasing his repertoire.

In 1858, James Bethune hired Blind Tom out to a Georgia planter named Perry Oliver, who exhibited him as "the musical prodigy of the age: A Plantation Negro Boy." His first known New York concert was on January 15, 1861, just before the outbreak of the Civil War.

Sadly, after the war began, Thomas was forced to give concerts for the same Confederate soldiers who were fighting to keep him and other African Americans enslaved. Blind Tom remained under Bethune's authority even after slavery and the war ended.

Bethune declared himself Tom's legal guardian and continued to collect whatever money the teenager earned.

Wherever Blind Tom played other musicians and nonbelievers in the audience would constantly test his competence. During his concerts, the audience would call out names of selections for him to play.

Blind Tom Bethune knew how to play nearly 7,000 musical selections. He could play all types of music, from marches, dances, operas, and ballads to plantation songs. He even composed his own music, and published some under his name and others under the pseud-onyms J.C. Beckel and Francois Sexalise. His best-known original piece was "Battle of Manassas" named after a Civil War battle.

Many came up on stage and played original work for him to repeat. Each time, Blind Tom would play back perfectly everything he had heard. "Once, while performing at the White House, he played correctly a twenty-page piece a short time after hearing it."

Today, Thomas Bethune would be recognized as a master musician. But in a time when most European Americans believed African Americans to be inferior and less than human, his superior musical abilities made many consider him a freak. Some historians believed he suffered from a form of mental illness. What Thomas Bethune's feelings were about his life may never be known. He never reaped the financial rewards to which he was entitled, but he continued to perform for many years.

He gave concerts throughout America under the legal guardianship of James Bethune. After James Bethune died, his son, and then the son's widow continued to reap the final rewards of Thomas's talents.

Blind Thomas Bethune died in poverty in 1908 in Hoboken, New Jersey. The Bethune family never freed their "human mockingbird." A marker placed where he was born near Columbus, Georgia, is on the list of state historic landmarks.

Chapter Sixty
Millie-Christine McCoy

(1851-1912)

Millie-Christine McCoy (sometimes spelled McKoy) were famous African American Siamese twins who dazzled and amazed the world with their songs. The were known as Millie-Christine.

The twins were born as slaves on July 11, 1851, in the rural Welches Creek community near Whiteville, North Carolina. Their parents, Monemia and Jacob McCoy, were the slaves of plantation owner Jabez McCoy.

McCoy sold the babies for $1,000 to John C. Purvis, who then sold them to J.P. Smith. Over the next several years, greedy European American profiteers kidnapped them at least three times. At one time, the twins were stolen and were missing for three years before Smith finally found them in England. After a lengthy court trial that established Smith as their legal owner, the children were returned to him.

The little girls were subjected to numerous medical examinations. They were joined in the area of the hip and lower spine, but each child had the use of her own arms and legs. They possessed above-average intelligence, and played and acted like other children their age. In conversation, each preferred using "I" rather than "we" when referring to themselves.

Millie-Christine enjoyed private tutors. They learned to dance and sing, and were well educated.

On posters and handbills, they were often billed as the "Carolina Nightingale" or the "United African Twins" with Christine singing soprano and Millie alto. They sang with "rich, sweet voices" such popular songs of their time as "Old Black Joe," "The Whip-poor-will's Song." and "Listen to the Mocking Bird." Millie-Christine were fluent in seven languages and sang not only in English but in French as well.

By the end of the Civil War, Millie-Christine had gained their freedom but kept J.P. Smith as their manager. Circus showman P.T. Barnum was also one of their promoters. At the peak of their singing career, they performed before England's Prince of Wales and Queen Victoria, who was so impressed by their talents that she gave them matching diamond brooches.

They sang before all the royal families of Europe, and visited forty-six American states, at one time earning more than $600 week. When Millie-Christine were not traveling, they lived in a large house they had built on part of the old McCoy family homestead in Welches Creek, where they were born.

Described as charitable, religious, and gentle, Millie-Christine sang at fairs, in circuses, and at special activities until 1880, when they retired from full-time performing. They helped to establish an African American school in the Welches Creek community and gave generously to other North Carolina schools. Warm and friendly to everybody, the twins had special get-togethers with other African Americans on Sunday afternoons on their front porch.

In 1909, their beloved home burned to the ground. The twins lost nearly all of the large collection of memorabilia they had collected on their travels around the world, including the brooches given to them by Queen Victoria. They spent their remaining years in a nearby six-room cottage. On October 8, 1912, at age sixty-one, Millie died of tuberculosis. Christine died several hours later.

Millie-Christine had feared that after their death they would be dissected or placed on exhibit, so they requested that the bodies be cremated. Instead, they were buried in the family cemetery near their home. For nearly a year, guards remained near the cemetery to discourage grave robbers.

Over the years, most people forgot about the famous twins. In 1969, interest in Millie-Christine was renewed. With the assistance of the Columbus County Historical Society, the North Carolina Sate Department of Archives and history, and relatives, the twins' remains were moved during a ceremony to the Welches Creek Community Cemetery, three miles outside of Whiteville. Inscribed on their tombstone are the words "A soul with two thoughts. Two hearts that beat as one."

A historical marker on North Carolina Highway 74-76 outside of Whiteville also honors the twins' achievements.

When Millie-Christine received visitors on their front porch in North Carolina, they liked to recite a poem they had composed about their life. The final lines were

> I'm happy quite, because content,
> For some wise purpose I was sent;
> My Maker knows what he has done,
> Whether I'm created two or one.

References

Reprinted by permission from:

Before The Mayflower: A History Of Black America by Lerone Bennett Jr. - Johnson Publishing Company, Inc., (ISBN# 0-87485-091-6) Copyright (c) 1961, 1969, 1988, by Johnson Publishing Company, Inc. and Lerone Bennett Jr.

Chapter 1) The African Past (Pages 3-26)

Chapter 2) Before The Mayflower (Pages 28-52)

Chapter 4) The Cotton Curtain (Pages 83-105)

Dreams From My Father: A Story of Race and Inheritance by Barack Obama - Three Rivers Press, Member of the Crown Publishing Group, A Division of Random House, Inc., (ISBN# 1-4000-8277-3) Copyright (c) 1995, 2004 by Barack Obama.

Chapter 19) - (Pages 396-402

Black Stars - African American Military Heroes by Jim Haskins - John Wiley and Sons, Inc., (ISBN# 0-471-14577-7) Copyright (c) 1998 by Jim Haskins.

Introduction - (Pages 1-3)

Part One - The Early Years

Chapter 1) - Private Peter Salem - 1750-1816 - (Pages 7-10)

Chapter 2) - Private Austin Dabney - ? - (Pages 11-13)

Chapter 3 - Private Lemuel Haynes - 1753-1833 - (Pages 14-18)

Chapter 4) - Deborah Sampson - 1760-1827 - (Pages 19-23)

Chapter 5) - Seaman John Bartan Vashon - 1792-1854 - (Pages24-26)

Pioneers In Protest by Lerone Bennett Jr. - Johnson Publishing Company, Inc., (ISBN# 87485-026-6) (Library of Congress Catalog No. 68-55366) Copyright (c) 1968 by Johnson Publishing Company., Inc.

Black Stars - African Women Writers by Brenda Wilkerson / Jim Haskins, General Editor - John Wiley & Sons, Inc., (ISBN# 0-471-17580-3) Copyright (c) 2000 by Brenda Wilkerson.

Part One - The Early Years

Chapter 1) - Phillis Wheatley - 1753-1784 - (Pages 9-15)

Chapter 2) - Sojourner Truth - 1797-1883 - (Pages16-21)

Part Two - The Civil War Years and Reconstruction

Chapter 1) - Harriett Jacobs - 1813-1897 - (Pages 25-29)

Chapter 2) - Frances E. W. Harper - 1825-1911 - (Pages 30-34)

Chapter 3) - Ida B. Wells-Barnett - 1862-1931 - (Pages 35-39)

Black Stars - African American Inventors by Otha Richard Sullivan / Jim Haskins, General Editor - John Wiley & Sons, Inc., (ISBN# 0-471-14804-0) Copyright (c) 1998 by Otha Richard Sullivan.

Introduction - (Pages 1-3

Part One - The Early Years.

Chapter 2) - Norbet Rillieux - 1806-1894 - (Pages 14-19

Chapter 3) - Benjamin Montgomery - 1806-1877 (Pages 20-24

Part Two - The Civil War Years and Reconstruction.

Chapter 1) - Elijah McCoy - 1843-1929 - (Pages 27-30)

Chapter 2) - Leis Howard Latimer - 1848-1928 - (Pages 31-38)

Chapter 3) - Andrew Jackson Beard - 1849-1941 - (Pages 39-42)

Chapter 4) - Jan Earnst Matzeliger - 1852-1889 - (Pages 43-48)

Chapter 5) - Daniel hale Williams, M.D. - 1856-1931 - (Pages 49-54)

Chapter 6) - Granville T. Woods - 1856-1910 - (Pages 55-59)

Black Stars - African American Entrepreneurs by Jim Haskins - John Wiley & Sons, Inc., (ISBN# 0-471-14576-9) Copyright (c) 1998 by Jim Haskins.

Introduction - (Pages 1-3)

Part One - The Early Years

Chapter 1) - Marie-Therese Metoyer - 1742-1816 - (Pages 7-11)

Chapter 2) - Paul Cuffe - 1759-1817 - (Pages 12-16)

Chapter 3) - James Forten - 1766-1842 (Pages 17-20)

Chapter 4) - Pierre Toussaint - 1766-1853 - (Pages 21-24)

Chapter 5) - "Free Frank" McWorther - 1777-1854 - (Pages 25-30)

Black Stars - African American Healers by Clinton Cox / Jim Haskins, General Editor - John Wiley & Sons, Inc., (ISBN# 0-471-24650-6) Copyright (c) 2000 by Clinton Cox.

Black Stars - African American Musicians by Eleanora E. Tate / Jim Haskins, General Editor - John Wiley & Sons, Inc., (ISBN# 0-471-25356-1) Copyright 2000 by Eleanora E. Tate.

About the Author

Tony Rose is the Publisher and CEO of Phoenix, AZ based, Amber Communications Group, Inc., the nation's largest African-American Publisher of Self-Help Books and Music Biographies; The 2013 44th Annual NAACP *Image Award Winner for Outstanding Literature*; The Los Angeles Leimert Park Book Fair / Jessie Redmon Fauset Book Awards, *"2014 African American Book Publisher of the Year"*; and The Harlem Book Fair / Phillis Wheatley Book Awards *"2013 African American Book Publisher of the Year"*.

ACGI's imprints include: The NAACP Image Awards winning, Amber Books Publishing; Amber Classics Books—Self-Help Reference Books; Colossus Books - Music Biographies; Amber/Wiley Books—Self Help and Financial Books Co-Published with John Wiley & Sons Inc.; Joyner/Amber Books—Co-Publishing with the Tom Joyner Foundation and Desmoon Books—Fiction.

Tony Rose led the movement towards modern Independent Book Publishing for the African American Self-Publisher and Independent Book Publisher as we know it today.

In 2000 he responded to the needs of the growing market of self-publishers and founded Quality Press, the nation's largest "African American Book Packager", in order to accommodate authors who wished to self-publish their books, and placed the Quality Press Self-Publishers Book Division under the direction of Yvonne Rose who is also an Associate Publisher for Amber Communications Group, Inc. and the Director of Quality Press.

In 2004 Tony Rose co-founded and became the Executive Director of The African American Pavilion at BookExpo America bringing together as exhibitors and attendees a community of thousands of African American book publishers and book publishing industry professionals, a feat that had been unprecedented in the over 100-year history of BookExpo America. In 2005 Rose founded the Katrina Literary Collective, which has been responsible for collecting and donating over 90,000 books for the Hurricane Katrina Survivors, he serves as a founding Director of the Harlem Book Fair National and The Harlem Book Fair/Roxbury, Mass.

He is noted as the first African American Independent Publisher to ink a multi-book, multi-year, Co-Publishing/Imprint deal with a major book publisher (John Wiley & Sons, Inc.), and the first book publisher to have titles licensed by Black Expressions Book Club with thirty five titles signed to date. In addition, Rose has acquired/licensed paperback rights from: Simon and Schuster, Harper Collins and Hyperion Books for publishing and distribution by ACGI.

He has also, successfully negotiated numerous world-wide partnerships, licensing and eBook licensing deals for ACGI in the United States, South Africa, Canada, Europe and Asia, recently setting the pace, signing a seven book exclusive eBook international licensing rights deal with K-Tel International for Colossus Books.

On February 1, 2013, Amber Books, the award winning imprint of Phoenix, AZ based, Amber Communications Group, Inc., was announced as an NAACP Image Award winner for "Outstanding Literary Work—(Youth/Teens)"—for its title, *Obama Talks Back: Global Lessons—A Dialogue With America's Young Leaders* by Gregory J. Reed, Esq. (Amber Books), and has earned an NAACP Image Award for Literature at the 44th Annual NAACP Image Awards Show, Shrine Auditorium, Los Angeles, CA.

On July 19, 2013, Tony Rose, Publisher/CEO, Amber Communications Group, Inc., was announced as the Harlem Book Fair / Phillis Wheatley Book Awards *"2013 African American Book Publisher of the Year"* at the 15th Anniversary of the Harlem Book Fair, in the Langston Hughes Auditorium, Schomberg Center for Research in Black Culture, New York City, NY.

Tony Rose was born in Roxbury (Boston) Massachusetts, raised in the Whittier Street Housing Projects, was honorably discharged from the U.S. Air Force after serving in the Vietnam War, and attended the University of Massachusetts, the University of California in Los Angeles and the New England Conservatory of Music, Boston, MA. He was employed as a production assistant at the Burbank Studios (Warner Brothers and Columbia Pictures), in the accounting and sales division at Warner/Electra/Atlantic Records (WEA), an accounts representative at Warren Lanier Public Relations and as an A & R representative at RCA Records, Los Angeles, California.

Rose returned to Boston and along with record producer Maurice Starr became the primary architect of that, which in the late 70's and 80's would be called "The Boston Black Music Scene" a movement that ultimately led to the discovery of the international blockbusters Prince Charles and the City Beat Band, The Jonzun Crew, New Edition and New Kids on the Block. In 1979 he formed Solid Platinum Records and Productions and in 1982 he was named one of the "Top Ten Record Producers in the World". Rose in the 80's held recording / production deals with Virgin Records, Atlantic Records and Pavilion / CBS/Sony Records.

Rose was a successful Executive Producer, Record Producer, Record Company Owner, Personal Manager, Music Publisher, Recording Studio Owner, Recording Engineer, Song Writer and Composer for more than fifteen years. His Solid Platinum Records and Productions was the first African American production company to have a production deal with Virgin Records. In 1983, albums produced by Rose *"Gang War"* and *"Stone Killers"* by Prince Charles and the City

Beat Band reached Gold Album status and shared the charts with Michael Jackson's Thriller for six consecutive months in the number one, two and three positions throughout the world and his legendary "Prince Charles and the City Beat Band" albums *"Gang War"*, *"Stone Killers"*, *"Combat Zone"* and singles, have accounted for more than Four Million sold worldwide. Rose's many music awards include "Gold" and "Platinum" Albums and "Ampex Golden Reel" Awards for recording and engineering New Kids on the Block. Rose, has also penned *Before the Legend – The Rise of New Kids on the Block and ...A Guy Named Maurice Starr – The Early Years,* published August 2008.

Rose is the recipient of several publishing awards including: The 2013 44th Annual **NAACP Image Award Winner for Outstanding Literature**—Best Literary Work (Youth / Teens), *Obama Talks Back: Global Lessons—A Dialogue With America's Young Leaders* (Amber Books); The Los Angeles Leimert Park Book Fair / Jessie Redmon Faust Book Awards, *"2014 African American Book Publisher of the Year"*; The 2014 Blacks In Government-Greater Orange County CA Chapter Award for *"Outstanding Contributions and Service to the African American Publishing Community"*; The Harlem Book Fair / Phillis Wheatley Book Awards *"2013 African American Book Publisher of the Year"*; The City of Phoenix, Arizona—Office of the Mayor *"Official Resolution for Fifteen Years of Successful Book Publishing & the 2013 NAACP Image Award for Outstanding Literature"*, The City of Boston and the Boston City Council *"Official Resolution for Success in the Music/Recording Industry and the Book Publishing Industry"*; The 2008 Harlem Book Fair / Phillis Wheatley Book Awards *"For Literary Work That Transcends Culture, Boundary and Perception"*; The Chicago Black Book Fair and Conference *"Independent Publisher/Press Award"*; The BlackBoard Bestseller's *"African-American Publisher of the Year Award"*; The American Library Association *"Reluctant Reader"* Award; The 1st YOUnity Book Reviewers, Disilgold Soul Magazine *"Publisher of the Millennium"* Award; The Diamond Literary Festival *"Certificate of Appreciation Award"*; The Harlem Book Fair, Boston/Roxbury *"Charles C. Yancey"* Literary

Award; The Commonwealth of Massachusetts, House of Representatives, *"In Recognition of Promoting the African American Experience Through the Literary World"* Award; The City of Boston *"Continuous Promotion of African American Authors"* Resolution; The Black Caucus of The American Library Association (BCALA) *"Appreciation Award"*; The BookExpo America *"Founders Award"*; The Haki R. Madhubuti *"Independent Publisher of Note Award"*; The City of Los Angeles, State of California, Leimert Park Village Book Fair, *"Certificate of Appreciation, For Extraordinary Contributions to the African American Literacy Legacy Award"*; The Los Angeles Black BookExpo, Certificate of Appreciation *"Outstanding Contributions in Promoting Black Literature Award"* and The Cape Verdean News *"Millennium Award for Book Publishing Excellence"*.

He also has served as a Literary Sub-Committee Member in the Category of Non-Fiction Literature and Instructional Literature for the 2007 (38th), 2008 (39th), 2009 (40th), 2011 (42nd) and 2012 (43rd) NAACP Image Awards (Show); the Co-Founder and Executive Director of the African American Pavilion at BookExpo America, the Nation's Largest Book Publishing Trade Show from 2004-2010 and the Founder of Amber Communications Group, Inc.'s African American Pavilion Booth at BookExpo America, 2011, 2012, 2013.

Among ACGI's most notable and diverse titles are *Grow Thinner and Lose Weight While You Sleep; Yoga Meditation and Spiritual Growth for the African American Community-If You Can Breathe, You Can Do Yoga and Find Inner and Outer Peace-The Ultimate Yoga Book for Beginners and the Young at Heart; Lady Gaga: Born to Be Free; Beyoncé-Before the Legend: The Rise of Beyoncé and Destiny's Child, The Early Years; Kanye West-Before the Legend: The Rise of Kanye West and the Chicago Rap & R&B Scene, The Early Years; Obama Talks Back: Global Lessons—A Dialogue with America's Young Leaders; The African American Criminal Justice Guide-Staying Alive and Out of Jail; The African American Scholarship Guide-Thousands of Scholarships and Grants for African American Students; The African American Employment Guide-Finding and keeping a Job; Ageless Beauty: The*

Ultimate Skincare and Makeup Book for Women and Teens of Color; The Revised Second Edition-Is Modeling For You? The Handbook and Guide for the Young Aspiring African American Model; Tom Joyner Presents: How To Prepare For College; African Americans and the Future of New Orleans; Beautiful Black Hair—Real Solutions To Real Problems; The African American Family's Guide to Tracing Our Roots; TheAfro-Centric Bride—A Style Guide; African American History In The United States of America, An Anthology-From Africa To President Barack Obama, Volume One; Born Beautiful: The African American Teenagers Complete Beauty Guide; The African American Guide to Real Estate Investing; Lil Wayne: An Unauthorized Biography; Jay Z and The Roc-A-Fella Records Dynasty; How To Get Rich When You Ain't Got Nothing: The African American Guide To Obtaining and Building Wealth; Pay Yourself First: The African American Guide to Financial Success and Security; Aaliyah – An R & B Princess in Words & Pictures; Destiny's Child: The Complete Story; God Made Dirt: The Life and Times of Ol' Dirty Bastard; Memoirs of a Superfreak – The Confessions of Rick James; and Before the Legend: The Rise of New Kids On The Block and....A Guy Named Maurice Starr, The Early Years; Eminem and the Detroit Rap Scene: White Kid in a Black Music World; Amy Winehouse: Too Young To Die...Too Old To Live and Nicki Minaj: The Woman Who Stole the World.

Tony Rose is the editor of numerous books and the co-writer of the national best-seller, *Is Modeling For You: The Handbook and Guide For The Young Aspiring Black Model,* written with Yvonne Rose, he has penned the critically acclaimed, best-seller, *Before the Legend: The Rise of New Kids On The Block and A Guy Named Maurice Starr, The Early Years* and written, compiled, edited and published the award winning, *African American History In The United States of America—An Anthology—From Africa To President Barack Obama, Volume One*, a Top Ten Best African American Book and has recently penned the critically acclaimed *America: The Black Point of View (1950's and 1960's) – An Autobiography of Short Stories – Essays and Poems.*

ORDER FORM

Please Mail Checks or Money Orders to:

Amber Communications Group, Inc.
1334 East Chandler Boulevard – Suite 5-D67
Phoenix, AZ 85048

Please send ___ copy(ies) of *African American History in the USA* ($17.95)

Please send ___ copy(ies) of *Obama Talks Back: Global Lessons—A Dialogue for America's Young Leaders* ($19.95)

Please send ___ copy(ies) of *America: The Black Point of View (1950's and 1960's)—An Autobiography of Short Stories—Essays and Poems* ($16.95)

Name: _____

Address: _____

City: _____State: _____Zip:_____

Telephone: (___) _____ / (___) _____

Email: _____

I have enclosed $_____, plus $5.00 shipping per book for a total of $_____.

For Bulk or Wholesale Rates, Call: **602-743-7211**

Or email: *Amberbk@aol.com*

Please visit: WWW.AMBERBOOKS.COM

www.ingramcontent.com/pod-product-compliance
Lightning Source LLC
Chambersburg PA
CBHW052027090426
42739CB00010B/1816